CHILDREN OF ALCOHOLICS

The John D. and Catherine T. MacArthur Foundation
Series on Mental Health and Development

CHILDREN OF ALCOHOLICS

A Critical Appraisal of Theory and Research

Kenneth J. Sher

THE UNIVERSITY OF CHICAGO PRESS/CHICAGO AND LONDON

KENNETH J. SHER is associate professor in the Department of
Psychology at the University of Missouri, Columbia.

The University of Chicago Press, Chicago 60637
The University of Chicago Press, Ltd., London
© 1991 by The University of Chicago
All rights reserved. Published 1991
Printed in the United States of America

00 99 98 97 96 95 94 93 92 91 5 4 3 2 1

ISBN (cloth): 0-226-75271-2

Library of Congress Cataloging-in-Publication Data

Sher, Kenneth J.
    Children of alcoholics : a critical appraisal of theory and
research / Kenneth J. Sher.
        p. cm. — (The John D. and Catherine T. MacArthur Foundation
series on mental health and development)
    Includes bibliographical references and index.
    1. Children of alcoholics—United States. I. Title. II. Series.
HV5132.S53 1991
362.29'2—dc20   91–2414

The University of Chicago Press gratefully acknowledges a subvention from the
John D. and Catherine T. MacArthur Foundation in partial support of the costs of
production of this volume.

To Holly and Hannah

Contents

	Acknowledgments	ix
1	Introduction	1
2	Genetic and Environmental Influences	16
3	Other Psychological Disorders Associated with a Family History of Alcoholism	34
4	Mediators and Moderators of Risk: Conceptualizing Vulnerability and Protective Factors	41
5	Cross-sectional and Prospective Research on COAs: Rationale and Methodological Issues	53
6	Psychological Characteristics	72
7	Biological Characteristics	93
8	Responses to Alcohol	106
9	Models of Vulnerability	121
10	Moderating Variables	140
11	The Clinical Literature WITH PHIL MOTHERSEAD	148
12	Concluding Comments	171
	References	176
	Index of Names	211
	Index of Subjects	218

Acknowledgments

I would like to express my deep appreciation to Terry Wilson and Peter Nathan for providing me with the opportunity to write a position paper for the Health and Behavior Network of the MacArthur Foundation on the state of knowledge concerning children of alcoholics which served as the basis of this book, and to Judith Rodin and Peter Nathan for encouraging me to expand the manuscript into a monograph for the John D. and Catherine T. MacArthur Foundation Series on Mental Health and Development. Without that opportunity and encouragement, this book would not have been written.

The influence of many colleagues can be found throughout this volume. However, I would like to acknowledge specifically my deep indebtedness to Laurie Chassin, John Donovan, and David Newlin for contributing to the development of many of the ideas presented in the following pages. A sabbatical leave at the University of Washington during 1989 provided me with the opportunity to discuss numerous ideas with Alan Marlatt and his colleagues and graduate students, and to teach a seminar on children of alcoholics, all of which greatly assisted me in organizing my thinking about COAs.

Phil Mothersead coauthored chapter 11 (on the clinical literature) and his expertise is greatly valued. Kim Walitzer and Kathy Biggers provided extensive bibliographic assistance in the beginning stages of this book. Jeannette Johnson provided a number of important references that I doubt I would have come upon on my own. John Donovan contributed many helpful comments on the original position paper written for the John D. and Catherine T. MacArthur Foundation meeting on children of alcoholics. Eric Martin and Tammy Workman provided extensive copyediting and pointed out areas in need of greater clarification in earlier drafts of the manuscript. Corby Magner, Renee Perrigo, Gail Raskin, and Trish Vandiver all helped out in numerous ways, especially when something needed to be done in a hurry.

I am grateful to the National Institute on Alcohol Abuse and Alcoholism for providing many valuable opportunities for professional development including a predoctoral National Research Service Award to Indiana University (where I did my graduate work), financial support of my research at the University of Missouri (research grants AA6182 and AA7231), the opportunity to serve as a member on the Psychosocial Research Review Committee (Epidemiology and Prevention Subcommittee), and to participate in several technical reviews and workshops.

Finally, I would like to express my deep appreciation to Holly, Hannah, Kim, Tom, and Lizette for their love, support, and encouragement.

1 Introduction

We are currently witnessing an explosion of interest in children of alcoholics (COAs) among mental health workers and the general public. Unsubstantiated generalizations about COAs have become popularized through the media and the mental health profession. One influential writer, Black (1982, p. 27), boldly states that "all children raised in alcoholic homes need to be addressed. All children are affected." A number of clinicians such as Black (1982), Wegscheider (1977), and Woititz (1983) view COAs as the unfortunate victims of an alcoholic family environment characterized by disruption, deviant parental role models, inadequate parenting, and disturbed parent-child relationships. Special attention is often paid to the central role of alcohol in the family, the multitude of ways the alcoholic parent disrupts family life, and the various adaptations employed by other family members in order to stabilize family process. These family environment variables are thought to contribute to ongoing distress and impaired functioning in COAs and to have enduring effects into adulthood. From this clinical perspective, being a COA is often thought to be a problem in its own right (although influential writers disagree on the extent to which all COAs are negatively affected). Along with this problem focus, the clinical literature describes a number of approaches to intervention in both childhood and in adulthood.

In addition to this "clinical" interest in COAs, there has been a dramatic increase in attention to COAs from a more basic (i.e., less applied), research perspective. The accumulating evidence supporting a genetic etiology in at least some forms of alcoholism has led to an interest in COAs as a group at high risk for later alcoholism, and numerous recent investigations have attempted to establish a wide range of correlates of being a COA, in order to detect variables potentially relevant for understanding the etiology of alcoholism. Although not usually addressing the issues raised by the clinical literature, these research investigations have generated a large empirical data base concerning the nature of correlates of parental alcoholism and have considerable clinical relevance. The research literature also has highlighted a number of methodological issues which are critical to a scientifically valid assessment of COA deficits and problems.

In two influential reviews published over a decade ago, El-Guebaly and Offord (1977, 1979) documented the wide range of problems encountered across the lifespan by COAs, ranging from fetal alcohol syndrome first manifested in infancy, emotional problems and hyperactivity in childhood, emotional problems and conduct problems in adolescence, to alcoholism in adulthood. Since the time of those early reviews, research has advanced on several fronts and has helped to clarify the problems facing COAs. These empirical studies have begun to identify specific environmental and biological variables that may be responsible for the development of these problems. A major purpose of this book is to summarize our current state of knowledge concerning COAs, relying primarily on the scientific literature. In addition to reviewing what is currently known, I attempt to elucidate basic models concerning the nature of deficits in COAs and their relevance to the etiology of alcoholism and other disorders. Although the present book necessarily overlaps with some of the other recent reviews published on this topic (MacDonald and Blume 1986; Russell, Henderson, and Blume 1985; Windle and Searles 1990; Woodside 1983, 1984), I hope to build on earlier reviews by focusing more extensively on areas particularly in need of further research and theoretical development. Particular attention will be given to methodological issues in research on children of alcoholics. Methodological sophistication is critical for evaluating the validity of available research and for designing studies which will expand our current knowledge.

The Pathological Use of Alcohol

Before examining the research on children of alcoholics, I shall briefly review what is meant by the terms "alcoholism" or "alcoholic." Unfortunately, scrutiny of the vast literature on the definitions and diagnosis of *alcoholism* and *alcohol problems* generally reveals a number of diverging viewpoints and controversies. For present purposes, I will sidestep these controversies and focus on the major distinctions and definitions used by contemporary clinicians and researchers.

In conceptualizing the degree to which a person's life has become disrupted by his or her use of alcohol, it is helpful to distinguish between *alcohol-related consequences or problems* and *alcohol dependence* (Edwards 1986). The term *alcohol-related consequences* refers to a variety of negative life events that are directly the result of alcohol consumption. These consequences include social problems (physical or verbal aggression, marital difficulties, loss of important social relationships), legal problems (arrests for driving while intoxicated, public inebriation), vocational problems (termination from employment, failure to achieve career goals), and medical problems (physical injury, liver disease, central nervous system disease). The term *alcohol dependence* refers to a syndrome comprising a variety of signs and symptoms that signify the importance of alcohol consumption in the life of the drinker. These signs and symptoms include what Edwards (1982, 1986; Edwards and Gross 1976) describes as "a narrowing of the drinking repertoire" (a tendency for drinking patterns to become fixed, less influenced by environmental cues or contingencies, and motivated by the avoidance or escape from withdrawal symptoms), "salience of drinking" (alcohol comes to play a more and more central role in the life of the drinker relative to other life tasks and challenges), increased tolerance of alcohol, withdrawal symptoms (especially autonomic hyperactivity and mood disturbance) upon cessation of drinking or reduction of alcohol intake, drinking to escape or to avoid withdrawal symptoms, "subjective awareness of the compulsion to drink," and rapid reinstatement of dependence symptoms after a period of abstinence.

Both alcohol-related consequences and the alcohol dependence syndrome can be viewed as dimensional constructs that can be graded in intensity from absent to severe. Missing from these descriptions is reference to the *amount* of alcohol consumed. Although individuals who drink excessive amounts of alcohol are more likely to incur alcohol-related problems and alcohol dependence symptoms, current diagnostic practice focuses more on the consequences of drinking and on the psychological and physiological significance of drinking to the individual than on the quantity or frequency of consumption per se.

Diagnostic Criteria

Although a number of approaches to the diagnosis and classification of pathological alcohol use have been proposed (Feighner et al. 1972; Jellinek 1960; National Council on Alcoholism 1972), at present the most widely adopted criteria in North America are those established by the American Psychiatric Association (1987) in the *Diagnostic and Statistical Manual of Mental Disorders* (third edition-revised) (DSM-III-R). DSM-III-R proposes two major classifications of alcohol use disorders: *alcohol abuse* and *alcohol dependence*. As can be seen in Table 1.1, the criteria for alcohol dependence incorporate a number of the characteristics described by Edwards and roughly correspond to what many would call "alcoholism." The criteria for alcohol abuse focus more on alcohol-related problems and approximate the more general term "problem drinking." (Note that in DSM-III-R alcohol dependence takes diagnostic precedence over alcohol abuse [see criterion C of alcohol abuse]).

Table 1.1 DSM-III-R Diagnostic Criteria for Alcohol Abuse and Dependence
Alcohol Dependence

A. At least three of the following:
   (1) alcohol often taken in larger amounts or over a longer period than the person intended
   (2) persistent desire or one or more unsuccessful efforts to cut down or control alcohol use
   (3) a great deal of time spent in activities necessary to get the alcohol, consuming the alcohol, or recovering from its effects
   (4) frequent intoxication or withdrawal symptoms when expected to fulfill major role obligations at work, school, or home (e.g., does not go to work because hung over, goes to school or work "high," intoxicated while taking care of his or her children), or when alcohol use is physically hazardous (e.g., drives when intoxicated)
   (5) important social, occupational, or recreational activities given up or reduced because of alcohol use
   (6) continued alcohol use despite knowledge of having a persistent or recurrent social, psychological, or physical problem that is caused or exacerbated by the use of alcohol (e.g., keeps using alcohol despite family arguments about it, alcohol-induced depression, or having an ulcer made worse by drinking)
   (7) marked tolerance: need for markedly increased amounts of alcohol (i.e., at least 50% increase) in order to achieve intoxication or desired effect, or markedly diminished effect with continued use of the same amount
   (8) characteristic withdrawal symptoms
   (9) alcohol often taken to relieve or avoid withdrawal symptoms
B. Some symptoms of the disturbance have persisted for at least one month, or have occurred repeatedly over a longer period of time.
Criteria for Severity of Psychoactive Alcohol Dependence:
   Mild: Few, if any, symptoms in excess of those required to make the diagnosis, and the symptoms result in no more than mild impairment in occupational functioning or in usual social activities or relationships with others.
   Moderate: Symptoms or functional impairment between "mild" and "severe."
   Severe: Many symptoms in excess of those required to make the diagnosis, and the symptoms markedly interfere with occupational functioning or with usual social activities or relationships with others.
   In Partial Remission: During the past six months, some use of alcohol and some symptoms of dependence.
   In Full Remission: During the past six months, either no use of alcohol, or use of alcohol and no symptoms of dependence.
Alcohol Abuse
A. A maladaptive pattern of alcohol use indicated by at least one of the following:
   (1) continued use despite knowledge of having a persistent or recurrent social, occupational, psychological, or physical problem that is caused or exacerbated by the use of alcohol
   (2) recurrent use in situations in which use is physically hazardous (e.g., driving while intoxicated)
B. Some symptoms of the disturbance have persisted for at least one month, or have occurred repeatedly over a longer period of time.
C. Never met the criteria for Alcohol Dependence.

Source: adapted from *Diagnostic and Statistical Manual of Mental Disorders,* Third Edition-Revised (DSM-III-R; American Psychiatric Association, 1987), with permission of the author.

It needs to be stressed that although the distinction between alcohol dependence (in varying severity) and alcohol abuse might be important both clinically and theoretically, most of the published research on COAs fails to employ this distinction. Indeed, the diagnostic methods of a large proportion of studies are often vague and poorly specified. Consequently, although many authorities might restrict the term "alcoholic" to those individuals who evidence moderate to severe alcohol dependence, in practice much of the research on COAs examines offspring of individuals with a range of severity of alcohol problems and dependence symptoms. Consequently, the terms "alcoholic" and "children of alcoholics" are used in a broad and imprecise sense throughout this book.

Epidemiology

Prevalence of Alcoholism

Direct estimates of the prevalence of alcoholism in the United States vary considerably as a function of definition, assessment techniques, and sampling strategies (Helzer 1987; Warheit and Auth 1985). Consequently, there is a certain arbitrariness to any set of estimates. The results of the Epidemiology Catchment Area survey (ECA; Regier et al. 1984), however, are particularly informative and represent a useful reference point. The ECA data are based on a large, diverse, multisite sample of community dwelling and institutionalized adults assessed with a reliable diagnostic interview (the Diagnostic Interview Schedule; DIS) and summarized in terms of widely accepted diagnostic criteria (DSM-III). Lifetime prevalence for alcohol abuse and dependence combined was found to be approximately 25 percent for men and 4–5 percent for women (Robins et al. 1984). (Some caution needs to be expressed about these rates since the sampling strategy was not truly representative of the U.S. population and because the DIS does not require a clustering of alcoholic symptoms in time. This latter issue could result in these estimates being somewhat inflated.) Nevertheless, these prevalence figures illustrate both the high rates of alcohol problems in the U.S. and the large difference in the prevalence of these problems across gender.

Although the prevalence of COAs has never been directly assessed on large, representative samples, Russell et al. (1985) estimate (based on figures available from the 1979 Drinking Practices Survey and the 1980 Census) that there are approximately 6.6 million COAs under the age of 18 and 22 million aged 18 and above. Although it is possible to derive other estimates from various definitions of parental alcoholism, Russell et al.'s estimates are reasonable ones and indicate that a large proportion of the U.S. population can be considered COAs.

Cohort Effects

An interesting finding to emerge from the ECA study is that, in two of the three sites reported on in 1984, the *lifetime* prevalence of alcohol abuse/dependence was higher in younger adults (less than 45 years of age) than in older adults (45 years of age and older) (Robins et al. 1984). These findings raise the possibility that alcoholism is becoming more prevalent in persons born in recent years (i.e., younger cohorts). Recently, Reich et al. (1988) reported data derived from a large sample of alcoholics in treatment in several clinical settings and from a register of convicted felons on probation and parole in the St. Louis area and their relatives. These researchers were able to demonstrate that indeed the lifetime prevalence of alcoholism is increasing in younger cohorts and that this trend is clearly evident for both males and females. The estimated functions relating year of birth to lifetime population prevalence are presented in Figure 1.1 (Reich et al. 1988, fig 5).

Reich et al. (1988) were also able to demonstrate strong cohort effects in the age of onset of alcoholism, with more recently born cohorts of both males and females demonstrating an earlier age of onset, and this trend was particularly marked for females. For example, the modal age of onset of alcoholism decreased approximately four years (from 24 to 20 years of age) for males and eight years (from 32 to 24 years of age) for females, for subjects born in 1953 compared to subjects born in 1938. These data suggest that the well-documented differences in age of onset of alcoholism across gender (Lex 1985) have been narrowing dramatically in recent years.

Reich et al. (1988) also showed that the *transmissibility* of alcoholism is also increasing in more recently born cohorts. Although alcoholism was found to be more transmissible in men, both males and females evidence increasing transmissibility over the years of birth surveyed. This suggests that (1) the increased prevalence of alcoholism in younger cohorts is not due to variables acting independently of genetic and environmental factors associated with a family history of alcoholism, and (2) that a family history of alcoholism is a more significant risk factor for the development of alcoholism in younger as opposed to older persons. Furthermore, as Reich et al. (1988) note, the cohort effects noted "have occurred too rapidly to be accompanied by genetic changes" (p. 463).

In short, Reich et al.'s findings indicate the prevalence of alcoholism has been increasing in recent years, that alcoholism is becoming a disorder with a younger age of onset, and that COAs appear to be especially vulnerable to these changes. More generally, these findings illustrate the changing nature of the epidemiology of alcoholism and demonstrate that a complete understanding of the intergenerational transmission of alcoholism ultimately requires an understanding of broad social factors associated with secular change.

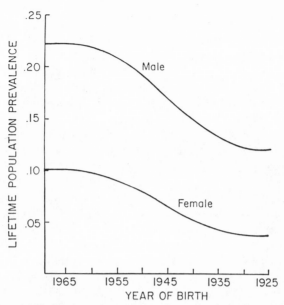

Figure 1.1. Expected lifetime population prevalence of alcoholism as a function of year of birth. Reprinted from Reich et al. (1988) with permission of the authors and the Research Society on Alcoholism.

Heterogeneity of Alcohol Use Disorders

The distinctions between alcohol-related consequences and the alcohol dependence syndrome and between DSM-III-R alcohol abuse and alcohol dependence imply that clinically meaningful distinctions can be made among individuals with alcohol use disorders. That is, alcoholism might best be characterized as a heterogeneous rather than a homogeneous diagnostic entity. In recent years, there has been considerable interest in subtyping forms of alcoholism according to age of onset, course, and clinical characteristics in order to delineate specific forms of alcoholism that might be homogeneous in terms of etiology, response to specific treatments, and prognosis. Closely related to the concept of ''alcoholism subtypes'' is the concept of alcoholism comorbidity (or ''dual diagnosis'') which refers to the frequent finding that persons meeting diagnostic criteria for alcoholism also meet criteria for one or more additional DSM-III-R diagnoses. Thus, from a comorbidity perspective, alcoholism could be subtyped according to the presence of additional psychological disorders (especially antisocial personality disorder, panic disorder, and major depression). Important sources of heterogeneity are briefly reviewed below.

Approaches to Alcoholism Subtypes

During the past fifty years a number of authors have proposed that there are clinically meaningful subtypes of alcoholism and have either implied or explicitly stated that these subtypes differ in etiology, course, and outcome. Table 1.2 briefly describes several of these typologies by noting some of the key features that are thought to characterize the various subtypes associated with different authors' classification schemes.

The selected listing of typologies in Table 1.2 illustrates the range of strategies that different authors have adopted in their attempts to discern meaningful subtypes of alcoholism. For example, Knight's (1937) essential/reactive distinction is based on clinical evaluation of psychological characteristics (character pathology, early adjustment), whereas Jellinek's (1960) typology is primarily grounded in drinking patterns and dependence symptoms. Cloninger's (1987a) Type 1/Type 2 distinction is based on an amalgam of personality features, the presence of antisocial behavior when drinking, and dependence symptoms. Other classifications such as the familial/nonfamilial distinction are based on family history of alcoholism (Penick, Read, Crowley and Powell, 1978), with later investigators finding it useful to distinguish the lineality of the family history (i.e., matrilineal, patrilineal or bilineal; Hesselbrock, Hesselbrock, and Stabenau 1985a) or the depth and density of the family history (Finn and Pihl, 1987).

Some authors have attempted to use statistical techniques such as cluster analysis (Morey, Skinner and Blashfield 1984; Partington and Johnson, 1969) to empirically derive taxonomies of alcoholism. The general term *cluster analysis* refers to a collection of statistical techniques designed to identify relatively homogeneous clusters or types of subjects in a larger heterogenous sample (cf. Aldenderfer and Blashfield 1984). Most of the cluster analytic studies of alcoholism have attempted to cluster alcoholics by their responses to standardized personality inventories such as the Minnesota Multiphasic Personality Inventory (MMPI). The number and types of clusters found by different investigators vary considerably, although this should be expected given the range of cluster analytic techniques employed, the varying nature of the data bases subjected to clustering, and the diversity of subject samples studied. Nevertheless, there appears to be consistent evidence for *at least* two clusters which could broadly be termed a personality disorder cluster and a neurotic cluster (Morey and Blashfield 1981). The basic distinction between a primarily personality disordered alcoholic and a primarily neurotic form of alcoholism was made more than fifty years ago by Knight (1937) in his essential/reactive distinction and has recently regained prominence in Cloninger's (1987a) theory of the etiology and nature of alcoholism.

Table 1.2 Some Selected Typologies of Alcohol Use Disorders

Author(s)	Subtypes	Selected Characteristics
Knight (1937)	essential	early age of onset, personality disorder, poor prognosis
	reactive	later age of onset, good early adjustment, drinking to cope with psychological distress
Jellinek (1960)	alpha	excessive drinking for purely psychological reasons, no evidence of "tissue adaptation"
	beta	excessive drinking which has led to tissue damage with no physiological dependence
	gamma	excessive drinking with evidence of tolerance and withdrawal, marked "loss of control"
	delta	excessive drinking with evidence of tolerance and withdrawal, "inability to abstain"
	epsilon	binge drinking
Partington & Johnson (1969)	Type I	antisocial, emotionally unstable, and cognitively disorganized
	Type II	low antisociality, moderately high thought disturbance
	Type III	neurotic, socially stable, drinks steadily
	Type IV	low antisociality, denial of problems
	Type V	moderate levels of neuroticism and antisociality, high frequency of drinking occasions with excessive consumption
Penick et al. (1978)	Familial	family history of alcoholism, early age of onset, more severe social and psychological problems
	Nonfamilial	negative family history of alcoholism, later age of onset, less severe problems
Morey, Skinner, & Blashfield (1984)	Type A	"early stage problem drinkers," drinking problems without much evidence of dependence symptoms
	Type B	affiliative, moderate alcohol dependence
	Type C	schizoid, severe alcohol dependence
Cloninger (1987)	Type 1	later age of onset, "loss of control," guilt and fear about dependence, high on personality traits of harm avoidance and reward dependence
	Type 2	early age of onset, "inability to abstain", antisocial behavior when drinking, highly genetic, high on personality trait of novelty seeking
Zucker (1987)	antisocial	early onset, antisocial behavior, highly genetic, poor prognosis, predominately male
	developmentally cumulative	cumulative extension of adolescent problem drinking and delinquency, genetic diathesis more environment-mentally mediated that antisocial type
	developmentally limited	extension of adolescent problem drinking, problem spontaneously resolves in early adulthood, infrequent treatment entry
	negative affect	more frequently middle class and female, use of alcohol to cope with role strain and dysphoria, family history of affective disorder

Note: Authors' own descriptors were used whenever feasible.

Cloninger (1987a) has proposed that there are two *prototypic* types of alcoholics, the Type 1 and the Type 2. Major characteristics of each of these prototypes are summarized in Table 1.3. Cloninger has proposed that certain constellations of personality traits predispose an individual to specific types of alcoholism. These personality traits (novelty seeking, harm avoidance, and reward dependence) are thought to be independent, moderately heritable, and to correspond to basic motivational tendencies. Novelty seeking can be viewed as predisposing to impulsivity and distractibility, harm avoidance as predisposing to anxiety and shyness, and reward dependence as predisposing to emotional dependence, persistence, and social sensitivity. These temperamental differences are thought to lead to different motivations for alcohol use. The Type 1 alcoholic can be thought to use alcohol to escape dysphoric reactions (negative reinforcement) while the Type 2 alcoholic can be thought to use alcohol primarily for its appetitive effects (positive reinforcement). As we will see later, Cloninger has found that Type 1 and Type 2 alcoholism differ in their patterns of inheritance and has speculated that "what is transmitted" is the underlying personality pattern.

The notion that there are fundamentally different types of alcoholism has profound implications for the study of COAs. It implies, at the least, that it is misleading to think of COAs as a homogeneous group and that it may be important to think of COAs subtyped on the basis of the form of their parent's alcoholism. While there are probably a number of other important, identifiable sources of heterogeneity among COAs, the issue of the form of the parental alcoholism has been largely unexplored.

Table 1.3 Distinguishing Characteristics of Two Types of Alcoholism

Characteristic features	Type of Alcoholism	
	Type 1	Type 2
Alcohol-related problems		
Usual age of onset (years)	After 25	Before 25
Spontaneous alcohol-seeking (inability to abstain)	Infrequent	Frequent
Fighting and arrests when drinking	Infrequent	Frequent
Psychological dependence (loss of control)	Frequent	Infrequent
Guilt and fear about alcohol dependence	Frequent	Infrequent
Personality Traits		
Novelty seeking	Low	High
Harm Avoidance	High	Low
Reward Dependence	High	Low

Source: from Cloninger (1987a) with permission of the author and the American Association for the Advancement of Science.

Comorbidity

Individuals diagnosed as alcoholics (in both clinical and community settings) often have other "diagnosable" psychological disorders. For example, Hesselbrock, Meyer, and Keener (1985b) examined the prevalence of lifetime psychopathology (using DSM-III) in a sample of 321 hospitalized alcoholics. It is important to note that the diagnostic instrument used by Hesselbrock et al. to assess psychopathology, the DIS, does not assess all DSM-III disorders and so certain categories of disorder were not evaluated. Table 1.4 displays some of the major findings from this study. As can be seen in Table 1.4, 77 percent of the alcoholics had at least one additional DSM-III diagnosis, with the most common additional diagnoses being substance abuse, antisocial personality disorder, depression, and phobia. These general findings are consistent with those of a number of other investigators (Halikas, Herzoq, Mirassou, and Lyttle 1981; Mendelson, Babor, Mello, and Pratt 1986; Powell, Penick, and Othmer 1982; Ross, Glaser, and Germanson 1988; Tyndel 1974; Wolf et al. 1988).

It can be argued that treatment status per se might be related to the finding of high comorbidity since persons with problems in addition to alcoholism would be expected to enter treatment more than those with alcoholism as a sole problem. That is, the high comorbidity found in treatment samples might be atypical of alcoholics more generally, most of whom never enter treatment. There is an empirical basis for this expectation; alcoholics in treatment typically show higher levels of psychiatric symptomatology than alcoholics who do not seek treatment (Woodruff, Guze, and Clayton 1973). Consequently,

Table 1.4 Lifetime and Current Prevalence of Psychopathology Among Hospitalized Alcoholics (in percentages)

	Males (n = 231)		Females (n = 90)		Total (N = 321)	
No additional psychopathology[1]	25		20		23	
Antisocial personality disorder[2]	49		20		41	
Substance abuse	45	(8)[3]	38	(13)	43	(9)
Depression	32	(18)	52	(38)	38	(23)
Phobia	20	(15)	44	(29)	27	(18)
Obsessive-compulsive disorder	12	(4)	13	(7)	12	(5)
Panic disorder	8	(5)	14	(9)	10	(6)
Mania	5	(2)	3	(1)	4	(2)
Somatization	1	(1)	2	(2)	1	(1)
Schizophrenia	2	(2)	3	(1)	2	(2)

Source: Adapted from M. Hesselbrock, Meyer, and Keener (1985) with permission of the authors and the American Medical Association.

[1]Diagnoses are without exclusion criteria.
[2]Diagnosis of antisocial personality was modified to exclude two items that are related to abuse.
[3]Percentages in parentheses indicate current diagnosis.

community-based studies examining the prevalence of comorbidity are informative in more generally characterizing the relationship between alcoholism and other psychopathology.

In a recent study, Helzer and Pryzbeck (1988) examined the relationship between a diagnosis of alcohol abuse/dependence and other DSM-III disorders in the ECA study (mentioned earlier). Some of the key findings from this study are summarized in Table 1.5. As Table 1.5 illustrates, persons diagnosed with alcohol abuse or dependence were more likely to have additional psychopathology than subjects in the total sample. This was true for virtually all of the disorders examined but particularly true for other substance (drug) abuse and antisocial personality disorder. Although comorbidity was common in men (44 percent of the male subjects had a second diagnosis), it was especially common in women (66 percent). Also, the presence of diagnoses in addition to alcohol use/dependence increased the likelihood that the subject had utilized treatment services. The ECA data indicate that comorbidity with alcoholism appears to be a prevalent phenomenon in both the clinic and the community.

Primary vs. Secondary Alcoholism

The relation between alcoholism and comorbid diagnoses can be conceptualized in a number of ways. First, some degree of comorbidity is expected by chance. However, the rates of comorbidity found in the general population exceeds chance expectation for several selected diagnoses. Second, a common factor (e.g., personality characteristics) might *directly* predispose an individual to develop both alcoholism and one or more other disorders. Third, primary alcoholism could cause or contribute to the development of a secondary psychological disorder (e.g., by disrupting biological processes or exposing the individual to alcoholism-related stressors) or a primary psychological disorder could lead to secondary alcoholism (e.g., by leading to excessive alcohol for self-medication).

The distinction between primary and secondary alcoholism is typically based on the temporal ordering of age of onset for alcoholism and comorbid diagnoses. For heuristic purposes, alcoholism can be considered *primary* if its onset precedes that of another diagnosis, or *secondary* if its onset succeeds that of another diagnosis. Although, in a strict sense, the primary/secondary distinction is usually made on a temporal basis, it is often assumed that this temporal relation implies an etiological or causal relation. Although perhaps a reasonable assumption when considering grouped data, establishing a causal relation in individual cases is fraught with difficulties. Establishing the temporal ordering of diagnosis onset sometimes proves problematic. Insidious onset of either alcoholism or another psychological disorder can often make it difficult to confidently date ages of onset, and retrospective reports spanning

Table 1.5 The Lifetime Prevalence of Key Diagnoses in Respondents with Alcohol Abuse or Dependence Compared to the Total ECA Population (5-site ECA data, weighted to U.S. population, in percentages)

	Total Population		Those with Alcohol Abuse and/or Dependence	
Diagnosis	Males	Females	Males	Females
Drug abuse and/or dependence	7	5	19	31
Antisocial personality disorder	4	0.81	15	10
Phobic disorder	9	16	13	31
Major depression	3	7	5	19
Panic disorder	1	2	2	7
Somatization disorder	0.02	0.2	0.07	0.87
Mania	0.3	0.4	1	4

Source: Adapted from Helzer and Pryzbeck (1987) with permission of the authors and the *Journal of Studies on Alcohol*.

many years are subject to errors of recall and distortion. Even when temporal ordering can be confidently established, spurious association or third-variable causation can usually not be excluded.

However, subtyping alcoholics on the basis of the primary/secondary distinction has often proved useful. Early support for etiological significance of this distinction came from a family study of 259 alcoholic patients reported by Winokur, Rimmer, and Reich (1971). These authors examined the prevalence of alcoholism, depression, and sociopathy (a diagnostic category very similar to DSM-III-R antisocial personality disorder) in the first-degree relatives of three groups of alcoholics: (1) primary alcoholics, (2) alcoholics with primary depression, and (3) alcoholics with primary sociopathy. Perhaps the most significant finding to result from this study was that "in first degree family members, alcoholism (was) more frequently seen for the primary alcoholism group, depression for the depression alcoholism group and sociopathy for the sociopathy alcoholism group" (p. 531). That is, there appears to be a fair degree of specificity between family history and the *primary* psychiatric diagnosis. The more recently reported findings that alcoholism, depression, and antisocial personality "breed true" (e.g., Cloninger, Reich, and Wetzel 1979; Merikangas, Leckman, Prusoff, Pauls, and Weissman 1985) are consistent with etiological importance of primary diagnoses among alcoholics.

The primary/secondary distinction has implications for course and outcome as well as presumed etiological influences. Schuckit (1985a) studied four groups of patients from an alcoholism treatment program at a VA hospital: (1) a group of patients with primary alcoholism, (2) a group of patients with primary drug abuse and secondary alcoholism, (3) a group of patients with primary antisocial personality disorders and secondary alcoholism, and (4) a group of patients with primary affective disorders and secondary alcoholism. These groups were found to differ on a number of background characteristics (antisocial behavior, drug use, prior suicide attempts, family history of different psychiatric disorders). Perhaps most important, data from a follow-up evaluation at twelve months after treatment revealed that the four groups differed in their social functioning, their employment history, and their drug use. These data suggest that the primary/secondary distinction has important implications for the course of disorder and (by implication) for the experience, genetic loading, and outcome of offspring.

Summary

It is clear that alcohol abuse and dependence are prevalent phenomena in our culture, especially for men. A direct implication of this is that a significant proportion of individuals are offspring of alcoholics. Although estimates of the numbers of COAs in the United States will vary as a function of the definition of alcoholism employed and the sampling strategy, reasonable estimates suggest that at least 10 percent of the population can be considered to be "children of alcoholics." The increasing prevalence of alcoholism in more recently born cohorts suggests that the proportion of COAs in the general population has been increasing in a corresponding fashion. Furthermore, the finding of increased transmissibility of alcoholism in recently born cohorts suggests that a family history of alcoholism is becoming a more significant risk factor for alcoholism than for earlier-born cohorts.

Although much of the clinical and research literature considers COAs to be a relatively homogeneous group (at least with respect to the basic nature of parental alcoholism), a number of lines of research and theory suggest that there is more than one type of alcoholism, and thus the category "Children of Alcoholics" is misleadingly broad. The optimal way of subtyping alcoholism is a matter of current debate, and at present there is no clear consensus. Many, if not most, researchers and clinicians consider the presence of additional psychopathology (comorbidity) an important basis on which to classify alcoholics. Additionally, the extent to which the comorbid psychopathology appears to be either primary or secondary to alcoholism may also be important. However, even within a group of alcoholics considered "primary," significant clinical heterogeneity remains, and it may be useful to think of subtypes of primary alcoholics. A number of subtypes of alcoholics have been proposed over the years and no one classification system has been embraced by the field. One distinction that has found expression in a number of different subtyping schemes is that between a more personality disordered alcoholic (with early age of onset, poor impulse control, and poor social adjustment) and a more neurotic form (with later age of onset, proneness to affective disturbance, and generally good social adjustment). Cloninger's currently influential Type 1/Type 2 dichotomy is generally consistent with this distinction. Although most researchers appear to appreciate the potential importance of comorbidity and alcoholism subtypes, these potential sources of heterogeneity have been largely ignored in most studies of COAs. Diagnostic imprecision and a lack of attention to important sources of heterogeneity have undoubtedly reduced our acuity in discerning important characteristics of children of alcoholics. The general concept "children of alcoholics" is too imprecise for many research questions. Despite this considerable vagary, quite a bit is known about COAs as a group, and scientific knowledge is accumulating at a rapid rate. In the following chapters, what is known and not known about COAs is systematically reviewed, with the goal of providing multiple frameworks for understanding the intergenerational transmission of alcoholism and related problems.

2 Genetic and Environmental Influences

Overview of Genetic Studies

A number of recent reviews suggest that alcohol use and alcohol abuse/dependence are genetically determined (Cloninger, Sigvardsson, Reich, and Bohman 1986; Goodwin 1988; Grove and Cadoret 1983; Gurling and Murray 1984; NIAAA 1985; Peele 1986; Schuckit 1985a; Schuckit, Li, Cloninger, and Dietrich 1985). The weight of current evidence suggests that genetic factors play an important role in some forms of alcoholism. However, the nature and extent of genetic mediation and its interaction with various environmental influences have yet to be specified. Even though Peele (1986), Gurling and Murray (1984), Searles (1988) and others have argued that the importance of genetic factors has been overstated and that reviewers have glossed over inconsistencies that exist across studies, these critics still do not contest the idea that genetic factors do play an etiologic role in the development of alcoholism.

Because the data supporting a genetic etiology for some forms of alcoholism have been so often reviewed recently, only a brief overview will be presented here.

Family Studies

Family studies consistently find a high prevalence of alcoholism in the first-degree relatives of alcoholics (cf., Cotton 1979; Goodwin 1988). Although there is some variability across studies, on average, offspring of alcoholics are approximately 3 to 5 times more likely to develop alcoholism themselves than offspring of nonalcoholics (Cotton 1979). A recent meta-analysis of the relation between sex-of-parent and sex-of-offspring on the transmission of alcoholism (Pollock, Schneider, Gabrielli, and Goodwin 1987) indicates that, across family studies, paternal alcoholism is associated with increased rates of alcoholism in both sons and daughters and maternal alcoholism is associated only with increased rates of alcoholism among daughters. Although such results are consistent with a genetic etiology, they are equally consistent with environmental transmission. In order to establish definitively a role for genetic influence, behavior genetic strategies that can partition genetic and environmental sources of variance are necessary. Two behavior genetic strategies that have been profitably employed in studies of humans are the twin study and the adoption study.

Twin Studies

Twin studies provide a much stronger test of the hypothesis of genetic transmission because they permit a quantitative assessment of genetic heritability (that is, the proportion of variance in heritability that is accounted for by genetic factors). Because monozygotic (MZ; identical) twins have 100 percent of their genetic makeup in common and dizygotic (DZ; fraternal) twins have only 50 percent of their genetic makeup in common, if a trait is genetically determined then MZ twins should be more concordant (more similar to each other) than DZ twins. With respect to alcoholism, this means that the concordance rate for alcoholism should be significantly higher in MZ twins than DZ twins. However, in order to make valid inferences concerning heritability from concordance rates, a number of assumptions must be made. For example, biological factors associated with twinning should not be related to risk for alcoholism (being a twin should not, by itself, be associated with risk for alcoholism). Also, the shared environment of MZs should be no more similar than the shared environment of DZs. At present, it does not appear that twins per se are at heightened risk for alcoholism. However, there is some evidence to suggest that MZ twins may share more common environment than DZ twins. For example, Kaprio et al. (1987) found that MZ twins spent more time together than DZ twins. However, even when assumptions of the classic twin method are violated, statistical adjustments for violation of these assumptions can be made (see Kaprio et al. 1987).

Although heritability estimates derived from various twin studies differ considerably, MZ twins are generally found to have higher concordance rates (or intraclass correlations) than DZ twins with regard to alcoholism (Hrubec and Omenn 1981; Kaij 1960; Pickens and Svikis 1988), although one study (Gurling, Murray, and Clifford 1981) failed to show higher concordance among MZ than DZ twins. A summary of these data is presented in Table 2.1. These studies of patients meeting diagnostic criteria for alcoholism are basically consistent with the hypothesis that there is a heritable component in alcoholism, *at least for men;* but the considerable variation in the reported findings limit confidence in the robustness of these effects.

In addition to the above studies of alcoholism, a number of recent studies have used the twin study method to examine the genetic contribution of selected aspects of drinking behavior in nonclinical samples (Cederlof, Friberg, and

Table 2.1 Concordance Rates (in percentages) for Alcoholism in Monozygotic and Dizygotic Twins

Investigator	MZ	DZ
Kaij (1960)		
Chronic alcoholism (N = 174 male pairs)	71	32
Drinking problems (N = 174 male pairs)	28	15
Gurling et al. (1981)		
(N = 56 male and female pairs)	21	25
Hrubec & Omenn (1981)		
(N = 715 male pairs)	26	12
Pickens & Svikis (1989)		
(n = 93 male pairs)	70	43
(n = 46 female pairs)	29	36
(N = 139 total pairs)	55	41

Source: table adapted (and updated) from Grove and Cadoret (1983) with permission of the authors and Plenum Press.

Lundman 1977; Clifford, Fulker, Gurling, and Murray 1981; Gabrielli and Plomin 1985; Jardine and Martin 1984; Jonsson and Nilsson 1968; Kaprio et al. 1987; Loehlin 1972; Partanen, Bruun, and Markkanen 1966; Pederson 1980), attitudes about alcohol (Perry 1973), willingness to drive when drunk (Martin and Boomsma 1989), and self-reports of intoxication following a challenge dose of alcohol (Neale and Martin 1989). Although most of these studies appear to show that aspects of drinking are under genetic control, in many of the studies employing multiple measures of drinking behavior, heritability was found only for certain variables (e.g., Gabrielli and Plomin, 1985; Loehlin 1972; Partanen et al. 1966). Perhaps the most accurate summary of the twin-study data is that a number of dimensions of alcohol-related behavior appear to be under genetic influence, but only to a modest degree. This directly implies that environmental factors and gene X environment interactions both play an important role.

Inconsistencies in the results across these studies (cf. Murray, Clifford, and Gurling 1983; Peele 1986; Searles 1988) may reflect methodological differences (how variables were assessed, twin ascertainment strategies, recruitment success, age and sex composition of samples), historical differences related to the years that the study surveyed, and population differences.

A variant of the twin method that has yet to be reported in the area of alcoholism is to study the offspring of MZ twins discordant for alcoholism, a design that has been profitably employed in the study of schizophrenia (Fischer 1971; Gottesman and Bertelsen 1989). For example, offspring of alcoholic fathers could be compared with their "cousins" who are the offspring of their alcoholic fathers' nonalcoholic cotwins. Although sociologically cousins, these two groups of offspring could be considered genetic half-siblings because they have genetically identical fathers. Finding no difference in the rates of alcoholism (or other relevant variables) between these two groups of offspring would constitute very strong evidence for the importance of genetic factors in alcoholism. Such a design could also be used to examine the importance of a number of environmental variables.

Adoption Studies

The strongest data supporting a genetic etiology for alcoholism come from adoption studies conducted in the last twenty years in Denmark (Goodwin, Schulsinger, Hermansen, Guze, and Winokur 1973; Goodwin et al. 1974; Goodwin et al. 1977), Sweden (Bohman, 1978; Bohman, Cloninger, von Knorring, & Sigvardsson 1984; Bohman, Sigvardsson, and Cloninger 1981; Cloninger, Bohman, and Sigvardsson 1981a), and Iowa (Cadoret, Cain, and Grove 1980; Cadoret and Gath 1978; Cadoret, Troughton, and O'Gorman 1987). (An early adoption study by Roe [1945] failed to find evidence of genetic transmission, but methodological shortcomings have led most reviewers to discount her findings.) The major findings of the adoption studies are reported in Table 2.2.

These adoption studies clearly demonstrate the significant contribution of biological relatives' alcoholism (or alcohol-related problems) to alcoholism in male adoptees. This generalization is also supported by the half-sibling study reported by Schuckit, Goodwin, and Winokur (1972).

Although the adoption studies implicate genetic factors, the results of these studies differ in the extent to which environmental variables are implicated, female adoptees are affected, or gene X environment interactions are present. Although some of these inconsistencies can probably be attributed to methodological differences among the studies (ascertainment of psychopathology in adoptees and their biological and adoptive parents, age of samples, etc.) and to population differences, the work of Cloninger, Bohman and their colleagues suggests that etiological heterogeneity might also represent an important but previously neglected issue. This research group delineated two types of alcoholism among adoptees, *milieu-limited* (also termed Type 1) and *male-limited* (also termed Type 2). The more common, milieu-limited alcoholism, is found both in male and female adoptees, is associated with mild alcohol abuse and minimal criminality in the biological parents, and has a usually mild but possibly severe course (depending largely on postnatal factors). Male-limited alcoholism, on the other hand is associated with severe alcohol abuse, criminality, and an extensive treatment history in the biological fathers of male adoptees, a moderate to severe course, and relatively little environmental moderation. (Because of the relative paucity of Type 2 female

Table 2.2 Prevalence of Alcoholism (in percentages) in Adopted Relatives of Alcoholics

Investigator	Adopted Relatives of Alcoholics		Adopted Relatives of Nonalcoholics		Non-adopted Relatives	
	Male	Female	Male	Female	Male	Female
Goodwin et al. (1973)	18		5			
Goodwin et al. (1974)	25				17	
Goodwin et al. (1977a)		2		4		
Goodwin et al. (1977b)		2				3
Cadoret et al. (1980)	53		20			
Cadoret et al. (1987)	31		9			
Cloninger et al. (1985)						
Male probands	22	4	15	3		
Female probands	26	10	15	3		
Male & female probands	33	9	15	3		

Source: table adapted (and updated) from Grove and Cadoret (1983) with permission of the authors and Plenum Press.

alcoholics in the Swedish studies, little is known concerning the liability of their offspring.) Females in the families of male-limited alcoholics were not found to have an excess of alcoholism, but were found to have an excess of a type of somatizing called diversiform somatization (characterized by relatively low frequency of diverse physical complaints and rare psychiatric complaints). Diversiform somatization appeared to be etiologically distinct from high-frequency somatization (characterized by frequent disability from abdominal, back, and psychiatric complaints), which is related to alcohol abuse, criminality, and low occupational achievement in the biological relatives of female adoptees. Although the findings from the Swedish studies are of great potential importance, two brief comments are in order. First, as is true for any research study, replication on independent samples is needed. Second, the relation between Type 2 alcoholism and antisocial personality disorder (with secondary alcoholism) needs to be clarified. In Cloninger's (1987a, 1987b) writings, there is a clear statement that the temperamental underpinnings of Type 2 alcoholism and antisocial personality disorder are similar if not identical. The basic distinctiveness of primary alcoholism and antisocial personality disorder is an issue addressed later.

Nevertheless, the findings of the Swedish group strongly suggest that even at the grossest level it is hazardous to consider COAs as a homogeneous group with a presumed unitary liability. The importance of obtaining detailed family history data that go beyond alcohol-related disabilities is clear, if possible sources of heterogeneity among COAs are to be addressed.

Genetic Linkage Studies

Another approach to studying the genetic basis of disorders such as alcoholism is linkage analysis. Because a detailed consideration of the logic and methods of linkage analysis is beyond the scope of the present discussion, only an outline of this approach will be given here. General introductions to the use of linkage analysis in psychiatric research can be found in several recent publications (Cox and Suarez 1985; Rieder and Kaufmann 1988; Suarez and Cox 1985).

Basically, the locus of a gene (the place on the chromosome where a specific gene or allele resides) for alcoholism is said to be linked to the locus of a genetic marker if the occurrence of both alcoholism and the genetic marker co-occur *in a given family* more than would be predicted by chance expectation. Linkage between alcoholism and a genetic marker implies that the locus for the gene for alcoholism is located on the same chromosome and close to the locus of the genetic marker. This is because genes at loci in close proximity are more likely to ''stay together'' during meiosis than those that are far apart. (Loci on different chromosomes cannot be linked.) *It needs to be emphasized that linkage implies a correlation between alcoholism and the marker in a given family (kindred), but not in the general population.* Because even genes at tightly linked loci will show some evidence of crossing-over (recombination), the distributions of alcoholism and the genetic marker in the population at large could be independent. (Traits, even biochemical characteristics under a high degree of genetic control, that correlate with alcoholism in the general population should be referred to as *biological markers,* reserving the term *genetic marker* to its use in linkage studies.)

In order to conduct linkage analyses, generally large families with multiple generations, multiple offspring, and a high density of alcoholism are needed to determine reliably whether genetic markers and alcoholism are ''passed down'' together from one generation to the next. However, linkage analysis based on large numbers of sibling-pairs is also possible and offers some unique advantages (Cox and Suarez 1985; Suarez and Cox 1985).

Linkage analysis offers considerable promise for research on the genetic basis of alcoholism and has important preventive and clinical applications as well. First, convincing demonstration of linkage is powerful evidence for the genetic basis of a disorder. Second, for certain families at least, it might be possible to identify individuals with genetic susceptibility for alcoholism. (At present, it is not possible to distinguish offspring of alcoholics with and without genetic susceptibility.) Third, with the continuing development of molecular genetic techniques for creating new genetic markers with known locations throughout the human genome, the possibility exists that the exact location of specific genes for (some forms of) alcoholism can ultimately be identified. Identification of such genes can lead to further analysis of their products, function, and their causal relation to alcoholism. Knowledge of how specific genes work to cause susceptibility to alcoholism would have profound implications for prevention and treatment. Fourth, the issue of heterogeneity could be addressed by subtyping forms of alcoholism on the basis of linkage to specific loci.

Although linkage analysis hold promise for the future, at present there are no widely accepted findings linking alcoholism to specific genetic loci. Although linkage of specific genetic markers (such as those related to blood type) to alcoholism have been reported, inconsistency and nonreplication plague existing studies (Hill, Goodwin, Cadoret, Osterland and Doner 1975; Hill, Aston, and Rabin 1988; Kojic et al. 1977; Swinson and Madden 1973; Tanna, Wilson, Winokur and Elston 1988; Winokur et al. 1976). While the development of new genetic markers using molecular genetic techniques offers hope to those attempting to isolate the gene or genes for alcoholism, undue optimism may be unwarranted. McGue and Gottesman's (1989) recent comments on the application of linkage analysis to schizophrenia are relevant to the study of alcoholism. Perhaps most important, a multifactorial (or polygenic) model of alcoholism appears to fit available data better than a single-gene model (cf. Grove and Cadoret 1983). Such polygenic models offer challenges to linkage analysis, especially when many loci are involved and the effects of the various polygenes are equal and small. While linkage methods are being developed to deal with polygenic inheritance (e.g., Lander and Botstein 1989), successful application to etiologically complex and heterogeneous disorders such as alcoholism has yet to be demonstrated. Indeed, as of this time, although reports of genetic linkage between several psychological disorders and genetic markers have been reported, none have been clearly replicable. In the near future, results from linkage studies now underway will provide more definitive data concerning the genetics of alcoholism.

Mention should also be made of a recent study of genetic association (not linkage) by Blum et al. (1990). These investigators reported a strong association between alcoholism and a specific allele (A1) that codes for an important type of dopamine receptor (D_2) in an analysis of brain tissue obtained from a sample of alcoholics and nonalcoholics. While this finding is of great potential importance and suggests that a single gene might be responsible for a large proportion of cases of alcoholism, this study has already been criticized by a number of researchers (Roberts 1990). Pending replication, it is difficult to determine the degree of confidence that should be put in the findings relating clinical alcoholism to the occurrence of a specific allele at a single genetic locus.

Genetic Animal Models

Human studies assessing the genetics of alcoholism have a number of limitations. Beyond the obvious limitation of expense, studies on humans are unable to control mating patterns and exposure to a host of potentially important environmental factors. In addition, assessment of drinking behavior in humans is rarely based on direct observation by researchers but instead must often rely on reports of subjects, their relatives, or on institutional records. Furthermore, direct experimentation designed to assess the interaction of genetic and environmental factors or to examine presumed biological indices and mechanisms of vulnerability are, by necessity, restricted in humans because of ethical concerns.

There are a number of approaches to studying the genetic basis of alcoholism in animals (cf. Crabbe 1989). For example, two or more existing inbred strains can be compared on their response to alcohol; differences in ethanol effects imply that these effects are under genetic control. Inbred strains can be crossed, and the response to alcohol of their offspring can be compared to the response of their respective inbred parents; the distribution of the responses can be used to infer certain patterns of inheritance such as single-locus control. Perhaps most intriguing, animals can be selectively bred for the expression of certain biological or behavioral characteristics related to alcohol.

In recent years, it has been shown that animals (rats and mice) can be bred for sensitivity to behavioral effects of alcohol (e.g., duration of the loss of righting reflex after alcohol consumption [McClearn and Kakihana 1981]) or for voluntary alcohol-seeking behavior (Li, Lumeng, McBride, and Waller 1981). Table 2.3 displays a number of alcohol-related characteristics that have been selectively bred in rodents. These selective breeding experiments demonstrate that certain alcohol effects and alcohol-seeking behavior can be controlled by genetic factors. Furthermore, the availability of these selectively bred animals for experimental purposes permits analysis of biological mechanisms that might mediate the genetically transmitted effects. The relevance of these types of studies to understanding human alcoholism is presently an open issue that will ultimately be decided upon on the similarity between the phenomenon of human alcoholism and the characteristics of the selectively bred lines. However, genetic animal studies have considerable potential for understanding the genetic basis of alcoholism.

Taken together, the family, twin, adoption, and half-sibling studies suggest that genetic factors play a significant role in susceptibility to the development of alcoholism. Although it appears that some forms of alcoholism may be highly heritable, these data also suggest that environmental factors play an important role, operating independently as well as in interaction with genetic factors. Before we move on, a caveat is in order. Careful analysis of the major twin and adoption studies (Murray, Clifford, and Gurling 1983; Searles 1988) suggests that each of these studies suffers from potentially important weaknesses that limit confidence in specific findings, and some may argue that

Table 2.3   Animal Studies of the Genetics of Alcoholism: Lines Selected for Ethanol-related Traits

Selection phenotype/species	Line
Long/Short Sleep Mice (LS/SS)	Duration of loss of righting reflex after ethanol
High/Low Alcohol Sensitive Rats (HAS/LAS)	Duration of loss of righting reflex after ethanol
Preferring/Nonpreferring Rats (P/NP)	Preference for 10% ethanol solution
High/Low Alcohol Drinking Rats (HAD/LAD)	Preference for 10% ethanol solution
Withdrawal Seizure Prone/Resistant Mice (WSP/WSR)	Severity of handling-induced convulsions after chronic ethanol
ALKO Alcohol/Nonalcohol Rats (AA/ANA)	Preference for ethanol solutions
ALKO Tolerant/Nontolerant Rats (AT/ANT)	Ethanol impairment of tilting-plane performance
Severe/Mild Ethanol Withdrawal Mice (SEW/MEW)	Severity of withdrawal on a multivariate index
COLD/HOT Mice	Acute ethanol hypothermia
FAST/SLOW Mice	Ethanol stimulated activity
Taste-Aversion Prone/Resistant Rats (TAP/TAR)	Cycolphosphamide-induced conditioned taste aversion
High/Low Stress Rats	Stress-induced plasma catecholamines
Diazepam Sensitive/Resistant Mice (DS/DR)	Diazepam induced rotarod ataxia

Source: table adapted from Crabbe (1989) with permission of the author and the Research Society on Alcoholism.

the case for genetic mediation of alcoholism is far from proven. Nevertheless, there appears to be sufficient consistency across studies to state that genetic transmission is a good working hypothesis with substantial empirical support.

Although the mode by which genetic transmission occurs has not been established, most theorists believe a multifactorial model best describes the available evidence (e.g., Murray and Gurling 1980). Also, the extent to which the above data can be explained in part by fetal alcohol effects (in the case of maternal alcoholism) and effects of alcohol on the genetic material of the male and female gametes prior to fertilization has not been determined (cf. Russell et al. 1985). It is clear however, that preconception effects of alcohol can effect reproduction in rodents (Abel 1989) and future research will, one hopes, clarify this underresearched area. Continuing research into the genetics of alcoholism, especially the application of molecular genetic techniques in linkage studies, holds promise for delineating the genetic contribution to alcoholism more precisely.

Family Environment and Psychosocial Influences

Family, twin, and adoption studies imply an important role for environmental factors in the development of alcoholism and psychiatric morbidity associated with a family history of alcoholism. For example, family studies document that many alcoholics do not have alcoholic near-relatives. MZ concordance rates for alcoholism (and intraclass correlations for continuous measures of alcohol-related behavior) do not approach unity. Adoption studies indicate gene X environment interactions, for at least one form of alcoholism, and some alcoholics do not have alcoholic biological parents. If we move away from genetically focused studies, the large cultural, occupational, and religious variations in alcohol use and abuse strongly suggest that there is a variety of important psychosocial determinants influencing the development of alcoholism (Goodwin 1988). However, specific environmental variables that may contribute to the development of alcoholism and other forms of dysfunctional behavior among COAs have not been well delineated. In this section, we will review factors that are posited to characterize the alcoholic home and that have potentially pathogenic effects on the child.

Two important issues should be stressed at the outset. First, although certain environmental conditions may characterize alcoholic homes, this does not imply that such conditions are necessarily related to the development of alcoholism. In order to show a relationship with later alcoholism (or other psychopathology), variation in the environment should be related to outcome. Second, even when environmental factors are correlated with offspring maladjustment, causal connections cannot be assumed. The appearance of environmental causation can be created by "third" variables (e.g., when there is significant gene/environment covariation [Plomin, Defries, and Loehlin 1977]). Furthermore, the direction of causality can be difficult to determine; children's behavior can influence parents' psychological adjustment and the nature of their parenting behaviors (Greist, Forehand, Wells, and McMahon 1980; Patterson 1982). A recent analog study (Lang, Pelham, Johnston, and Gelertner 1989) has demonstrated that interactions with oppositional children can lead to increased alcohol consumption in adult caretakers. Consequently, when a dysfunctional pattern of parental or family behaviors is observed in alcoholic families, determining the cause of the dysfunction is not a straightforward procedure.

The following discussion of environmental effects of parental alcoholism will rely heavily upon the findings from several recent extensive reviews of this area.

Child and Spouse Abuse

Many clinicians and writers assume a strong relation between family violence and parental alcoholism: recent reviews of the empirical literature (Hamilton and Collins 1985; Orme and Rimmer 1981; Russell et al. 1985; Steinglass and Robertson 1983; West and Prinz 1987) however, paint a less clear-cut picture. The muddled picture is largely due to the lack of methodological rigor in this area. Major methodological problems include: (1) weak ascertainment of family violence (child abuse and spouse abuse), (2) weak ascertainment of alcohol abuse and alcoholism in parents, (3) sampling problems (sampling from populations likely to have high rates of both familial alcoholism and violence), and (4) lack of appropriate control groups.

Given these methodological problems, it is not surprising that few consistent findings emerge or that some reviewers (e.g., Orme and Rimmer 1981) state that no firm conclusions can be made. Rates of parental alcoholism among families with reported child abuse range from 0 to 92 percent. If we assume a population prevalence of alcoholism of 5–10 percent, the majority of studies suggest increased prevalence of alcoholism among parents who abuse children (Hamilton and Collins 1985). Furthermore, although several psychological disorders (especially depression) have also been related to child abuse, existing research suggests alcoholism is more strongly related than other disorders (Famularo et al. 1986). The relation between alcoholism and spouse abuse appears stronger than the relation with child abuse, but similar cautions must be made concerning research in this area.

Although not firmly established, there are some data suggesting that alcohol-related family violence is related to social class, with a stronger relation noted for the lower social classes, and that episodic drunkenness is more strongly related to family violence than is continuous or near-continuous drunkenness (Steinglass and Robertson 1983). The assumption that COAs are more likely to be abused than nonCOAs still remains a viable one despite the continued need for a convincing empirical demonstration employing methodological improvements. Additionally, the parameters governing the association between alcoholism and family violence need to be systematically studied.

A potentially important, but little researched, area concerns the relation between paternal alcoholism and sexual abuse (incest). Although several studies report very high rates of alcoholism among the parents of incest victims, much additional research in this area is needed (Russell et al. 1985).

Data from a number of studies indicate that exposure to the father's abuse of the mother and the experience of being abused tend to be associated with a range of childhood behavior problems, especially conduct problems in boys (cf. Russell et al. 1985). Although the direction of causality is unclear in these studies, they do suggest that family violence may be one path by which parental alcoholism has a negative impact on offspring.

Family Environment and Family Interactions

A number of recent reviews have summarized the empirical research on the characteristics of alcoholic families (Jacob, Favorini, Meisel, and Anderson 1978; Jacob and Seilhamer 1987; Russell et al. 1985; Seilhamer and Jacob 1990; Steinglass and Robertson 1983; West and Prinz 1987; Wilson and Orford 1978) and the following tentative conclusions seem warranted.

Self-reported family environment. Studies of alcoholic families using the self-report Family Environment Scale (FES) (Clair and Genest 1986; Filstead, McElfresh, and Anderson 1981; Moos and Billings 1982; Moos and Moos 1984) reveal a number of differences between alcoholic and nonalcoholic families. If we consider just those findings replicated in at least one independent study, alcoholic families, compared to nonalcoholic, control families, reported higher levels of conflict and lower levels of family cohesion, expressiveness, independence, intellectual-cultural orientation, and active-recreational orientation. However, it would appear that much of the family disruption may be due to the alcoholic parent's ongoing drinking problems, since the family environment of recovered alcoholics did not differ significantly from that of nonalcoholic control families (Moos and Billings 1982). These studies utilizing the FES demonstrate that the milieu of alcoholic and nonalcoholic families differ on several dimensions, some of which relate to the current drinking status of the alcoholic parent. Recent studies using other self-report measures of family functioning (Benson and Heller 1987; Callan and Jackson 1986) support this conclusion.

Behavioral observations of family interaction. Several studies have examined the interactions among the members of alcoholic families, using a variety of direct observational methods (reviewed in detail by Jacob and Seilhamer 1987, and Steinglass and Robertson 1983). The generalizability of all these studies is limited by their small and possibly unrepresentative samples. They are important, however, because they demonstrate the feasibility of directly studying the interactions in alcoholic families in the laboratory and in the home environment, and they provide intriguing preliminary data.

Perhaps the best-known work in this area is the research program of Steinglass and his associates (Steinglass 1979, 1981a, 1981b; Steinglass, Davis, and Berenson 1977; Steinglass, Weiner, and Mendelson 1971). Major findings from this programmatic research effort support the notions that: (1) alcohol serves a variety of adaptive functions in different families (e.g., permitting the expression of certain behaviors and the inhibition of others), (2) behavioral observations of alcoholic families both at home and in the laboratory do show differences between families characterized by continued abstinence, by continued drinking, or by a mixed/transitional pattern (i.e., phases of alcoholism), and (3) there is a great deal of heterogeneity in the interaction patterns among alcoholic families. Although a number of more specific findings could also be cited, the most important generalizations that can be drawn from this research are that drinking can serve adaptive functions and that there is considerable heterogeneity among alcoholic families.

Studies comparing the family interactions of alcoholic and nonalcoholic families in the laboratory setting (Billings, Kessler, Gomberg, and Weiner 1979; Jacob and Krahn 1988; Jacob and Leonard 1988; Jacob, Ritchey, Cvitkovic, and Blane 1981; O'Farrell and Birchler 1985) demonstrate that alcoholic families show impaired problem-solving and more negative and hostile communications relative to nonalcoholic families. An important finding to emerge from those studies that included control groups of nonalcoholic distressed couples (Billings et al. 1979; Jacob and Krahn 1988; O'Farrell and Birchler 1985) was that disturbed family interaction was not specific to alcoholic families (at least when the alcoholic is not intoxicated) and tended to characterize other problem families.

Effect of alcohol on family interaction. In addition to Steinglass's early work, a number of recent studies have examined the effect of alcohol on family interaction in the laboratory among alcoholic and nonalcoholic families (Billings et al. 1979; Jacob et al. 1981; Jacob and Krahn 1988; Jacob and Leonard 1988; Frankenstein, Hay, and Nathan 1985). Only one of these studies provided strong support for the hypothesis that alcohol consumption serves an adaptive or reinforcing role in the family (Frankenstein et al. 1985), although a difficult to interpret interaction in the Jacob and Krahn (1988) study suggested that more positive (i.e., more adaptive) interactions occurred when a daughter (as opposed to a son) was present. Additional analysis of this study indicated that alcohol consumption had more of an adverse effect on marital interaction among episodic than stable drinkers (Jacob and Leonard, 1988). Furthermore, a recent longitudinal study of drinking in a small sample of male alcoholics characterized by either in-home drinking or out-of-home drinking (Dunn et al. 1987) demonstrated that the effect of drinking on marital functioning appears to differ as a function of the locale of typical alcohol consumption. For in-home drinkers, drinking was associated with increased marital satisfaction. For out-of-home drinkers, both drinking and the anticipation of further drinking were associated with decreased marital satisfaction. These findings suggest that the adaptive point of view might apply to only a subset of alcoholic families.

Great caution is needed in generalizing from laboratory studies (especially those involving alcohol consumption) of family interaction to the general population of alcoholics. In the influential research program of Jacob and his colleagues, several issues need to be recognized. The alcoholic families were volunteers from the community and it is not clear how a voluntarism bias might have influenced the obtained findings. This may be an especially important issue given that alcohol consumption was an integral part of the experimental procedures, and presumably many alcoholic families would decline participation in studies such as these. Also, Jacob screened out subjects with significant comorbidity (antisocial personality disorder, other substance abuse, depression). As we have already seen, comorbidity in alcoholic populations is high, and the exclusion criteria of other psychological disorders could have profound influence on generalizability. Finally, family interaction studies conducted to date rely on intact nuclear families, and the family stability of research participants might be higher than would be expected in the general population. Some of these factors that might limit generalizability should not be necessarily viewed as methodological weaknesses. For example, excluding subjects with coexisting psychopathology makes it easier to attribute group differences to alcoholism per se when an appropriate control group is used (which is important theoretically). However, this practice reduces the value of these findings for the clinician.

Family variables associated with the intergenerational transmission of alcoholism and other dysfunction. In general, the research on family environment and family interaction just reviewed does not address the relation between family variables and offspring adjustment. The study by Moos and Billings (1982) found that offspring adjustment was related to whether or not the alcoholic parent was recovering or relapsed, with only relapsed alcoholic fathers having offspring who were more symptomatic than controls were. A recent study by Chassin, Rogosch, and Barrera (1990) partially replicated this finding by showing that offspring of "recovering" alcoholic fathers (defined as having no symptoms of alcoholism in the past three years) were intermediate in their level of psychopathology compared to offspring of nonalcoholic and current/recent alcoholics. These studies suggest that the ongoing stress of having an "actively" alcoholic parent is an important contributor to offspring adjustment among COAs and that a parent's recovery brings with it an improvement in the psychological status of children. It can be argued that more severe forms of alcoholism are less likely to remit and that it is severity of alcoholism, not recovery, that is the crucial variable. That is, the seeming benefits of recovery might be an artifact of the cross-sectional designs of the studies to date. As more prospective data find their way into the literature, this issue should become resolved.

A limitation of the Moos and Billings (1982) and Chassin et al. (1990) studies is the failure to relate family variables to long-term outcome among COAs. However, several relevant studies do exist and we will turn to those now.

One of the few studies to examine the relation between family variables and later alcoholism was reported by Wolin and his colleagues (Wolin, Bennett, and Noonan 1979; Wolin, Bennett et al. 1980) and is of considerable potential importance. Using semistructured interviews, Wolin et al. (1979, 1980) assessed the extent to which "family rituals" (e.g., celebrating holidays, taking vacations) were disrupted by the drinking of the alcoholic parent. On the basis of these interviews, families were classified as "distinctive" (little or no disruption of family rituals), "subsumptive" (family rituals subsumed by alcoholism), or "intermediate" (some family rituals subsumed by drinking while others spared). Wolin et al. found that subsumptive families and, to a lesser extent, intermediate families tended to produce alcoholic offspring while distinctive families did not. Furthermore, Bennett, Wolin, Reiss, and Teitelbaum (1987) found that COAs who exhibited high levels of "deliberateness" in establishing and maintaining rituals in their own marriage were less likely to become alcoholic themselves. Although these findings are potentially of great importance, they clearly need replication in a larger sample of families. Additionally, third-variable explanations need to be rigorously excluded and detailed characterization of the effects of disrupted family rituals on the offspring *prior* to the development of alcohol problems need to be conducted (to establish the appropriate temporal ordering).

There is some evidence based on prospective (Miller and Jang 1977; Werner 1986) and retrospective (Clair and Genest 1986) studies that family disruption is related to difficulties in adult adjustment among COAs. However, Drake and Vaillant (1988) found that both "environmental disruption and adolescent adjustment were remarkably unrelated to subsequent alcoholic drinking" (p. 803) in their sample of 174 adult male COAs in a thirty-three-year follow-up of subjects originally assessed as adolescents. Additional prospective longitudinal research is needed to determine the parameters governing this relation and to rule out third-variable explanations.

Roles adopted by COAs. Mention should be made of the writings of several clinicians emphasizing the specific types of roles adopted by COAs (Black 1982; Deutsch 1982; Scott 1970; Wegscheider 1977), some of which are postulated to be related to birth order. One role, termed the "superachiever," the "responsible one," or the "family hero," is thought to characterize the older children in the family who assume responsibility for household chores and for rearing the younger children in addition to performing at an above-average level in school. Another role, termed the "problem child," the "acting out child," or the "scapegoat," describes COAs who attempt to divert attention from their parent's drinking problem by getting in trouble with the police or other authority figures. In addition to these two extreme types, other roles COAs are thought to adopt include the "adjuster," who finds relief by changing to fit the demands of the situation, the "placator," who confronts stress by trying to please everyone, and the "family pet" or "mascot," who tends to cope by using humor and by exhibiting endearing behaviors. These roles are thought to persist into adulthood and to result in adverse psychological and interpersonal consequences.

Although the roles described by Black, Wegscheider, and others have appeared to gain the status of fact in the clinical literature, I am not aware of any well-controlled studies that demonstrate that such typologies validly portray the full range of behaviors engaged in by COAs. In a preliminary attempt to identify role types among COAs, Burk (1985) cluster analyzed retrospective reports of childhood coping strategies in a group of college-student COAs. Although there was some support for the notion of "placator" and "adjuster" roles, the retrospective nature of the data and the limited number of coping strategies asked about render these findings tentative. The study, however is important because it demonstrates that these clinical conceptions of childhood roles can, in principle, be tested empirically. Even though clinicians may find the descriptions of COAs to be helpful in their therapeutic endeavors, research supporting the validity of these role types is lacking.

Parental Modeling of Alcohol Use

One of the most straightforward hypotheses concerning the transmission of alcoholism from parent to child is that children's consumption patterns are acquired through imitative social learning or modeling. Although the data from the half-sibling and adoption studies would appear to discount the importance of this type of social learning (and suggest that apparent modeling represents gene/environment covariation), modeling of parents' drinking could in principle represent an important causal pathway for at least some alcoholics. Zucker (1976) reviewed the literature on parental influences on drinking behavior in offspring and noted that a number of intrafamilial as well as extrafamilial factors need to be considered when examining and conceptualizing modeling effects. Parental alcohol use has been shown to be an important correlate of alcohol use in adolescence (cf. Glynn 1981; Russell et al. 1985), but the enduring nature of parental drinking patterns on offspring when they reach adulthood has not been as thoroughly studied. One recent study (Harburg, Davis, and Caplan 1982) examining the correlation between parents' and adult-offspring alcohol consumption found evidence for a significant linear relation between parent and offspring alcohol use but noted a significant quadratic effect (departure from linearity among "very heavy" drinking parents as well as abstaining parents). In general, it appeared that sex-specific (father-son, mother-daughter) modeling was stronger than opposite-sex modeling. Additionally, a number of variables (e.g., education, gender composition of the family) appeared to moderate the general relations. In general, the magnitude of parent-offspring correlations was quite modest (both the linear and quadratic trends account for less than 4 percent of the variance).

Although simple parent-offspring correlations might be rather modest, parental modeling might exert its effects through interaction with other variables related to the family (Russell et al. 1985; Zucker 1976). The importance of such moderator variables has recently been demonstrated by McCord (1988), who showed that father-son transmission of alcoholism was more likely when the alcoholic father was held in high esteem by the mother. In addition, parental values concerning the use of alcohol and other alcohol-related social influence variables might exert important and somewhat independent effects (cf. Glynn 1981).

Special note should be made of a recent experimental study (Chipperfield and Vogel-Sprott 1988) which found that young adult male COAs were especially vulnerable to modeling effects. More specifically, COAs were prone to drink heavily in the presence of a heavy-drinking model, but not in the presence of a light-drinking model.

Although it is clear that alcoholic families are characterized by a negative milieu which appears to have negative psychological effects on family members, available data suggest that most of the morbid effects of alcoholism are temporally specific to periods of active alcoholism. Despite theorizing to the contrary (e.g., Deutsch 1982), families of recovering alcoholics simply are not markedly discriminable from families of nonalcoholics. Furthermore, active alcoholism appears to have the same effect on the family environments that is found with other forms of parental psychopathology. Given the early stage of research on family process in alcoholism, these conclusions must be seen as tentative.

Much additional work needs to be done to determine what family factors relate to the intergenerational transmission of alcoholism. The work of Wolin and his associates represents an important, preliminary step in this direction. Further research on the possible relationship between parental alcoholism and forms of child and spouse abuse is also needed to clarify the nature of any relations and their implications for offspring adjustment. It bears repeating that one cannot infer a causal relationship from data showing that environmental features predict later disorder. An interesting illustration of this is provided by a recent study which replicated the frequently observed correlation between parental divorce and conduct problems in children (Lahey et al. 1988). However, these authors discovered that when antisocial personality disorder in parents was statistically controlled, the association between divorce and conduct disorder disappeared. At least in these data, it appears that both family disruption and child outcome were related to the same factor (parental psychopathology) and that their correlation was spurious.

Clearly, work on family factors in alcoholism is in an embryonic stage and the empirical data base is limited. A particular limitation of the existing data concerns the lack of data on children growing up in one-parent families and step-families. Because family interaction researchers are interested in family dynamics, they have tended to focus on intact families. As demonstrated recently by Hops et al. (1987), environmental correlates of substance use differ between one-parent and two-parent families. Consequently, research examining COAs growing up in one-parent families (which will typically be with a nonalcoholic mother) is needed.

Most of the work has been guided by conceptual frameworks such as family systems and social learning theory, ignoring possible genetic contributions to ostensibly "environmental" influences. Where possible, behavior genetic strategies (e.g., extended twin studies) could be attempted in an effort to more accurately partition environmental and genetic sources of variance.

3 Other Psychological Disorders Associated with a Family History of Alcoholism

In addition to alcoholism and somatizing disorders in offspring, parental alcoholism has been linked to a variety of childhood and adult psychological disorders. As noted earlier, El-Guebaly and Offord (1977) reviewed a range of psychological problems and disorders affecting COAs across the lifespan. Earls (1987), Russell et al. (1985), and West and Prinz (1987) have recently reexamined this extensive literature in greater detail. Consequently, this section will only summarize the major conclusions of these recent reviews except where additional discussion is needed to highlight controversial or complex areas, and when certain topics (e.g., adult anxiety disorders) were not covered in the earlier reviews.

In general, parental psychopathology is associated with a wide range of behavior disorders and offspring maladjustment. Consequently, although COAs might be at risk for a variety of negative outcomes, this does not imply that such outcomes are specific to COAs. Related to this, the high degree of comorbidity found in alcoholics raises the possibility that some of the excess of psychopathology found in offspring might be more a function of comorbid disorder than alcoholism itself. Furthermore, the increased prevalence of psychopathology among COAs does not imply that all offspring of alcoholic parents are affected. In most studies, only a minority of COAs are diagnosed as having specific psychological disorders. Additionally, child psychopathology is often discontinuous with adult psychopathology, and COAs experiencing problems in childhood do not inevitably progress to adult forms of psychopathology. In fact, Drake and Vaillant (1988) found that various ratings of adolescent adjustment correlated weakly (and more typically not at all) with adult alcoholism and personality disorder. Finally, because research on COAs is often designed to assess dysfunction rather than healthy or positive functioning, the literature can be thought of as having an implicit bias in characterizing COA outcomes. An extended discussion of this bias can be found in Heller, Sher, and Benson (1982).

Nevertheless, an appreciation for the range of negative outcomes affecting COAs is important for documenting the extent of risk associated with parental alcoholism and for determining the services needed for this population.

Fetal Alcohol Syndrome (FAS)

It is clear that high levels of maternal alcohol consumption can result in a range of deficits in the infant including dysmorphic facial feature, growth retardation, intellectual impairment, and disrupted behavior patterns such as hyperactivity (cf. Abel 1981; Steinhausen and Spohr 1986; Streissguth, Landesman-Dwyer, Martin, and Smith 1980). There appears to be a subset of FAS children who show a pattern of improvement over time on some features of the syndrome, although academic difficulties, attention deficits and hyperactivity appear to persist for the vast majority (Steinhausen and Spohr 1986). The degree to which low and moderate levels of maternal ethanol consumption have lasting effects on the child and the extent that paternal alcohol consumption results in teratogenic effects have not been clearly resolved.

Drug Abuse

Although the literature on substance abuse in COAs has tended to focus on alcohol abuse rather than drug abuse, a number of recent studies have suggested that COAs are also at risk for drug use and abuse (Chassin et al. 1990; Hesselbrock and Hesselbrock 1986; Johnson, Leonard, and Jacob 1989; Pandina and Johnson 1989; Schuckit 1982a; Schuckit and Sweeney 1987; Sher, Walitzer, Wood, and Brent, in press). A recent adoption study (Cadoret, Troughton, O'Gorman, and Heywood 1986) found that drug abuse in adoptees was related to alcohol problems in the biological relatives, suggesting some genetic contribution to the excess of drug abuse in COAs.

Given Cadoret et al.'s findings, it is of particular interest that a recent study (Ciraulo, Barnhill, Ciraulo, Greenblatt and Shader 1989) found that male COAs experienced a greater euphoriant effect from alprazolam (a benzodiazepine) than nonCOAs. These findings suggest that the vulnerability for alcoholism in COAs may be more general than originally thought. However, it would be premature to conclude that a single liability underlies vulnerability to alcoholism and other forms of substance abuse/dependence. At least two family studies of alcoholism and other drug abuse (Hill, Cloniger, and Ayre 1977; Meller, Rinehart, Cadoret, and Troughton 1988) yielded findings suggestive of independent familial transmission. Additional work is needed to resolve this issue.

Attention Deficit Hyperactivity Disorder (ADHD)

ADHD (formerly termed hyperactivity and minimal brain dysfunction) is a disorder with onset in childhood and is characterized by fidgetiness, distractibility, attentional problems, and impulsivity. Although most studies suggest that there is a link between parental alcoholism and ADHD, numerous methodological issues preclude any firm generalizations concerning this relation (cf. Russell et al. 1985; Walitzer 1990; West and Prinz 1987). This association appears to be stronger when: (1) alcoholic parents serve as the probands (i.e., the index cases) than when ADHD children serve as the probands, and (2) when antisocial fathers are excluded from the analysis.

A major problem in this area is the frequent failure to differentiate ADHD children who do and do not exhibit conduct problems. Since conduct problems appear to be associated with parental alcoholism (see below) and conduct problems frequently coexist with ADHD (cf. Hinshaw 1987), any observed relation between childhood ADHD and parental alcoholism could be attributable to their joint relationship with conduct problems. Conversely, the failure of Drake and Vaillant (1988) to find an association between "hyperactivity" and parental alcoholism could be due to their exclusion of subjects who evidenced delinquency during adolescence.

Although the focus of this discussion is on the extent to which ADHD is related to paternal alcoholism, it should be noted that only ADHD adolescents with coexisting conduct disorders appear to be at risk for later alcoholism and other forms of substance abuse/dependence (Gittelman, Mannuzza, Shenker, and Bonagura 1985; Loney 1980). This suggests that if ADHD (either full-blown or subsyndromal) represents the expression of familial risk for alcoholism as some have suggested (e.g., Tarter 1988), it is only those ADHD individuals who develop conduct problems that are at risk. That is, it is not attention deficits by themselves that appear critical.

Childhood Conduct Problems and Delinquency

As just noted, most research indicates a relation between parental alcoholism and conduct problems (physical aggression, truancy, lying, stealing) in childhood. This relation appears to hold both for diagnosed conduct disorder, as well as for specific conduct problems such as lying, stealing, fighting, truancy, school behavior problems, and police contacts (West and Prinz 1987). To some extent, the relation may be attributable to parental divorce and other problems associated with parental alcoholism. When these environmental variables are statistically controlled, the relation between parental alcoholism and conduct problems is attenuated or eliminated (Offord, Allen, and Abrams 1978; Robins, Murphy, and Breckenridge 1968; Schuckit and Chiles 1978). West and Prinz (1987) suggest that these analyses support the hypothesis that parental alcoholism imposes risk on offspring to the extent that it causes environmental disruption, which is the true causal mechanism. Although this is certainly possible, the alternative hypothesis that the family disruption is a case of gene/environment covariation is also viable. That is, one can legitimately ask the question "Is the relationship between parental divorce and other family stressors and conduct problems still significant after parental alcoholism has been controlled?" In order to answer this question, behavior genetic strategies are necessary.

Childhood Anxiety and Depressive Symptoms

A number of studies show that COAs report higher levels of symptoms of generalized distress such as low self-esteem, high levels of anxiety and depression (see West and Prinz 1987). However, the designs of these studies make it difficult to attribute offspring maladjustment specifically to parental alcoholism. Confounding factors include family disruption and psychiatric comorbidity in the parents.

Adult Anxiety Disorders

A number of family studies have demonstrated a relation between family history of alcoholism and the prevalence of alcoholism. Early studies of "anxiety neurotics" (Cloninger et al. 1981b; Cohen and White 1951; Crowe, Pauls, Slymen, and Noyes 1980; Noyes, Clancy, Crowe, Hoenk, and Slymen 1978) found high rates of alcoholism in the first-degree relatives. More recent studies examining the relation between a family history of alcoholism and specific anxiety disorders (Munjack and Moss 1981; Noyes et al. 1986) suggest that this relationship is found for panic disorder with agoraphobia and social phobia but not simple phobias or uncomplicated panic. A recent review of the literature on the comorbidity of alcoholism and anxiety disorders (Kushner, Sher, and Beitman 1990) notes a similar specificity. Additionally, the general association between anxiety disorders and alcoholism cannot be accounted for by anxiety-related comorbidity in alcoholic relatives (Merikangas et al. 1985). The exact nature of the intergenerational link between alcoholism and anxiety disorders is not yet clear, however. Merikangas et al. propose that individuals vulnerable to anxiety might drink to self-medicate their symptoms. This issue is discussed in greater depth in chapter 8.

Adult Depression

There is considerable comorbidity between alcoholism and depression (at least in females), and increased rates of depression among COAs (Russell et al. 1985). However, the relation between alcoholism and depression is complex. The hypothesis that alcoholism and depression share an underlying genetic diathesis (Winokur, Reich, Rimmer, and Pitts 1970) manifested as alcoholism in male COAs and as depression in female COAs has not been supported by recent data (Cloninger, Reich, and Wetzel 1979; Merikangas et al. 1985). Furthermore, findings from the Danish Adoption Study (Goodwin et al. 1977) suggest that increased depression among (especially female) COAs is most likely environmentally mediated. A number of influences could account for the observed relations between alcoholism and depression, including assortative mating between alcoholics and depressives, depressive comorbidity in the alcoholic parent, family stressors, etc. (Russell et al. 1985).

Antisocial Personality Disorder (ASP)

One of the most interesting and confusing issues in alcoholism research concerns the relation between alcoholism and ASP. Although individuals with ASP frequently abuse alcohol (and could be considered "secondary alcoholics"), and alcoholics frequently act in "antisocial" ways (e.g., Schuckit 1973), at present the dominant view on this relation is that alcoholism and ASP are clinically and conceptually distinct entities (Cadoret, Troughton, and Widmer 1984; Rimmer, Reich, and Winokur 1972; Schuckit, Rimmer, Reich, and Winokur 1970; Winokur et al. 1970, 1971). To make matters more confusing, the behavioral antecedents of both alcoholism and ASP share a number of similarities (e.g., the presence of aggressive traits in childhood) although prospective studies (McCord 1981; Vaillant 1983) suggest differing patterns of early antecedents for the two disorders. Furthermore, adoption data appear to indicate that these disorders are genetically unrelated (Bohman 1978; Cadoret, O'Gorman, Troughton, and Heywood 1985). Consequently, although there is an excess of COAs having ASP (cf. Russell et al. 1985), it is very possible that this excess is due to primary ASP diagnoses in the parent, not to parental alcoholism per se. A further complexity is that antisocial behaviors, not necessarily culminating in ASP, may characterize a subset of COAs.

Although the dominant view is that primary alcoholism and ASP are etiologically and clinically distinct disorders, Cloninger's (1987b) theory of personality disorders posits that the underlying temperamental makeup of ASP is "high novelty seeking, low harm avoidance, and low reward dependence" (p. 584), the same pattern of characteristics that underlie the form of alcoholism he labels Type 2 (Cloninger, 1987a). In a similar vein, other theorists (e.g., Gorenstein 1987; Gorenstein and Newman 1980) have hypothesized that alcoholics and psychopaths share a common underlying deficit.

At present, it is difficult to resolve the issue of the basic distinctiveness of a form of primary alcoholism (e.g., Type 2) and ASP. Although clinical practice and family studies suggest that these are basically distinct disorders, there are many potentially important commonalities and well thought-out theoretical positions linking these disorders to a similar etiological process. Furthermore, at least one study has failed to find differences between offspring of primary alcoholics and offspring of patients with ASP (Earls, Reich, Jung, and Cloninger 1988).

A limitation of existing research is that family and diagnostic studies have not only failed to consider heterogeneity in primary alcoholism but also heterogeneity in ASP. This contrasts sharply with earlier work on psychopathy which distinguished "primary" or "true" psychopathy from "secondary" or "neurotic" psychopathy (e.g., Hare 1970). Related to this, a recent study by Smith and Newman (1990) indicates that alcoholism is related to only one dimension of psychopathy. Using Hare's (1985) two-factor Psychopathy Checklist (PCL) in a sample of institutionalized criminal offenders, Smith and Newman found that lifetime substance abuse (both alcohol abuse and drug abuse) was strongly related to PCL-factor 2 (the general social deviance factor) but unrelated to PCL-factor 1 (the factor assessing the core personality features of psychopathy such as callous egocentricity), indicating the importance of considering heterogeneity among subjects classified as antisocial. At this point, additional data that not only accounts for the heterogeneity of alcoholism but of ASP, and that examines the unfolding of ASP and alcoholic symptomatology over the lifespan, will help resolve this issue.

Interpersonal Difficulties

The clinical literature on COAs (Black 1982; Deutsch 1982; Seixas and Youcha 1985; Woititz 1983) describe a number of interpersonal problems encountered by COAs. These include problems in developing trust in relationships and in becoming overly self-reliant or overly dependent. These clinical writers have characterized COAs as having high levels of guilt, shame, insecurity, fear, and anger—characteristics likely to lead to interpersonal difficulties. Although the clinical literature is rich with descriptions of the difficulties COAs encounter in the interpersonal sphere, the research literature addressing this issue is scanty. West and Prinz (1987) recently concluded in their review that the "paucity of empirical data in this area makes it impossible to state unequivocally what impact parental alcoholism has on children's interpersonal functioning" (p. 210). Variability in sample composition and lack of consistency of findings plague the few relevant studies. Significantly, none of the studies in this literature used behavioral observations or sociometric techniques or other objective methods of determining interpersonal functioning. (However, Burk and Sher 1990, have recently shown that adolescents attribute a number of negative stereotypes to

COAs.) A recent study by Black, Bucky, and Wilder-Padilla (1986) demonstrated that adult COAs report a number of interpersonal problems including problems in trusting people, problems in identifying feelings, problems in expressing feelings, dependency problems, work-relationship problems, and intimacy problems. Although this study is noteworthy for the large samples employed and the range of behaviors assessed, the highly selected nature of the COA and nonCOA samples limits confidence in the generalizability of these findings. Given the importance that clinical workers attach to the interpersonal problems of COAs, additional research is needed to clarify the interpersonal consequences of having an alcoholic parent.

Summary

It is clear that COAs are at increased risk for a variety of negative outcomes. However, there are a number of important issues raised by the literature; the most important, perhaps, is specificity. Although certain disorders may be found in excess among COAs, some of this observed relation might be related to parental deviance (psychiatric comorbidity in the proband or the spouse, family disruption, parental separation), which may be a more important determinant of psychopathology than any underlying genetic diathesis specific to alcoholism.

A recent study by Jacob and Leonard (1986) illustrates a number of these important issues. First, although as a group male and female COAs appeared more dysfunctional on parent ratings on the Child Behavior Checklist (CBCL) than children of parents with no ostensible pathology, relatively few evidenced high levels of dysfunction and most appeared to be well-functioning. Second, when COAs were compared to a group of children of depressed parents (COD), few differences were found, indicating that the problems COAs experience are not unique to that group. Third, COAs, CODs, and control-group children could not be distinguished on teacher ratings of these groups, suggesting that some of the problems of COAs might be specific to the home content, which would not be reflected in teacher ratings. Fourth, among COAs, degree of dysfunction was related to the severity of both parental psychopathology and drinking problems. This last point is amplified by a recent study (Moos and Billings 1982) which found that childhood behavior problems varied as a positive function of the alcoholic parent's current drinking status; child behavior problems were higher in relapsed, but not in recovering, alcoholic families. Of equal interest, disruption of family structure and functioning correlated with the level of the child's emotional disturbance. Future research on psychopathology among COAs needs to pay more attention to these issues.

4 Mediators and Moderators of Risk: Conceptualizing Vulnerability and Protective Factors

This chapter will review several important conceptual distinctions, especially those related to processes that mediate and moderate risk. The emphasis is conceptual, and empirical data are not reviewed. Later chapters will describe the extent to which various mediating and moderating processes are supported by available research.

The Concept of Vulnerability

In the chapters to follow, numerous studies exploring possible differences between COAs and nonCOAs are reviewed. The scientific motivation underlying most of these studies is the desire to identify characteristics that predispose COAs to develop specific outcomes, particularly alcoholism and related problems. These predisposing characteristics can be termed vulnerability factors. Vulnerability refers to an increased likelihood of developing disorders, not the presence of expressed or manifest disorder. This distinction between vulnerability and expressed disorder has critical theoretical and methodological importance.

First, it needs to be stressed that not all COAs should be assumed to possess significant genetic vulnerability. Under most conceivable genetic models, only a proportion of COAs are expected to have substantial vulnerability. Vulnerability can be conceptualized as being either continuously distributed in the population (e.g., along a normal distribution as illustrated in Figure 4.1) or as discretely distributed (e.g., as two groups: nonvulnerable and vulnerable). Although Figure 4.1 illustrates that as a group COAs possess greater vulnerability than nonCOAs, there is considerable overlap between the vulnerability distributions of COAs and nonCOAs. Some COAs appear to have relatively little vulnerability, some nonCOAs appear to have substantial vulnerability.

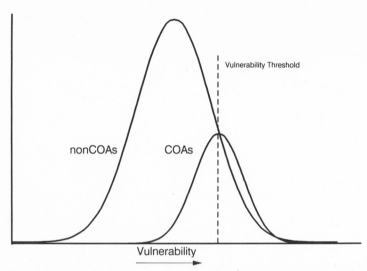

Figure 4.1. Hypothetical distribution of vulnerability in COAs and nonCOAs. Figure illustrates the overlap of vulnerability between COAs and nonCOAs as well as the high proportion of COAs expected to possess substantial vulnerability.

Conceptualizing vulnerability in discrete terms, we can view individuals above the "vulnerability threshold" marked in Figure 4.1 as possessing significant vulnerability and those below the threshold as possessing virtually no vulnerability. We can then compare the proportions of COAs and nonCOAs who possess vulnerability. In the hypothetical example in Figure 4.1, approximately 50 percent of the COAs could be considered vulnerable compared to only 10 percent of the nonCOAs. This is a large difference and suggests that COAs are, other factors being equal, approximately five times more likely to become alcoholic than nonCOAs. *However in this example, because there are many more nonCOAs, the majority of individuals with significant vulnerability are nonCOAs.*

The reasonable assumption that not all COAs possess significant vulnerability means that the failure of some COAs to develop alcohol or other problems does not necessarily indicate that some special "protective" factor was at work mitigating the harmful effects of parental alcoholism. Although protective factors are undoubtedly important (as discussed later in this chapter), good outcomes among some COAs are likely to occur simply because these individuals never inherited vulnerability. Even within the same family, one child might inherit vulnerability while his/her sibling does not (unless of course the siblings are MZ twins). Consequently, discordance for alcoholism or other problems among COA siblings does not imply that the "spared" sibling was exposed to more benign environmental factors than the affected sibling, although some writers have inferred this.

It is also important to note that *not all individuals with vulnerability will develop alcoholism or other problems*. Vulnerability implies only increased likelihood for developing problems, not the inevitability of problems.

Identifying Mediators of Risk

Closely related to the concept of vulnerability is the concept of a *mediator* of risk. According to Baron and Kenny (1986), a mediating variable is one which accounts for the relation between a predictor and a criterion variable. Extending this definition to research on COAs, we can view a *mediator* as a variable that "accounts for" the relation between alcoholism in a parent and the eventual development of alcoholism or related problems in the offspring. By "accounting for," we mean describing the mechanism of how alcoholism in a parent leads to problems in the offspring. In order for a variable to be a candidate for a mediator, three zero-order, bivariate conditions must be met: (1) family history must be correlated with the outcome variable (e.g., alcoholism), (2) family history must be correlated with the presumed mediator, and (3) the presumed mediator must be correlated with the outcome variable. These three bivariate conditions are schematically illustrated in the top panel of Figure 4.2. (More detailed discussions of the concept of mediation in behavioral research and, more specifically, in research on COAs, can be found in two recent papers [Baron and Kenny 1986; Rogosch, Chassin, and Sher 1990]).

In the case of complete or "perfect mediation," the *entire* relation between family history and the outcome variable can be statistically explained by the mediator. This is illustrated by the path diagram in the middle panel of Figure 4.2. In this figure, the direct path between family history of alcoholism and alcoholism in the offspring is no longer significant when the indirect path (through the mediator) is taken into account. However, for a number of reasons (including the heterogeneity of alcoholism, measurement error, etc.), it is unlikely that perfect mediation will ever be found. Partial mediation, however, can be identified when the three bivariate conditions are met, but a significant direct path between family history of alcoholism and offspring alcoholism remains after statistically accounting for the indirect path involving the mediator. That is, the mediator accounts for *part of* the relation between family history and the outcome measure.

These concepts can be illustrated more concretely by providing numerical examples. Using hypothetical data, Figure 4.3 gives an example of what perfect mediation might look like. In this example, all the explainable variance in the family history of alcoholism/offspring alcoholism relation is accounted for by the mediator. That is, the semipartial correlation between family history of alcoholism and offspring alcoholism (after taking out the

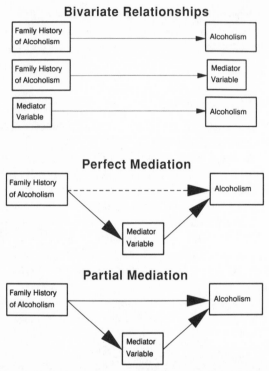

Figure 4.2. Schematic illustrating the necessary bivariate conditions for demonstrating mediation, and the paths implied by perfect and partial mediation. Solid lines represent significant simple and semipartial correlations, and dashed line represents a nonsignificant semipartial correlation.

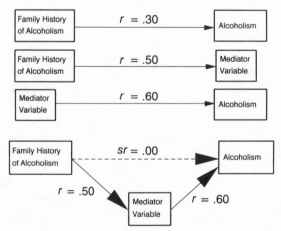

Figure 4.3. Hypothetical example of perfect mediation. Note that the mediator completely accounts for the relation between family history of alcoholism and offspring alcoholism.

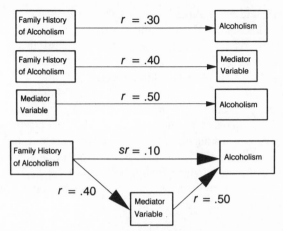

Figure 4.4. Hypothetical example of partial mediation. Note that the mediator explains the majority of the relation between family history of alcoholism and offspring alcoholism, but that a significant amount of variance in offspring alcoholism remains unaccounted for.

effect of the mediator on offspring alcoholism) does not differ significantly from zero.

Figure 4.4 similarly portrays an example of partial mediation. In this case, although some of the relation between family history of alcoholism and offspring alcoholism is accounted for by the mediator, the direct path (the semipartial correlation between family history of alcoholism and offspring alcoholism) remains significant but is smaller than the simple correlation between family history of alcoholism and offspring alcoholism. Although these are hypothetical data, the simple correlation between family history of alcoholism and offspring alcoholism is probably close to the $r = .30$ assumed here.

As suggested earlier, error in the measurement of the presumed mediator will tend to lead to an overestimate of the direct path between family history of alcoholism and offspring alcoholism. That is, unreliable measurement will preclude the ability of the mediator to account for the entire relation between the predictor and outcome variable. If there is adequate power to detect small effects, then the direct path will remain significant and only "partial" mediation will be demonstrated. Structural-equation modeling with latent variables can be used to address the problems of measurement error when multiple indicators of each type of variable are available (Hayduk 1987).

Multiple Mediators

Up until this point, only the case of single mediators has been considered. However, we can easily consider multiple mediators of risk. For example, it has been suggested that COAs possess vulnerability on multiple, independent dimensions of temperament (Cloninger 1987a; Tarter, Alterman, and

Edwards 1985) and on multiple, independent measures of ethanol sensitivity (Schuckit and Gold 1988). Consequently, we can consider the case of multiple mediators of risk by extending the basic model as illustrated in Figure 4.5. The notion of polygenic (or more generally, multifactorial) transmission suggests (but does not dictate) that multiple mechanisms may be responsible for intergenerational transmission of risk in alcoholism. Multiple mechanisms are also implicated by theories positing that different alcoholism subtypes are associated with unique underlying mechanisms. However, for evaluating mediational hypotheses surrounding different subtypes, testing of hypothesized mediational mechanisms in separate groups of offspring from parents with different forms of parental alcoholism (e.g., Type 1 vs. Type 2), rather than considering parental alcoholism a homogeneous construct in a single analysis, would be most appropriate.

Mediational Chains

The research on differences between COAs and nonCOAs has identified a range of possible differences at varying levels of biopsychosocial organization. For example, studies have reported differences related to neurotransmitter functioning, behavioral effects of alcohol, and self-reported expectancies of reinforcement from alcohol. Rather than identifying independent deficits, it is plausible that research efforts on these seemingly disparate variables are identifying a set of related phenomena. It is possible that individual differences in neurotransmitter functioning mediate the magnitude of reinforcement from alcohol which, in turn, mediates formation of favorable expectancies of alcohol consumption (by providing the direct experience critical to the devel-

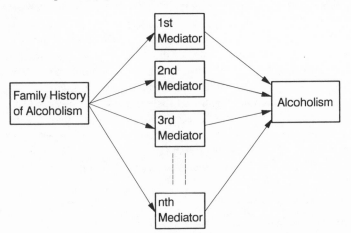

Figure 4.5. Schematic illustrating how family-history risk can be conceptualized as being mediated by multiple mechanisms.

opment of expectancies), which mediate alcohol-seeking behavior. These mediational chains can also be modeled as illustrated in Figure 4.6. Presumably, as interdisciplinary research on COAs progresses, researchers will be able to conceptualize complex causal chains across levels of biopsychosocial organization. However, at present, the data base for attempting such modeling is extremely limited.

The Moderation of Risk: Protective and Exacerbating Factors

In addition to considering variables that appear to mediate risk, we can also think of variables that *moderate* risk. According to Baron and Kenny (1986), "a moderator is a . . . variable that affects the direction and/or strength of the relation between a . . . predictor variable and a . . . criterion variable" (p. 1174). In terms of COA research, we can think of a moderator variable as one that attenuates or magnifies the relation between parental alcoholism and offspring adjustment; that is, a variable that demonstrates a significant interaction with family history in predicting offspring adjustment.

At first glance, it might appear to be important to distinguish moderators that exacerbate risk from moderators that protect against risk. However, in most cases the distinction is more apparent than real. For example, assume that the quality of family communication moderates the effect of parental alcoholism on offspring adjustment. Would it make more sense to say that good family communication skills are a protective factor or that poor skills are an exacerbating factor? Similarly, most possible moderators can be described as either a protective factor or an exacerbating factor. Consequently, the term "moderating factor" is probably more descriptive and less value laden then the more commonly used term "protective factor."

Simple Moderation

The distinction between variables that mediate and moderate risk has been clearly described by Rutter (1987). "The crucial difference between . . . protection processes and risk mechanisms is that the latter lead directly to disorder (either strongly or weakly), whereas the former operate indirectly

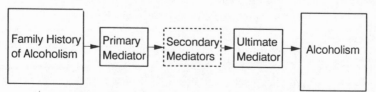

Figure 4.6. Schematic illustrating how mediational processes can be conceptualized as involving a series of causally linked (chained) processes.

with their effects apparent only by virtue of their interactions with the risk variable" (p. 319). The idea that a variable can moderate the effect of parental alcoholism on offspring adjustment is graphically illustrated by hypothetical data in the top panel of Figure 4.7. In this example, the likelihood of parental alcoholism leading to offspring alcoholism is relatively high for individuals high on the moderating variable but not for those individuals who are low. In contrast, the moderator variable had no effect on offspring alcoholism for individuals who lacked a family history of alcoholism. Interactive patterns such as the one depicted here indicate a moderator type relation.

Moderated Mediation

Although it is important to identify factors that moderate the relation between parental alcoholism and offspring outcomes, it needs to be reemphasized that not all COAs can be assumed to be at risk for alcoholism and other negative outcomes; not all COAs are vulnerable. Ultimately, we wish to be able to identify variables that moderate the relation between *vulnerability* and outcome; that is, variables that moderate the effect of the mediator. This is illustrated in the bottom panel of Figure 4.7.

Comparison of the top and bottom panels of this figure reveals two important principles: (1) classification of subjects on the basis of their true vulnerability should yield a more accurate prediction of who is likely to develop negative outcome than classification based on family history, and (2) the magnitude of the interaction involving the moderating variable should be stronger when it involves true vulnerability than when it involves family history alone.

The idea of moderating the influence of true vulnerability (based on the mediating variable), as opposed to the more distal predictor variable (i.e., family history), has been termed *moderated mediation* (Baron and Kenny 1986). A primary goal of research on COAs is to be able to specify mediational (risk) processes and how they might be moderated by any of a number of biopsychosocial variables.

Issues Surrounding the Heterogeneity of Alcoholism

As discussed earlier with respect to mediating variables, an implication of heterogeneity of alcoholism is that different moderator models may need to be developed for different forms of alcoholism. For example, Cloninger (1987a) appears to have shown that one form of alcoholism (Type 1) demonstrates significant moderation by social class while the other major form (Type 2) does not. This discrepancy points to the need to take heterogeneity into account when developing and testing etiological models of alcoholism.

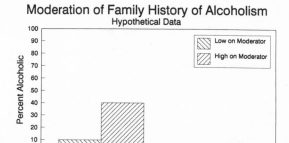

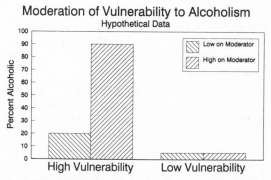

Figure 4.7. Hypothetical illustration of simple moderation (top panel) and moderated mediation (bottom panel).

Confusion between Mediators and Moderators

As previously described (Rogosch et al. 1990), a number of recent investigations have failed to employ appropriate methodologies for establishing mediation or moderation. Werner's (1986) prospective study of temperament and infant-caregiver interaction and Wolin et al.'s (1979, 1980) retrospective studies of family interaction variables are often viewed as documenting personal and family variables that serve protective functions. However, in these studies, analyses focus on differences between transmitter and nontransmitter families with alcoholic parents. That is, these studies show a simple effect of a putative moderator among COAs. This approach is methodologically flawed because it is not capable of distinguishing between moderator and mediator variables; both types of variables (as well as independent risk factors) would be expected to show such simple effects. In order to distinguish mediator variables, moderator variables, and independent risk factors, control groups of nonCOAs are necessary.

Some Related Issues in Correlational Research

As is always true in correlational research, correlation does not demonstrate causation. Several problems for correlational research on COAs, specifically for research on mediators and moderators are described below.

Direction of Causality

In order to have confidence in a mediational model, the direction of causation must be unambiguous. In the case of simple mediation, this means that the outcome variable should be shown not to cause the mediator variable which in turn should be shown not to cause family history. Although it is difficult to imagine how a characteristic of the offspring could "cause" family history of alcoholism, a recent experimental study (Lang et al. 1989) illustrates this point. This well-controlled study demonstrated that noncompliant child behavior increased the drinking behavior of adults who were forced to interact with them. Extrapolating from these data, one can speculate that the stress of parenting oppositional or conduct-disordered children leads to excessive alcohol consumption in some parents. In a related vein, it has been suggested that behavior problems in offspring of alcoholics is mediated in part by family conflict and poor parental disciplining practices (cf. West and Prinz 1987). However, there is considerable evidence indicating that problem behavior in children can cause family disruption and severely challenge parenting ability. Although the generality of the Lang et al. (1989) study is an open question and there are independent reasons for believing that parental alcoholism *causes* certain forms of childhood disorder, existing data indicate that direction of causality can never be casually assumed.

Third Variables

In attempting to model mediator and moderator relationships, failure to consider so-called third variables can lead to erroneous conclusions. Third variables can be thought of as unmeasured variables that exert a causal influence on both the mediator (or moderator) and outcome variable. For example, suppose it were found that family conflict met the statistical criteria for mediating the relation between parental alcoholism and offspring alcoholism. Even if direction of causality could be shown to be consistent with a mediator interpretation of family conflict, it remains possible that a third variable related to parental alcoholism "caused" both family conflict and offspring alcoholism. It is possible that the third variable in this case is the alcoholic parent's aggressive personality traits which bring him into constant conflict with his spouse, causing family conflict. It is also possible that there is a heritable component to these characteristics which are passed on to offspring and in turn lead to alcoholism. In this case, the true mediator, a personality trait, is never discovered and a mediator role for exposure to marital conflict can be erroneously inferred.

This last example brings up a special class of third-variable problems that is particularly important when studying a disorder with a genetic component, *genotype-environment correlation* (Plomin et al. 1977). Genotype-environment correlation refers to the idea that environmental variables can be correlated with an individual's genetic makeup. Plomin et al. (1977) distinguish three separate types of genotype-environment correlation: (1) passive, (2) reactive, and (3) active. The *passive* type usually refers to the situation where genetically related individuals share a common environment. The earlier example of the correlation between aggressive personality traits and exposure to marital conflict represents a form of passive genotype-environment correlation. The *reactive* type refers to the situation where environmental phenomena are directly provoked by factors directly related to an individual's genetic makeup. For example, genetically related aggressive traits might elicit coercive responses from caregivers, or intellectual impairment might lead to increased likelihood of a number of psychosocial failure experiences. However, it should be stressed that reactive genotype-environment correlation need not be based on others' reactions to genetically related overt behavior. Genetically related physical characteristics (small stature, physical attractiveness) "pull" for different reactions from others in many situations. The *active* type refers to the situation where individuals will seek out specific environmental situations that are consistent with their genetic predisposition. Extraverts might preferentially seek out social situations over more solitary ones; sensation seekers might seek out various types of stimulating activities.

Although environmental correlates of specific genotypes can sometimes be thought of as spurious in a causal sense, this isn't necessarily the case. One can consider the situation where physical unattractiveness is related to adverse mental health outcomes such as depression. Genetically related unattractiveness might be correlated with social rejection, and it is quite possible that it is the social rejection, not unattractiveness per se, that is intimately linked to the development of depression.

The point of emphasizing the concept of genotype-environment correlation is to point out that conceptually distinguishing environmental from genetic sources of influence is not as straightforward as it might seem at first glance. A number of presumed environmental risk factors associated with parental alcoholism (parental separation and divorce, family conflict, poor parenting practices) might represent instances of genotype-environment correlation. Further discussion of the genotype-environment correlation and approaches to measuring it are provided by Plomin et al. (1977).

The above discussion has attempted to provide a basic overview of the concept of mediation and moderation using techniques based on what statisticians have termed the linear model. More extensive discussions of linear models can be found in texts on regression analysis (e.g., Cohen and Cohen

1983; Pedhazur 1982) and structural-equation modeling that employs latent variables (e.g., Hayduk 1987).

Summary

The concepts of mediation and moderation of risk are central to an understanding of risk and protective processes among COAs. Mediators can be thought of as variables that ''account for'' or explain the mechanism of how parental alcoholism leads to problems in offspring. Moderators can be thought of as variables that affect the strength and the direction of the effect of parental alcoholism on offspring problems. Basic strategies for assessing mediator and moderator relationships are described above. As is true in all correlational investigations, care must be taken to establish directionality and to eliminate third-variable explanations before great confidence can be placed in empirical findings. A special kind of third-variable problem, genotype-environment correlation, warrants special attention in research on COAs.

5 Cross-sectional and Prospective Research on COAs: Rationale and Methodological Issues

Family, twin, half-sibling, and adoption studies demonstrate strong familial transmission of alcoholism and indicate a role for genetic factors. An understanding of the etiology of alcoholism and other problems associated with a family history of alcoholism requires that the specific factors responsible for this transmission be identified and their etiologic roles be described. To date, the search for potential mediators of risk has focused on numerous variables at different levels of biopsychosocial meaning. For example, role modeling, personality variables, subjective responses to ethanol, and biochemical characteristics have each been studied in an effort to understand the etiological link between parental and offspring alcoholism. Nevertheless, it needs to be stressed that such cross-sectional, high-risk studies can show only that a variable is a *potential* mediator. Additional data may bolster the case for etiological relevance. For example, if the high-risk/low-risk ratio of a given characteristic approximates the relative risk associated with the risk factor, this suggests that the characteristic may index risk. However, proof of a mediating role requires establishing the correct temporal order (direction of causality), prospective prediction, statistically accounting for the relationship between family history and offspring outcome (as discussed at length in Chapter 4), and the logical exclusion of third-variable explanations.

The Rationale for the High-Risk Design

The basic rationale for the high-risk design was laid out more than twenty years ago in an influential article by Mednick and McNeill (1968). In reviewing the literature on schizophrenia, based primarily on cross-sectional and retrospective studies of schizophrenia, Mednick and McNeill concluded that existing research on the etiology of schizophrenia was severely limited. They based this conclusion on their observations that schizophrenics were so affected by their illness that studying them told us more about the consequences of schizophrenia than about its causes. Although they noted that use of childhood records (e.g., from archival sources) helped get around a number of problems, use of these records involves a number of sampling problems and data insufficiencies. To remedy this problem, they recommended the "longitudinal study of young children at high risk for schizophrenia" (p. 687). The recommendation for longitudinal designs stemmed from the need to distinguish antecedents from consequences of disorder using research-focused assessment strategies. The recommendation for utilizing high-risk subjects stemmed from the need to concentrate resources when studying an infrequent disorder such as schizophrenia (which is generally thought to have a lifetime prevalence < 1 percent). Additionally, Mednick and McNeill (1968) pointed out that, although prospective data are optimal, the high-risk method had cross-sectional utility in that "differences between the high- and low-risk groups may relate to factors predisposing to mental illness" (p. 689). Because the high-risk method has the potential to discover "predisposing" factors prior to the ultimate development of the disorder, it has been frequently employed in the study of psychopathology (especially schizophrenia), and in the last ten years numerous cross-sectional high-risk studies have been conducted in the area of alcoholism (these are the focus of the research reviewed in Chapters 6 and 7).

It needs to be reemphasized that high-risk vs. low-risk differences on a variable do not necessarily imply that the variable is etiologically important in the development of disorder (see Chapter 4). As McNeill and Kaij (1979) have pointed out, these differences "are most correctly interpreted as reflecting the characteristics, correlates and/or consequences of the risk criterion" (p. 548). Thus, high-risk vs. low-risk differences, by themselves, cannot be interpreted as reflecting either genetic or environmental causes, and demonstration of a mediational role involves the considerations discussed in Chapter 4 and prospective follow-up data.

It also needs to be emphasized that the high-risk method has a potentially important limitation for developing general theories of etiology for a disorder. If etiologically distinct familial and nonfamilial forms of disorder exist, the high-risk method may not tell us much about the etiology of the nonfamilial forms. This is particularly important in schizophrenia research, where the overwhelming majority of schizophrenics (approximately 90 percent) do not have schizophrenic relatives, and where the base rate of schizophrenia in control populations is so low that there would be insufficient cases of a nonfamilial form for adequate study. Fortunately, high-risk research in alcoholism is less likely to be limited in generalizability. Because at least one-third of alcoholics have family histories of alcoholism (Cotton 1979), if a familial form of alcoholism is etiologically distinct, high-risk research is likely to yield results of relevance for a substantial proportion of alcoholics. Also, the prevalence of alcoholism is sufficiently high that longitudinal follow-up of low-risk subjects can feasibly provide data concerning the antecedents of nonfamilial alcoholism.

Methodological Issues Surrounding Ascertainment

High-risk research on COAs has been plagued by numerous serious weaknesses. Although the state-of-the-art has been improving in recent years, a review of common problems in this area is important for evaluating existing empirical findings and designing future studies.

Ascertainment of Family History: Direct Assessment of Alcoholic Parents vs. Family History Method

The method of ascertainment of family history of alcoholism varies considerably across studies. A number of studies rely solely upon self-identification methods (asking subjects about parents' and other near-relatives' drinking behavior and consequences). This general approach of assessing family history on the basis of a subject's reports of his relatives' behavior is usually referred to as the *family history method*. In psychopathology research this method is found to show high test-retest reliability (Andreasen, Endicott, Spitzer, and Winokur 1977; Zimmerman, Coryell, Pfohl, and Stangl 1988). However, the family history approach tends to underestimate psychopathology in relatives (Andreasen et al. 1977; Andreasen, Rice, Endicott, Reich, and Coryell 1986; Thompson, Orvaschel, Prusoff, and Kidd 1982). These latter studies indicate that it is uncommon for an individual to indicate the presence of a disorder in a relative when none actually exists (i.e., specificity is high). This conclusion mirrors that of Cotton (1979) who reviewed existing family studies of alcoholism and concluded "that when a first-degree relative of an alcoholic is reported to be an alcoholic or have a psychiatric disease, it is almost certain to be true" (p. 108). However, false negatives are not uncommon (sensitivity is found to be only moderately good in most studies). That is, we can have less confidence in the denial of a subject concerning relatives' drinking behavior. This bias toward underreporting suggests that a limitation of the family history method is that some proportion of subjects deemed to have no alcoholic parents (i.e., low-risk subjects) will be misclassified. However, given the prevalence of alcoholism in the general population, it seems unlikely that this proportion of misclassified subjects would ever exceed 10 percent (using conservative assumptions).

The limitations of the family history method would appear to be magnified when additional diagnostic dimensions are being considered. For example, the ability to distinguish among alcoholism subtypes, determine the extent of comorbidity, and differentiate primary from secondary psychopathology is likely to be considerably less when relying on offspring reports than when having direct interviews with the target family member. Consequently, it is almost always desirable to obtain direct assessments of family members, especially when more extensive and subtle diagnostic information is required.

Direct evaluation of parents and other relatives is often impractical, if not impossible, however, because these relatives may be in distant locations, deceased, or otherwise unavailable. Even when relatives are available, direct assessments may be extremely intrusive for relatives and potential subjects, and may limit cooperation. Furthermore, even when direct interviews with relatives are obtained, the family history method can be used to supplement these direct assessments because, in some situations, the reporting of a relative might be more veridical than the direct reports of a targeted individual. Consequently, the family history method will probably continue to play a major role in identifying COAs.

Instruments for Assessing Family History

Although the family history method appears to be a viable strategy for identifying COAs, a number of different approaches to assessing family history have been employed, and these approaches appear to vary in their adequacy. Perhaps the most thoroughly researched technique is the Family History–Research Diagnostic Criteria (FH-RDC) interview developed by Endicott, Andreasen, and Spitzer (1978). An updated, similar instrument, the Family Informant Schedule and Criteria (FISC), has recently been introduced (Mannuzza, Fryer, Endicott, and Klein 1985). Strengths of both of these interviews are the referencing of assessments to established diagnostic criteria (Research Diagnostic Criteria [RDC] and DSM-III) and the inclusion of items assessing other diagnostic categories facilitating assessment of comorbidity.

As both clinical and research interest in COAs has increased in recent years, a number of new instruments have been developed to assist in efficiently screening large numbers of subjects for a history of alcoholism in parents and other relatives. Some of these instruments represent adaptations of instruments originally developed for direct screening for alcoholism. The 25-item Michigan Alcoholism Screening Test (MAST; Selzer 1971) and the 13-item Short MAST (SMAST; Selzer, Vinokur, and van Rooijen 1975) have been referenced to parents' drinking to yield measures of parental alcoholism. This approach shows moderate levels of validity when compared with parents' completion of the same form (Levenson, Oyama, and Meek 1987) and good reliability across siblings (Sher and Descutner 1986). Other approaches using similar screening inventories to assess parental alcoholism would appear to have similar characteristics (Mann, Sobell, Sobell, and Pavan 1985; O'Malley, Carey, and Maisto 1986; Vogel-Sprott, Chipperfield, and Hart 1985). In our experience of screening for a family history of alcoholism in college students and young adults, we have found it useful to validate subjects' family histories (both negative and positive) by administering a structured interview such as the FH-RDC to subjects passing an initial screen. A second assessment using an interview format permits an assessment of consistency across time and assessment format. Furthermore, greater probing and clarification is possible in the interview format. We also attempt to obtain direct assessments from parents. However, our experience is that a significant proportion of subjects (approximately 70 percent) refuse to give permission to contact parents, and of those parents we do attempt to contact, only about 60 percent agree to provide details on their own drinking problems.

In contrast to screening interviews that are based on items assessing alcohol-related consequences and dependence symptoms, the Children of Alcoholics Screening Test (CAST; Jones 1983) is referenced to the impact of a parent's drinking on the child. The CAST includes items such as "Have you ever lost sleep because of a parent's drinking?" "Did you ever feel like hiding or emptying a parent's bottle of liquor?" "Have you ever felt sick, cried, or had a 'knot' in your stomach after worrying about a parent's drinking?" Although it would appear highly likely that a child endorsing a sufficient number of CAST items would indeed have an alcoholic parent, there are at least three related limitations of this approach beyond those of the family history approach more generally. First, since many of the items are based on subjective reactions, the personality characteristics and the developmental level of the child during periods of active alcoholism cloud the distinction between the extent of parental drinking problems and offspring adjustment. Second, because the diagnosis of family history of alcoholism is based on the direct experience of the child, the scale may be relatively insensitive to parental alcoholism that has been in recovery since the time of the child's birth or that has occurred in an absent or noncustodial parent. Third, because the items of the CAST do not reference traditional criteria of alcohol abuse and dependence, the relationship between the CAST and more traditional diagnostic assessments is uncertain. Although validity data on the CAST are reported by Jones (1983), they are of limited utility. Even though the CAST was found to have excellent sensitivity, all family history positive subjects had a parent who had sought treatment for either their own or their spouse's alcoholism. Consequently, parental alcoholism was clearly a salient, well-defined entity in the family. Furthermore, the CAST appeared to have only moderate specificity. This pattern of findings is the opposite of those traditionally found using family history techniques and, therefore, is suspect. An additional limitation of the CAST is that specific consequences are not attributed to each parent separately. Consequently it is difficult to determine to what extent endorsed problems reflect paternal or maternal drinking.

Although the CAST would appear to be of limited use for high-risk studies and other research purposes seeking to determine a family history of alcoholism per se, it would appear to be a useful instrument for assessing specific life events a child may encounter because of a parent's drinking. As such it might be considered a COA-specific life-events measure, rather than a diagnostic instrument. In this light, it should also be noted that other measures for assessing COA-specific life events have also been developed (Roosa, Sandler, Gehring, Beales, and Cappo 1988).

In addition to multi-item self-report questionnaires for diagnosing family history of alcoholism, several investigators have relied on single items to identify COAs. These include: "Have you ever wished that either or both of your parents would drink less?" (DiCicco, Davis, Travis, and Orenstein 1983–84; DiCicco, Davis, and Orenstein 1984), "Has the drinking of either parent created a problem for you?" (Biek 1981), "Have you ever considered either of your biological parents to be an alcoholic?" and "Do you consider that either of your parents ever had a drinking problem?" (Claydon 1987), and finally, "(that a parent) may have had or may have an alcohol abuse problem" (Berkowitz and Perkins 1988). Although we have found that a global item assessing perceived paternal alcoholism shows adequate inter-sibling agreement (Sher and Descutner 1986), for most research purposes such vague and subjective assessments are clearly inadequate.

In summary, although direct assessment of alcoholism and other disorders in relatives is optimal, this is not always possible. Fortunately, the family history method is a reasonable, cost-effective technique that tends to show relatively high specificity but more modest sensitivity. Structured interviews for conducting family history interviews are available and are generally to be preferred over questionnaire assessments because of the ability to probe and clarify subjects' responses. However, several questionnaires are available which appear to show adequate psychometric properties and can be used cost-effectively to screen large numbers of subjects. Validation of screened subjects using additional assessments strengthens confidence in initial determinations. The use of single-item assessments and questionnaires such as the CAST should be discouraged in most research investigations when an accurate designation of diagnosable parental alcoholism is the goal.

Source of Sample

The source of the sample can have important implications for the types of inferences that can be made. For example, some studies have examined differences between COAs and nonCOAs in delinquent samples (Tarter, Hegedus, Goldstein, Shelly, and Alterman 1984). Failure to find between-group differences could be due to a host of factors (e.g., significant parental antisocial pathology in both groups or just the control group) and may not be generalizable to most groups of interest.

In general, sampling COAs who are themselves in treatment (e.g., the Tarter et al. 1984, study cited above) will tend to overestimate psychopathology among COAs. Sampling control subjects from clinical samples is similarly problematic. Perhaps less obvious are the problems that stem from studying COAs whose parents are (or were) in treatment. Although this may be a useful strategy for many investigations, there are many reasons to believe that these individuals are more likely to show signs of problems than COAs more generally. This "psychopathology bias" is discussed at length by Heller et al. (1982).

The problem of subject source relates not only to subjects drawn from clinical samples but to other types of samples as well. Selection of subjects from settings that require a high degree of intellectual or social competence (elite colleges, certain professional groups) implicitly filters out subjects with severe behavior problems; those who are most at risk may never be represented in a sample. So-called community volunteers responding to advertisements or other nonsystematic solicitations can differ from the general population in numerous ways that can severely limit generalization.

With the growth of the COA movement, many COAs have participated in various kinds of treatments (e.g., self-help and professionally led groups). Countless more have probably read newspaper features, magazine articles, and one or more of the dozens of trade books currently available (some of which have reached the top of the best-seller lists). The extent to which involvement with currently popular COA lore alters self-perception is not at all clear, but it is quite possible that extensive exposure to the COA literature and treatment movement could lead to reports of specific personality characteristics and interpersonal difficulties that are consistent with COA stereotypes. Consequently, for investigations focusing on characteristics that are popularized by the COA movement, exposure to these materials should be assessed so that their possible effects could be statistically evaluated.

Heterogeneity

As discussed in Chapter 1, alcoholics are a very heterogeneous group. There appears to be considerable variation with respect to the form of alcoholism, the coexistence of other disorders, and the degree to which the alcoholism appears to be primary or secondary to other disorders. Although it would be difficult for any single study to classify parents along all potentially relevant diagnostic distinctions, it is highly desirable to collect sufficient information to describe alcoholic parents according to subtype and to the extent and nature of other psychopathology. In addition, it is useful to assess the extent of family history of alcoholism in subjects' families beyond targeted parents. Some studies have shown differences between COAs with either no alcoholism or additional alcoholism in other first- and in second-degree relatives (e.g., Finn and Pihl 1987, 1988). That is, some COAs come from families with limited alcoholism in the extended family (e.g., father only) while others come from families with a higher density of alcoholism. At a minimum, the additional diagnostic information provides important information for sample description. More important, assessment of additional diagnostic information permits important types of analyses relating dimensions of heterogeneity to offspring outcome.

For a number of reasons, most research on COAs has focused on the offspring of alcoholic fathers. However, it is usually desirable to examine the effects of a history of maternal alcoholism. Furthermore, when maternal alcoholism is determined, it is extremely important to determine the extent that active alcoholism *or heavy drinking* was present during pregnancy in an effort to exclude those subjects likely to have had significant prenatal exposure to alcohol or to place those subjects in a separate group for analysis (or to employ some other method of statistical control). Subjects with extensive prenatal alcohol exposure may exhibit cognitive or behavioral dysfunction attributable to teratogenic effects of alcohol which will seriously complicate interpretation of obtained data.

The failure to consider significant sources of heterogeneity may be the single greatest methodological weakness plaguing research on COAs. Unfortunately, there is little research that systematically investigates the implications of clinically and theoretically meaningful sources of alcoholism heterogeneity on offspring.

Other Basic Design Issues

Spousal Psychopathology

A hidden confound in many studies of COAs concerns the nature of spousal psychopathology. If alcoholism in a parent is related to psychological disorder in the spouse, then comparisons between COAs and nonCOAs inadvertently are confounding parental alcoholism with spousal psychopathology. The literature on spousal psychopathology in alcoholics is complex and derives from both a clinical research tradition where concern has been for the nature and extent of psychopathology in spouses and the behavior genetic tradition where the concern has been for understanding the intergenerational transmission of alcoholism and the basis of the drinking pattern of both parents. Early clinical descriptions of the wives of alcoholics described them as "fragile, dissatisfied, insecure, interpersonally restricted, severely anxious and suspicious, sexually inadequate, abnormally angry, and profoundly unhappy people who feel unloved, resentful, and aggressive" (Paolino, McCrady, Diamond, and Longabaugh 1976). However, the subjective and anecdotal descriptions did not hold up to empirical test (Edwards, Harvey, and Whitehead 1973). Edwards et al. (1973) concluded that wives of alcoholics "have essentially normal personalities of different types, rather than of any one particular type.

They may suffer personality dysfunction when their husbands are active alcoholics, but if their husbands become abstinent and the periods of abstinence increase the wives experience less and less dysfunction'' (p. 130). Unfortunately, these early studies did not use modern diagnostic criteria and did not determine the extent to which active alcoholism in the spouse might create sufficient distress to result in diagnosable mental disorders. It does appear that the drinking patterns of husbands and wives are related and that this relationship between parental drinking patterns is primarily due to assortative mating for drinking pattern or social contagion of drinking after marriage (Hall, Hesselbrock, and Stabenau 1983a, 1983b). These data suggest that it is potentially important to assess the psychological functioning of both parents in studies of COAs.

Maternal Alcohol Consumption During Pregnancy

The literature on fetal alcohol syndrome demonstrates deficits (e.g., hyperactivity) that have also been associated with a history of paternal alcoholism. Obviously, when studying the children of alcoholic mothers, it is important to determine the extent of maternal drinking during pregnancy to assess the potential effects of drinking on the fetus. Also, to attribute deficits to paternal alcoholism in COAs, assessment of maternal drinking during pregnancy is necessary to evaluate the extent to which alcohol's effect on the fetus contributes to obtained findings.

Control Groups

There are numerous potential problems associated with the selection of control groups. When COAs are identified through parents in treatment, it is often difficult to find an appropriate control group. Matching on obvious variables (census tract, parent's SES, child's sex and age, family size, birth order, etc.), although helpful, does not solve all potential problems. To the extent that the stigma of receiving treatment for a behavior disorder extends to family members (a phenomenon Goffman [1963] refers to as a courtesy stigma), COAs might differ from children of nonstigmatized families on several dimensions. Although such social labeling processes may be irrelevant for studies on ethanol metabolism and stable, trait-like physical characteristics, they could be important for more state-like psychological characteristics (e.g., self-esteem) or for social consequences (e.g., delinquency).

More important, few studies have attempted to control for parental deviance/psychopathology in general. Thus, even in those areas where consistent relationships between COA status and specific variables appear established, it is usually not possible to infer that the relationship is attributable just to parental alcoholism and not to more general parental deviance or psychopathology. Research on children of depressed parents, for example, would appear to indicate that parental depression often shows effects on offspring similar to those associated with a family history of alcoholism.

The issues that go into the selection of a control group differ considerably as a function of the purpose of an investigation and the maturity of an area of inquiry. In most cases, offspring of parents with no substance abuse/dependence or other significant psychological disorder represent an important comparison group. In general, controls for parental psychopathology (or possibly other parental problems) are necessary if specific correlates of a family history of alcoholism are to be obtained. However, once we get beyond these two generalizations, issues in the selection of control groups get considerably more complex and must be determined by a careful analysis of the goals of the study and the particular inferences the investigators hope to be able to draw.

Inclusion/Exclusion Criteria

Certain control procedures may mask meaningful between-group differences. For example, some laboratories (especially those studying older subjects) screen out COAs who have already manifested drinking problems. Although there is a clear rationale for this (the study is concerned with risk or vulnerability, not manifest disorder), there is a very real possibility that vulnerable individuals are screened out. To illustrate this point, we (Sher 1985a) demonstrated that potentially meaningful group differences between COAs and nonCOAs on a personality measure were progressively reduced by increasing the severity of screening criteria on problem drinking. Personality differences noted between COAs and nonCOAs when all subjects were included vanished when analyses were limited to subjects who did not report possible alcohol abuse. Although in alcohol consumption studies it may be unethical to include alcohol abusing subjects, in general a reasonable strategy would be to avoid screening out manifest disorder (especially if it is overly represented in the high-risk group) and to statistically examine the influence of manifest disorder on between-group comparisons. As a caveat, in studies using extensive screening, it is possible that the resultant high-risk sample is composed largely of *invulnerable* subjects and not persons truly at risk!

Potential problems with exclusionary criteria are also illustrated in a recent study by Drake and Vaillant (1988). In their 33-year follow-up study of male COAs, subjects who evidenced delinquency in adolescence were originally screened out. Examination of the study reveals several findings that are inconsistent with most published data and that might be directly attributable to the exclusion of adolescent delinquents. First, the researchers failed to find an excess of "hyperactivity" and of impaired cognitive performance in their COAs. Second, they failed to find any subjects with antisocial personality disorder in adulthood (although 24 percent of their entire sample met criteria for a personality disorder). These anomalous findings are plausibly a direct function of the initial exclusion criteria. Consequently, researchers need to be keenly aware of the nature of both explicit and implicit screening that occurs when a sample is constructed, and, in prospective studies, screening that occurs through subject attrition.

Matching Procedures

A related issue concerns the approach to matching COA and nonCOA subjects used by a number of investigators. To the extent that COAs and nonCOAs are matched on variables that may be related to the distributions of vulnerability in the two populations, such matching could result in the elimination of meaningful between-group differences (e.g., a "low-risk" sample obtained by such matching may differ so much from its parent population that it no longer characterizes the "low-risk" population from which it was drawn). Although matching on key variables may permit certain types of inferences not possible with unmatched samples, the limitations of matching have not generally been appreciated and its widespread use should be questioned. An insightful discussion of the problems of matching subjects in psychopathology research that has relevance for any cross-sectional research on behavior disorders is presented by Chapman and Chapman (1973).

Age of Sample

Studies of COAs have targeted subjects across the life span. Although there are many good reasons to study COAs of different ages, the age variable becomes a major methodological issue when variables related to vulnerability are the focus of investigation. As subjects' ages move progressively further into the period of risk for alcoholism, comparisons between *nonalcoholic* COAs and nonCOAs become progressively less likely to yield psychological and biological markers of risk. This is because subjects remaining nonalcoholic become progressively less likely to possess significant vulnerability. Inferences based on high-risk vs. low-risk comparisons should be most valid when made prior to the onset of risk for subjects.

Sample Sizes

The small sample-sizes utilized in the majority of studies are a major problem. Small sample-size can represent a particular problem in high-risk studies due to the inherent heterogeneity within groups (Sher 1983). That is, only a proportion of subjects designated as high-risk can be expected to possess vulnerability. In general, the effect size of between-group comparisons can be expected a priori to be relatively low (because of substantial within-group variation of vulnerability in both COAs and nonCOAs), and designs with relatively small samples will suffer from limited statistical power. Because of the small samples characterizing many studies, it is likely that the literature is plagued with many Type 2 errors (failing to find differences when they truly exist).

Issues Surrounding Type 1 Errors

Because of the difficulty in constructing high-risk samples, many research groups conduct extensive assessments of their subjects. Although comprehensive assessments are often desirable, controlling for Type 1 (false positive) error when comparing high-risk and low-risk groups can be problematic when the number of dependent variables is large and the sample size is small. One recent study (Nagoshi and Wilson, 1987) reported 78 separate t-tests in a total sample of 35 high-risk and 35 low-risk subjects with no attempt to set the experiment-wise Type 1 error to a reasonable level. Consequently, interpretation of individual comparisons at the .05, .01, or even the .001 levels of significance is problematic (in this instance, use of the Bonferroni procedure would yield a .0006 rejection level). Unfortunately, failure to control Type 1 error for multiple comparisons has probably led to a number of spurious findings being reported in the literature. Overall, multivariate statistics are infrequently employed, even when required. In studies using repeated-measurement designs, it is rare for investigators to address the probable violation of the sphericity (compound symmetry) assumption and apply appropriate corrections to the degrees-of-freedom or, alternatively, employ the multivariate approach to repeated-measures analyses.

It also appears, although it is difficult to determine with certainty, that some researchers use the same sample to generate data presented in different publications (in one publication the findings concerning one variable are presented and in a subsequent publication other data collected at the same time are presented). This practice would serve to compound the problem of Type 1 errors.

Unfortunately, when investigators attempt to control Type 1 error by means of appropriate multivariate statistics or Bonferroni corrections, they run a risk of making Type 2 errors when the sample size is relatively small. For example, in one recent study of neuropsychological impairment among COAs, many moderate-sized effects were found (approximately .5 standard deviations) but did they not reach statistical significance (Workman-Daniels and Hesselbrock 1987). The only clear solution to the interrelated problems of Type 1 and Type 2 errors is to employ appropriate procedures for controlling Type 1 errors while insuring that samples are of sufficient size to detect effects of reasonable magnitude (reducing the likelihood of Type 2 errors).

Although the statistical analyses in many of the relevant studies are quite elegant, in general studies contrasting groups at high and low risk have tended to be unsophisticated. Fortunately, the appropriate use of statistical analysis has shown steady improvement in recent years. Nevertheless, much of the data published to date has been poorly analyzed.

Issues Surrounding "Differential Deficit"

Studies from several areas of research on COAs (e.g., the research on neuropsychological deficits reviewed in chapter 6) find that COAs are different from nonCOAs on a given measure (Task A) but not on a seemingly related measure (Task B) When this occurs, it is tempting to conclude that COA status is more associated with Task A performance than Task B performance. However, this conclusion is often not warranted. At the most basic level, differential performance on two or more tasks cannot be inferred unless the differences between COAs and nonCOAs on Task A are larger than those on Task B. In the simplest case, when data are on the same metric (or a legitimate statistical transformation can be used to scale task performance to the same metric) a 2 × 2, COA status (COA vs. nonCOA) × Task (Task A vs. Task B), repeated-measures analysis of variance (ANOVA), could be used to attempt to demonstrate a significant COA status × Task interaction. (This of course generalizes to more complex designs, including multiple groups and tasks.) A significant COA status × Task interaction implies significantly different performance between groups. In some cases, hierarchical discriminant analysis or logistic regression could be used to determine, if after *first* entering Task B performance, Task A performance significantly contributed to group prediction. These types of analyses could yield more clear-cut analysis of whether COA/nonCOA differences were significantly larger on one task than another.

However, the situation is more complex than might appear at first glance. Even when appropriate repeated-measures ANOVAs or other techniques are employed and the relevant statistical tests are significant, it cannot be confidently assumed that the *ability* underlying Task A performance is more related to COA status than the ability underlying Task B performance. In order to make this inference, additional assumptions must be met concerning the comparability of the discriminating power or true score variance of Task A and Task B. (Detailed discussion of this issue is beyond the scope of this text, and the interested reader is referred to the work of Chapman and Chapman [1973, 1978]). In the absence of data attesting to the psychometric comparability of two or more related tasks, definitive demonstration of "differential deficit" is impossible. Unfortunately, research on COAs has yet to reach the level of methodological sophistication where these issues are addressed.

The 2 × 2, Family History of Alcoholism ×
Alcoholism, Factorial Design

Beginning with a study by Schaeffer, Parsons, and Yohman (1984), several investigations have utilized a research design where family history of alcoholism (present vs. absent) is crossed with clinical alcoholism (present vs. absent) yielding four groups: (1) familial alcoholics, (2) nonfamilial alcoholics, (3) nonalcoholics with a positive family history of alcoholism, and (4) nonalcoholics with a negative family history of alcoholism. Although on the surface this appealing factorial design appears to offer the promise of disentangling the separate and interacting effects of clinical alcoholism and family history of alcoholism, careful consideration of this design suggests potential problems which can result in faulty inferences. The major problems can be summarized as follows.

First, if the sample is well into their period of risk for alcoholism (which it is by necessity since alcoholics are included), nonalcoholics with a family history of alcoholism might be relatively low in vulnerability to alcoholism. This would tend to reduce effects associated with a family history of alcoholism. Second, although nonfamilial alcoholics may not have any alcoholic near-relatives, they might still possess the same type of vulnerability that familial alcoholics possess (e.g., they might have had parents with unexpressed genotypes for alcoholism). This would also tend to reduce effects associated with a family history of alcoholism. Alternatively, nonfamilial alcoholics might possess a special form of vulnerability that makes them different from nonalcoholics with a negative family history, in ways other than the mere presence of alcoholism. The effects of this possibility are unclear. These potentially problematic issues suggest that data resulting from this design are difficult to evaluate and prone to misinterpretation.

Issues Surrounding Ethanol Challenge Studies

One major type of theory concerning COAs' vulnerability to alcoholism posits that they are affected differently by alcohol (either more or less) than non-COAs. Consequently, numerous studies have investigated whether COAs and nonCOAs respond differently to alcohol consumption (ethanol challenge). (These studies are reviewed in chapter 7.) However, use of ethanol challenges presents a number of special considerations, both methodological and ethical, which need to be appreciated in evaluations of the adequacy of planned and completed research. In addition to the discussion below, interested readers might wish to consult several additional articles that address methodological and ethical issues surrounding ethanol challenge studies (Connors and Maisto 1983; Lawson, Nathan, and Lipscomb 1980; Maisto, Connors, and Vuchinich

1978; Marlatt et al. 1981; National Advisory Council on Alcohol Abuse and Alcoholism 1989; Rohsenow and Marlatt 1981).

Importance of Setting

Few, if any, psychoactive drugs have reliable *psychological or behavioral* effects across situations. Research on the effects of alcohol on subjective experience (Kalin, McClelland, and Kahn 1965; Pliner and Cappell 1974; Sher 1985b; Warren and Raynes 1972) indicate that the effect of alcohol on mood is closely dependent upon the context in which drinking occurs. Consequently, simple generalizations concerning the effect of alcohol on mood, based on individual laboratory studies, can be problematic. Presumably, the effect of alcohol on some physiological parameters are less likely to be affected. However, the generalizability (or what is sometimes termed *external validity*) of a study can never be simply assumed.

Need for Placebo Controls

Several early ethanol challenge studies on COAs (e.g., Schuckit 1980a; Schuckit and Duby 1982) failed to include a placebo control group. Failure to control for placebo effects precludes the opportunity to attribute COA/nonCOA differences in alcohol effects to individual differences in alcohol. That is, it is not possible to determine if the COA/nonCOA differences are attributable to alcohol or if they would exist in a given experiment if alcohol wasn't consumed. Although some researchers (e.g., Finn and Pihl 1987) have included a no-beverage control condition to permit more confident inferences concerning differential response to ethanol, this still might not be adequate. Newlin (1985) has demonstrated that COAs and nonCOAs appear to differ in their response to an alcohol placebo. This implies that differences between COAs and non-COAs to an alcohol challenge might be more a function of response to the expected or conditioned effects of alcohol than to the pharmacological properties of ethanol. Consequently, in the absence of a placebo control, inferences concerning differential effects of alcohol consumption on COAs are limited. Furthermore, Newlin's (1985) work suggests that a no-beverage control provides additional valuable information. Amplification of these issues can be found in Marlatt and Rohsenow's (1980; Rohsenow & Marlatt 1981) discussion of the balanced placebo design in alcohol research and Newlin and Thomson's (1990) analysis of the placebo considerations in research on COAs.

Dose of Ethanol Employed

The dose of alcohol administered in an ethanol challenge study can be critical in determining whether or not an alcohol effect is documented. For example, in research on the so-called "tension-reducing" effects of alcohol, only studies employing a relatively high dose of alcohol (e.g., 1 g ethanol/kg body weight) show reliable effects with more inconsistent findings at lower doses (cf., Sher 1987b). Unfortunately, because multiple-dose studies are more time-consuming and expensive than single-dose studies, most human studies employ only a single dose of ethanol.

On a priori grounds, we can hypothesize that between-group differences in alcohol effects would be related to the dose of ethanol employed. At extremely low doses presumably no subjects might show a given effect of alcohol; at extremely high doses all subjects might be equally affected. Presumably, it is at "intermediate" doses that between-group differences are likely to emerge. (The reasoning underlying this speculation is based on research and theory on person × environment interactions [Magnusson and Endler 1977].) However, determining an intermediate dose for a given effect of alcohol is an empirical issue that undoubtedly varies across different effects of alcohol.

Although the idea that between-group differences in ethanol sensitivity are likely to emerge at certain doses is speculative, relevant empirical data appear to bear out this conjecture. For example, Schuckit (1984a) found that COA vs. nonCOA differences in subjective experience were most marked at an ethanol dose of .75 mL/kg, with relatively little (and nonsignificant) differences at 1.1 mL/kg and placebo conditions. Presumably, if Schuckit had studied only the higher-dose condition, COA vs. nonCOA differences would not have emerged. Consequently, multiple-dose studies with COAs are clearly desirable and negative findings derived from a single-dose level should not be generalized to other dose levels.

Limb of the Blood Alcohol Curve

Another important parameter when investigating alcohol effects is the limb of the blood alcohol curve. The ascending limb refers to the period of time following alcohol consumption when the blood alcohol level is rising; the descending limb refers to the subsequent period of time when the blood alcohol level is falling. It has often been observed that, even at identical blood alcohol levels, the ascending and descending limbs are associated with alcohol effects that differ in magnitude or even in direction (cf., Connors and Maisto 1983). Typically, the descending limb is associated with smaller-magnitude alcohol effects than the ascending limb, a phenomenon sometimes referred to as acute tolerance.

The limb of the blood alcohol curve may have critical importance for research on COAs. In a recent review, Newlin and Thomson (1990) have shown that the seemingly conflicting findings from ethanol challenge studies on COAs can be reconciled by considering the limb of the blood alcohol curve when measurements were taken. On the ascending limb, COAs appear more sensitive to alcohol; on the descending limb, COAs appear more tolerant (this issue is discussed further in chapters 8 and 9). Consequently, great attention needs to be paid to limb phenomena when designing experiments and evaluating findings.

It needs to be pointed out that within-study examination of limb effects involves a number of difficult methodological problems. For example, studies that involve human performance must be designed to unconfound repeated performance (which can be associated with learning, fatigue, and reactive inhibition) from limb effects. For virtually all studies, observation of descending-limb effects involves prolonged time in the laboratory, which can result in fatigue and boredom. Designing studies to avoid these confounds involves considerable thought and additional experimental conditions. However, at the least, sufficient monitoring of blood alcohol levels provides important information on blood alcohol curve limb which can assist interpretation of observed effects.

Inclusion/Exclusion Criteria Associated with Ethanol Challenge Studies

Administration of alcohol to human subjects involves a number of special considerations (cf. National Advisory Council on Alcohol Abuse and Alcoholism, 1989). First, under most circumstances, it is difficult to justify giving alcohol to subjects who: (a) are under the legal drinking age of a jurisdiction, (b) have never consumed alcohol before, (c) are deliberately abstaining from alcohol, (d) do not customarily drink alcohol in the amount dictated by the experimental protocol, (e) have psychiatric or medical conditions which contraindicate alcohol consumption, and (f) are alcoholic. (Of course there may be special circumstances where use of these subjects in any of these categories is justified because the risk/benefit ratio is deemed favorable and appropriate protections for human subjects are met.) Consequently, alcohol consumption studies typically exclude subjects falling into any of the above categories. To the extent that these exclusions are related to COA status, systematic bias enters into the study. Although there are some contradictory findings, there is certainly evidence to believe that both abstainers (e.g., Harburg et al. 1982) and alcohol abusers (e.g., Pandina and Johnson 1989; Sher 1985a; Walitzer 1990) are overrepresented in COAs by the time they reach legal drinking age and are eligible for alcohol consumption studies.

Time of Day

There is reason to suspect that circadian variations in the effect of alcohol exist, and the time of day when subjects are run can affect the outcome of alcohol consumption studies (Jones 1974). Although experimental work on COAs that varies the time of day of alcohol administration has not been reported, the work of Revelle, Humphreys, Simon, and Gilliland (1980) demonstrating three-way interactions among caffeine, time of day, and personality characteristics suggests that important individual differences in drug responses may emerge only at certain times of day. At present, there is considerable variability in the times of day that alcohol consumption studies on COAs are conducted, and Newlin and Thomson (1990) speculate that this may have had considerable impact on the outcome of specific studies.

Use of Within-Subjects Designs

In order to maximize the utility of relatively scarce subjects, a number of investigators use within-subject designs where the same subjects consume alcohol and placebo on different days. Within-subject designs often bring with them relatively high statistical power because subjects serve as their own control and, consequently, experimental error is reduced. However, the validity of these designs is compromised when undetected interactions between order of beverage administration and key independent variables (e.g., COA/nonCOA status) are present. When these interactions are present, interpretation of findings can be problematic. Furthermore, there is reason to suspect that such interactions do occur. In a recent study in my lab (Sher, Walitzer, Bylund, and Hartmann 1989), a number of higher-order interactions involving both COA/nonCOA status and order of beverage administration were found which defied simple description, and some of Newlin's recent work on novelty and tolerance development (cited in Newlin and Thomson, 1990) suggest that there is reason to suspect that these COA/nonCOA status × order interactions might be quite general. Ideally, if within-subject designs are used, they should be designed to include sufficient numbers of subjects to permit adequate statistical power when analyses are restricted to purely between-group comparisons (e.g., first session only) should order effects be found. Of course, some research goals (e.g., studies of the development of chronic tolerance and sensitization) require within-subjects designs. However, in those cases where the interest is on change in ethanol response over repeated occasions, researchers are less likely to mislead themselves because data are not likely to be collapsed across sessions.

Gender

Only two studies involving alcohol challenges with female COAs have been reported (Levenson et al. 1987; Lex, Lukas, Greenwald, and Mendelson 1988). However, it should be noted that alcohol consumption studies with women involve two special considerations: (1) protecting subjects against possible fetal injury (e.g., National Advisory Council on Alcohol Abuse and Alcoholism, 1989), and (2) controlling for possible fluctuations in alcohol metabolism and alcohol effects associated with the menstrual cycle (e.g., Connors and Maisto 1983).

The Reliability of Ethanol Effects

Finally, it needs to be emphasized that individual differences in certain effects of alcohol tend to be unstable, and there is considerable day-to-day variation in ethanol metabolism and in many alcohol effects, especially physiologic and behavioral effects (Nagoshi and Wilson 1988, 1989). Low temporal reliability suggests that response to alcohol might be less trait-like than is often assumed. The unreliability of alcohol effects suggests that individual studies may have difficulty in demonstrating COA/nonCOA differences in alcohol effects. More important, for researchers interested in correlating alcohol sensitivity with other variables, assessment of alcohol sensitivity on multiple occasions may be necessary in order to derive stable, trait-like indices. Aggregation of individual measurements over multiple occasions and/or situations has been shown to yield much better prediction of theoretically related criteria than individual measurements taken alone (Epstein 1979, 1980) and may be necessary to demonstrate a mediational role of alcohol sensitivity (or tolerance) in risk for alcoholism. However, repeated laboratory testing of subjects with alcohol challenges could involve sensitization and tolerance processes (cf. Newlin & Thomson, 1990) which would need to be taken into consideration when analyzing and interpreting experimental findings.

Summary

There are numerous methodological issues to consider in studies of COAs, and much of the published research shares a number of limitations. The point of raising these methodological issues is not to dismiss most of the published work but to illustrate the limitations of available data. All scientific research represents a compromise between the optimal and the feasible, and individual researchers should not be faulted for failing to conduct the perfect study. However, without appreciation of the methodological considerations, accurate appraisal and interpretation of existing data are impossible and our ability to design progressively better studies is limited.

6 Psychological Characteristics

In this chapter, studies examining differences between COAs and nonCOAs on psychological variables are reviewed. The goal of most of these studies is the discovery of psychological characteristics that may represent mediational links between a family history of alcoholism and later problems, especially alcoholism. Although the clinical literature has described a number of putative psychological characteristics of COAs (e.g., perfectionism, self-derogation), relatively little empirical work has been published attempting to validate these descriptions. Consequently, the reader familiar with the commonly described stereotypes of COAs may be surprised by the lack of attention to many of the generalizations popularized by the clinical and popular literature. The question of COA/nonCOA differences in psychopathology was addressed earlier (chapter 3), and thus will not be reviewed below.

Personality

The relationship between premorbid personality traits and later alcoholism has long been an area of heated debate. A number of personality characteristics known to characterize samples of clinical alcoholics appear to be consequences of alcoholism, not precursors (cf. Barnes 1983). Nevertheless, there appears to be consistent evidence for traits that are predictive of later alcoholism (i.e., prealcoholic traits; cf. Zucker and Gomberg 1986). Prospective and archival studies suggest that traits related to behavioral undercontrol (such as impulsivity, rebelliousness, and aggressiveness) appear to characterize the prealcoholic male (Cloninger, Sigvardsson, Reich, and Bohman 1988; Jones 1968; Loper, Kammeier, and Hoffmann 1973; McCord and McCord 1962; Robins, Bates, and O'Neal 1962; Robins et al. 1968). Limited data on prealcoholic females suggest that they may be characterized by different traits (Jones 1971). Recently, Cloninger (1987a) has suggested that personality traits may provide a mediational link between genetic risk for alcoholism and later alcoholism. Personality traits typically show heritability coefficients of approximately .50, and are thus consistent with models of transmission involving both significant genetic and environmental factors.

A difficulty in reviewing personality factors in COAs is determining what personality data are relevant. Commonly used clinical instruments such as the Minnesota Multiphasic Personality Inventory (MMPI) are sometimes used to assess personality dimensions, but MMPI scales contain items reflecting symptoms (e.g., somatic complaints, hallucinations, depressive thoughts). Behavioral data (e.g., referral to child treatment centers, involvement with juvenile courts for conduct problems) are often used to assess traits such as antisociality, but these behavioral outcomes are sometimes difficult to cast in basic personality terms and clearly are confounded with environmental variables (such as tolerance for deviance in the environment and social class). Even scales expressly developed to assess basic personality dimensions (such as the California Psychological Inventory) contain items that some would not consider "personality items" at all but rather instances of antisocial behavior. Nevertheless, it is possible to review relevant data and look for consistency and/or interesting leads.

Three broad domains of personality will be surveyed: (1) *behavioral undercontrol* (impulsivity, aggression), (2) *emotionality* (tendency to experience negative affective states, neuroticism), and (3) *sociability*. These three dimensions are similar, in most cases, to those discussed by a number of writers (Cloninger 1987a; Cattell, Eber, and Tatsuoka 1970; Eysenck 1978; Tarter 1988; Zuckerman, Kuhlman, and Camac 1988). In addition, findings concerning several additional traits that do not easily fit into one of these broad dimensions (activity level, locus of control, Type A behavior pattern, alexithymia, cognitive style) are also discussed. Although some reviewers have considered hyperactivity in discussions of personality in COAs (e.g., Tarter 1988), the link between hyperactivity as a diagnostic entity and activity level as described by temperament theorists (e.g., Buss and Plomin 1984) is not straightforward. Consequently, hyperactivity per se is not discussed in the following section although features commonly associated with hyperactivity (or ADHD) such as impulsivity, conduct problems, and activity are discussed.

Behavioral Undercontrol

Data from a number of sources indicate that COAs tend to be characterized by an undercontrolled behavioral style. Both Saunders and Schuckit (1981) and Knowles and Schroeder (1989) found that young, nonalcoholic adults with a positive family history of alcoholism score higher than controls on the MacAndrew (1965) alcoholism scale (MAC—an MMPI-derived scale that primarily samples undercontrolled traits such as aggressiveness, risk taking, and sensation seeking). It needs to be noted, however, that although these differences were statistically significant, they were small in absolute magnitude. Consequently, Alterman and his colleagues (Alterman, Bridges, and Tarter 1986a; Alterman et al. 1989) and Goglia's (1986) failure to find differences on the MAC between college men with and without a history of paternal alcoholism is not surprising given the limited sizes of their samples.

Data from our own laboratory (Mann, Chassin, and Sher 1987; Sher 1985; Sher, Walitzer, Wood, and Brent in press) indicate that both male and female COAs, in adolescence and young adulthood, appear to be more behaviorally undercontrolled on a number of personality measures. These measures include the Socialization scale of the CPI, the MacAndrew alcoholism scale from the MMPI, the Psychopathic deviate scale of the MMPI-168, the Novelty Seeking scale from the Tridimensional Personality Questionnaire (TPQ; Cloninger, 1987c), and the Psychoticism scale from the Eysenck Personality Questionnaire (EPQ; Eysenck and Eysenck 1975). Subjects' scores on all of these measures suggested relatively high levels of impulsivity and rebelliousness. However, in our most recent study involving 490 first-time freshmen at a large state university (Sher et al. 1990), the average effect size of the difference on undercontrolled traits which discriminated COAs and nonCOAs was approximately one-third of a standard deviation. An effect size of this magnitude can be conceptualized as indicating that 77 percent of the subjects in the two samples overlap. Thus, although there are clear significant differences between groups, there is also substantial group overlap.

A recent study (Alterman, Searles, and Hall 1989) comparing male college-student COAs and nonCOAs on a number of personality variables related to behavioral undercontrol (the Sensation Seeking Scale, the Childhood Problem Behaviors Checklist, the MacAndrew Scale, and an interview measure of adolescent antisocial behavior) reported statistically significant differences on only one of eleven scales or subscales studied. However, scrutiny of the data suggest that the findings were much stronger than these investigators indicated. When a ''middle'' risk group composed of subjects with second-degree and no first-degree alcoholic relatives is excluded from consideration, COA/nonCOA comparisons yield a mean effect size of approximately one-half a standard deviation. Even with the relatively small sample sizes employed, COA/nonCOA differences do reach conventional levels of statistical significance on the majority of measures related to behavioral undercontrol if the so-called ''middle risk'' group is excluded.

The prospective Danish study (Knop, Teasdale, Schulsinger, and Goodwin 1985; Schulsinger, Knop, Goodwin, Teasdale, and Mikkelson 1986) found that COAs tend to be rated as exhibiting more ''impulsivity'' and less ''antiaggression'' than nonCOAs by interviewers and more ''impulsive-restlessness'' by teachers. An early study by Aronson and Gilbert (1963) also found that COA boys were rated by teachers as more ''impulsive'' than nonCOA boys. Also consistent with these general findings is Alterman et al.'s (1986a) finding that young-adult male COAs report higher levels of antisocial behavior (e.g., problems at school, lying, cheating) during childhood and adolescence than nonCOAs. We are aware of one study which directly contradicts these findings; Tarter et al. (1984) found COAs less impulsive than nonCOAs. However, the subjects in that study were sampled from a delinquent population and all subjects would be expected to be highly impulsive and at elevated risk for substance use. Also, Berkowitz and Perkins' (1988) study of college students found no differences on the impulsivity scale of the Self-Identification Form.

Further support for the etiological relevance of behavior undercontrol in COAs comes from a recent prospective study (Werner 1986). Werner found that COAs who developed significant behavior problems by age 18 scored significantly lower than those who failed to develop such problems on the CPI scales of Socialization, Responsibility, and Self-Control when they were 10. These data suggest that behavior undercontrol not only distinguishes COAs from nonCOAs but also differentiates among COAs those likely to develop problems. Thus available data, although limited, suggest convergence between the literature on prealcoholic personality traits (Zucker 1987; Zucker and Gomberg 1986) and on the characteristics of COAs and would appear to provide a promising lead for further research.

Before we leave the topic of behavioral undercontrol, several issues warrant discussion. First, as we noted above, the average effect size of differences between COAs and nonCOAs on undercontrolled traits, although statistically significant, are rarely more than ''moderate'' (cf. Cohen 1977) in size. Second, the issue of heterogeneity is undoubtedly important. In our recent study (Sher et al. in press), when subjects with other parental psychopathology were excluded from COA/nonCOA comparisons, the effect size decreased substantially. This suggests that a large percentage of the relation between behavioral undercontrol and family history of alcoholism may be attributable to parental comorbidity. Presumably, other sources of heterogeneity could also affect generalizations about undercontrolled traits.

Third, it has been argued that the concept of undercontrolled behavior might be considered overly broad and the assumption that a common factor underlies a number of conceptually distinct variables (e.g., impulsivity, sensation seeking) can easily be challenged (cf. Windle 1990). Molina, Chassin, Sher, Crews, and Hepworth (1990) have recently shown that four traits that might be subsumed under the rubric of behavioral undercontrol (extraversion, rule breaking, sensation seeking, impulsivity), although highly correlated, are empirically distinguishable and appear to have different behavioral correlates. Also, a recent study by Smith and Newman (1990) has shown, in a sample of criminal offenders, that only one of Hare's (1985) two dimensions of psychopathy (the antisocial factor) correlated with alcohol abuse/dependence. The other factor, which samples personality traits such as interpersonal callousness, was not related to alcohol diagnosis. However, as pointed out recently by Zuckerman, Kuhlman, and Camac (1988), "the level at which one wishes to assess personality will depend on the goals of assessment . . . (and) if the goal is to predict broader observational judgments over longer periods of time, . . . the research indicates that broadly assessed traits will be the most useful" (pp. 105–6). There appears to be good reason to feel comfortable with the concept that behavioral undercontrol represents such a broadly assessed trait. In a recent factor analytic study of a number of commonly used personality scales (Zuckerman et al. 1988), a clearly defined behavioral undercontrol factor (labeled by the authors as *Impulsive Unsocialized Sensation Seeking*) marked by high loadings on scales measuring aggression, sensation seeking, impulsivity, and socialization emerged as a major dimension in a three-factor solution. Although there is currently considerable controversy on the number of basic dimensions of personality (Digman and Inouye 1986; Eysenck 1978; McCrae and Costa 1985; Mershon and Gorsuch 1988; Noller, Law, and Comrey 1987; Zuckerman et al. 1988), it is clear that traits subsumed under the behavioral undercontrol rubric appear to be correlated with each other, with alcohol use/abuse, and with family history of alcoholism.

Fourth, it can be argued that behavioral undercontrol is more accurately viewed as a behavior pattern rather than a personality trait (cf. Nathan 1988; Windle 1990). For example, the correlation between early antisocial behavior and later alcoholism could be conceived as merely reflecting a correlation between different aspects of norm-violating behavior. Knowing that someone frequently engages in antisocial behavior tells us nothing about the motives for the behavior, the context in which antisocial behavior is likely to occur, or the extent to which the behavior is related to fundamental aspects of the self. Whether or not a pattern of behavior such as persistent antisocial activity can be considered a personality trait as defined by certain personality theorists (cf. Nathan 1988) is a complex theoretical issue. What is not in doubt, however, is that COAs and prealcoholics tend to be undercontrolled in their behavior. Future research needs to determine why this appears to be the case.

Emotionality

Several lines of inquiry suggest that a tendency to experience negative affective states is associated with both clinical alcoholism and vulnerability to alcoholism (cf. Tarter 1988). (However, note that Tarter [1988] and several other theorists include impulsivity under the heading of emotionality, where we place it under behavioral undercontrol.) We do not challenge this basic position except to note that longitudinal studies of prealcoholics (cf., Zucker and Gomberg 1986) suggest that undercontrolled traits appear more predictive of alcoholism than traits related to emotionality, at least for males; the opposite may be true for females (Jones 1971).

A number of studies have employed measures related to the construct of emotionality. Finn and Pihl (1987) failed to find COA/nonCOA differences on the Emotionality scale of Buss and Plomin's (1984) Emotionality-Activity-Sociability (EAS) scale in a sample of young adults. Benson and Heller (1987) found that adult women COAs were more neurotic on the Langner Symptom Checklist than control nonCOAs with nondisturbed parents. Three studies employing the Neuroticism scale of the Eysenck Personality Inventory (EPI; Eysenck and Eysenck 1968) and the EPQ with young adults have yielded mixed results. Schuckit (1983) failed to find differences between male COAs and nonCOAs. However, Finn and Pihl (1987) found that young, adult males with multigenerational paternal alcoholism scored higher on the EPI-Neuroticism scale than controls, and Sher et al. (in press) found that both male and female COAs scored higher than nonCOAs on the EPQ-Neuroticism scale. Furthermore, in contrast to Sher et al.'s (in press) findings concerning undercontrolled personality traits, excluding subjects whose parents exhibited either antisocial personality disorder and/or depression resulted in *larger* magnitudes of COA/nonCOA differences. However, Benson and Heller (1987) found that the adult female COAs in their sample were not distinguishable from nonCOA controls whose fathers had been psychiatrically hospitalized, suggesting a lack of specificity to parental alcoholism per se. These more recent data suggest that the relation between a family history of alcoholism and neuroticism clearly warrants further evaluation but that it is extremely important to consider other domains of parental psychopathology when evaluating these data.

Finn and Pihl (1987) found that COAs with unigenerational paternal alcoholism scored higher on the Emotionality subscale of the EAS than subjects with either a multigenerational history of paternal alcoholism or nonCOAs. The differing patterns of findings obtained by Finn and Pihl (1987) on the Emotionality scale of the EAS and the Neuroticism scale of the EPI are hard to interpret. However, it appears that obtained differences on Emotionality reflect differences on the Anger subscale of the Emotionality score.

Several studies have compared COAs and nonCOAs on a variety of measures of both trait and state anxiety, all with negative findings. Bennett, Wolin, and Reiss (1988b) failed to find COA/nonCOA differences on the anxiety scale of the Conners (1970) Parent Symptom Rating Scale in a late childhood/early adolescent sample. Employing a similar sample, Jacob and Leonard (1986) also reported no differences on the tension-anxiety scale of the Conners (1969) Teacher Rating Form. Lund and Landesmann-Dwyer (1979) found no differences on the "anxious self-blame" scale of the Devereux Adolescent Behavior Rating Scale (Spivack, Spotts, and Haimes 1967) in a clinical sample of adolescents. Schulsinger et al. (1986) failed to find differences in rated anxiety in the Danish prospective study. Schuckit (1982b) reported no differences between COAs and nonCOAs on the Trait Form of the State-Trait Anxiety Inventory (Spielberger, Gorsuch, and Lushene 1970) in young men (primarily college students). Berkowitz and Perkins (1988) reported no differences between college-student COAs and nonCOAs on self-reported "lack of tension" on the Self-Identification Form (Borgatta 1965). Finally, in a college-student sample, Sher et al. (in press) failed to find differences on the Harm Avoidance scale of the TPQ and the Social Anxiety scale of the Self-Consciousness Scale (SCS; Fenigstein, Scheier, and Buss 1975). These negative findings are difficult to reconcile with the literature relating family history of alcoholism to the prevalence of anxiety disorders discussed in chapter 3, as well as the findings concerning neuroticism noted earlier.

Although numerous studies have examined differences between COAs and nonCOAs on various measures of depression (see chapter 3), it is difficult to relate these findings to personality per se. As noted earlier, the relationship between parental alcoholism and dysphoric symptoms appears to vary as a function of the stage-of-recovery of the alcoholic parent (Moos and Billings 1982). This suggests that the depression noted in COAs may not be sufficiently trait-like to view in personality terms. A possible exception to this is the finding reported by Clair and Genest (1987) indicating that COAs scored higher than nonCOAs on a measure of "proneness to moderate depression" which is conceptually distinct from the severity of current depression assessed by most clinical instruments.

Although there appears to be some evidence that COAs are characterized by higher levels of emotionality than nonCOAs (Benson and Heller 1987; Clair and Genest 1987; Finn and Pihl 1987; Sher et al. in press), the majority of negative findings in this area cast doubt on the robustness of emotionality as a reliable discriminator of COAs and nonCOAs. However, as noted by Sher et al. (1990), parental comorbidity may exercise a significant influence on the magnitude of COA/nonCOA differences, and future research needs to attend to this issue. Similarly, other sources of comorbidity can be expected to play a significant role in moderating the relation between family history of alcoholism and emotionality. Finally, a tendency to experience negative affective states might be of greater etiologic significance for females than males (Jones 1968, 1971).

Sociability

There is little evidence suggesting an important role for sociability in the etiology of alcoholism. Scales measuring sociability (e.g., the Extraversion scale of the EPI) fail to reliably differentiate alcoholics from nonalcoholics (Barnes 1983). Comparisons of COAs and nonCOAs similarly fail to show differences on the Extraversion scale of the EPI and EPQ (Finn and Pihl 1987; Schuckit 1983; Sher et al. 1990) and the Sociability scale of the EAS (Finn and Pihl 1987). It should be noted that descriptions of the prealcoholic suggest interpersonal facility and outgoingness (e.g., Jones 1968). However, as argued by Tarter (1988), it appears likely that the seeming sociability of some prealcoholics might be more a reflection of disinhibitory control rather than true sociability. This speculation appears sound; however Tarter's (1988) conclusion that the "prealcoholic is not normatively sociable" (p. 192) is not clearly supported by available data. The existing research most clearly supports the stance that the personality dimension of sociability is not related to a family history of alcoholism or to the phenomenon of clinical alcoholism.

Activity Level

Activity level appears to be a basic, heritable dimension of temperament (Buss and Plomin 1984). As noted earlier there appears to be a reliable association between ADHD (hyperactivity) and both clinical alcoholism and a family history of alcoholism. Tarter (1988) has equated these findings, suggesting that a high activity level is associated with risk for alcoholism. However, as noted in chapter 3, there is reason to believe that it is not hyperactivity alone but rather hyperactivity associated with conduct problems that is related to risk for alcoholism. Two studies directly comparing COAs and nonCOAs on measures related to activity level (Finn and Pihl 1987; Schulsinger et al. 1986) fail to find significant differences, while one recent study (Tarter, Kabene, Escallier, Laird, and Jacob 1990) found that adolescent male COAs reported higher activity level than nonCOAs on a self-report temperament instrument. Consequently, at present there is some evidence suggesting that activity level distinguishes COAs and nonCOAs, but the empirical data base is limited and somewhat contradictory.

Cognitive Style

Personality psychologists have identified several traits related to perceiving and organizing experience that appear to have important implications for personality and behavior. One of these traits, stimulus-intensity modulation or reduction-augmentation, refers to the tendency to modulate the intensity of what is perceived; augmenters tend to subjectively increase or overestimate their perceptual experience, and reducers tend to decrease or underestimate their perceptual experience (Petrie 1967). Measures of stimulus-intensity modulation can be derived by self-report, behavioral (psychophysical), and electrophysiological measures. In a recent review, Barnes (1983) concluded that there was "some support" for the notion that alcoholics tend to be augmenters relative to nonalcoholics but that the empirical base is small. Hennecke (1984) recently reported that a sample of young (10–12 year old) boy and girl COAs evidenced a higher number of augmenters than a matched sample of nonCOAs on a behavioral measure of stimulation-intensity modulation (the Kinesthetic Figural Aftereffect; Petrie 1967). Given the ability of alcohol to reduce perceptual experience (cf. Hennecke 1984), the findings on stimulus-intensity modulation suggest an intriguing psychobiologic link between presumed vulnerability and alcohol effects. Further exploration of this finding is clearly warranted.

Another aspect of cognitive style related to personality functioning is field dependence-independence (Witkin, Dyk, Faterson, Goodenough, and Karp 1962). The dimension of field dependence-independence refers to the degree to which individuals are able to distinguish figure versus ground relations. For example, field-dependent individuals have difficulty in perceiving discrete figures embedded in a complex background while field independent individuals show relatively little difficulty at such tasks. A number of investigations demonstrate that clinical alcoholics tend to be field dependent relative to other populations, but the extent to which the increased field dependence reflects a consequence of the chronic effects of alcohol on the central nervous system (CNS) versus a predisposing characteristic is uncertain (Barnes 1983). Six recent studies have compared COAs and nonCOAs on measures of field dependence-independence (either the Rod and Frame Test or the Embedded Figures Test) and five of these failed to find significant differences (Alterman et al. 1986a; Drejer, Theilgaard, Teasdale, Schulsinger, and Goodwin 1985; Hennecke 1984; Schuckit and Penn 1985; Tarter, Jacob, Hill, Hegedus, and Carra 1986), although one recent study (Whipple, Parker, and Noble 1988) did find poorer performance on the Embedded Figures Test by COAs. Given the diverse nature of the samples and differing assessment instruments, these studies offer equivocal support for the hypothesis that field dependence-independence contributes to COAs' vulnerability. However, the sound sampling and design of Whipple et al. (1988) suggests that further research on this variable appears justified.

Locus of Control

Another area of personality research on COAs concerns the personality dimension of locus of control. Locus of control refers to the extent to which an individual perceives control over his/her environment. Numerous writers have hypothesized that the chaos and inconsistency of living in an alcoholic home could lead to perceptions of uncontrollability among COAs. The relation between locus of control and clinical alcoholism is unclear; a number of contradictory findings appear in the literature (cf. Barnes 1983), and the same generalization can probably be made regarding the results to date with COAs. Prewett, Spence, and Chaknis (1981) and Kern et al. (1981) found that school-age COAs (ages 7–12) were significantly more external than controls.

However, Callan and Jackson (1986) failed to find differences between adolescent COAs (who were members of Alateen) and nonCOAs, and two studies (Churchill, Broida, and Nicholson 1990; Morrison and Schuckit 1983) failed to find any differences between young adults with and without a family history of alcoholism. The discrepancy among studies could result from the age differences in the samples (especially since the younger subjects were presumably still living in alcoholic environments), use of different instruments to assess locus of control, and control-group selection.

Self-esteem

COAs appear to have lower self-esteem than nonCOAs. This appears to be the case in school-age children (Bennett et al. 1988b), adolescents (Roosa, Sandler, Beals, and Short 1988), and college students (Berkowitz and Perkins 1988; Sher et al. 1990; but also see Churchill et al. 1990, for a failure to replicate). However, it is not clear whether these self-esteem deficits reflect a correlate of a basic personality dimension such as emotionality or transient depressive states.

Alexithymia

According to Finn and Pihl (1988), alexithymia describes a deficit in experiencing and expressing affect, and "alexithymic characteristics are thought to hinder an individual's ability to cope with stress due to an inability to identify an event as stressful and a tendency to cope by using action" (p. 746). Two recent studies have found that young, adult male subjects with bigenerational, paternal alcoholism exhibit higher levels of alexithymic traits (as assessed by the Schalling Sifneos Personality Scale [SSPS]; Apfel and Sifneos 1979) than subjects with unigenerational paternal alcoholism (Finn and Pihl 1988; Finn, Martin, and Pihl 1987) and subjects without a family history of alcoholism (Finn et al. 1987). However, Sher et al. (in press) failed to find a relation between paternal alcoholism and scores on the SSPS. Since alexithymia is related to autonomic hyperreactivity and a tendency to somatize, the data reported by Finn and his colleagues are somewhat puzzling, in that the data from the Swedish adoption study suggest that it is the female offspring of alcoholics (especially Type 2 alcoholics) who are prone to somatization. At this time, future research on alexithymia in COAs appears warranted, with particular attention to the role of gender in the expression of alexithymic traits.

Other Personality Dimensions

To date, a number of other personality traits have been studied in COAs or other individuals with a positive family history of alcoholism. Existing research has failed to show COA/nonCOA differences in assertiveness (Schuckit 1982b), Type A personality traits (Manning, Balson, and Xenakis 1986), or dispositional self-awareness (Chassin, Mann, and Sher 1988; Sher et al. in press).

Broad personality dimensions such as behavioral undercontrol and emotionality may characterize COAs as a group, and further research is needed to specify these effects more clearly. At present, there is little evidence to suggest that COAs differ from nonCOAs on other broad dimensions such as sociability and activity level. The relation between other personality variables such as alexithymia, augmentation-reduction and locus of control are intriguing and deserving of further research. Despite recent theorizing on the possible relationship between basic dimensions of temperament and risk for alcoholism (Cloninger 1987a; Tarter 1988; Tarter et al. 1985), there has been virtually no research on the extent to which cross-sectional differences in behavioral undercontrol and emotionality reflect genetic factors or the consequences of growing up in an alcoholic home or both. Although there have been a number of negative findings with several personality variables, it would probably be premature to rule out personality factors as being unrelated to family history of alcoholism. A host of factors including sampling strategies, small sample sizes, and the potential relevance of different personality dimensions at different ages might interact to obscure potentially meaningful results.

Future research on the relation between personality and family history of alcoholism needs to determine the empirical overlap between ostensibly different constructs (e.g., behavioral undercontrol, augmentation-reduction, alexithymia). Only by examining a number of these potentially relevant personality traits in a multivariate context can we determine common and unique variance contributions in the relation between personality and family history of alcoholism. Cloninger's (1987a) recent theory implies that different types of parental alcoholism will be associated with different types of personality styles in the offspring. In a sense, this notion is supported by recent studies on alexithymia (Finn et al. 1987; Finn & Pihl 1988) distinguishing COAs with bigenerational and unigenerational family histories of paternal alcoholism. Consequently, it is reasonable to suspect that failure to consider etiological heterogeneity may have obscured important group differences.

Although the study of personality traits appears to be a potentially promising area of inquiry on COAs, it needs to be remembered that personality traits are generally poor predictors of behavior (Mischel 1968). The isolation of COA/nonCOA group differences on various dimensions of personality does not, by itself, provide much of an advance in our understanding of the etiology of alcoholism.

An understanding of the interaction of personality variables with environmental variables has the potential to explain more variance in behavior than prediction based solely on personality variables (Magnusson and Endler 1977). With respect to COA research, the interaction of personality with alcohol effects appears to be a potentially promising research direction. Almost sixty years ago, McDougall (1929) hypothesized relations between various personality dimensions and alcohol effects. Research by Eysenck and his colleagues (Claridge, Canter, and Hume 1973; Eysenck 1957) suggest that although McDougall's speculations were overly simplistic, the study of personality X drug interactions is a valuable strategy in biopsychosocial research. Demonstration that certain personality traits might be related to increased reinforcement from alcohol (Levenson, Oyama, and Meek 1987; Sher 1986; Sher and Levenson 1982) suggests one possible pathway through which personality variables might relate to the development of alcoholism. The recent demonstration that the relation between behavioral undercontrol and alcohol involvement appears to be mediated by expected reinforcement from alcohol (Goldman 1989; Sher and Walitzer 1989; Walitzer 1990) supports this viewpoint. Cloninger's (1987a) model of the neurochemical substrate subserving basic personality/motivational systems, although speculative, suggests a number of testable hypotheses concerning the interactions of personality characteristics, environmental challenges, and drug effects.

Alcohol Expectancies

Individually held alcohol expectancies (i.e., anticipated alcohol effects) have been shown to be strongly correlated with drinking patterns in both adults (Brown, Goldman, Inn, and Anderson 1980) and adolescents (Christiansen and Goldman 1983; Christiansen, Goldman, and Brown 1985; Christiansen, Goldman, and Inn 1982). Recently, these expectancies have been shown to predict alcohol consumption and problem drinking prospectively in adolescents (Christiansen, Smith, Roehling, and Goldman 1989). Also, strong parent-offspring correlations in generalized expectancies for alcohol effects have been recently reported (Johnson, Nagoshi, Danko, Honbo, and Chau 1990). Although it has been argued that this intergenerational transmission of alcohol expectancies is culturally determined (Johnson et al. 1990), Perry's (1973) twin study of attitudes towards different types of drugs indicates moderate heritability of attitudes toward alcohol, suggesting that there may be a genetic contribution to alcohol expectancies.

Because of the demonstrated power of alcohol expectancies in predicting drinking behavior, several recent investigations have explored the relation between family history of alcoholism and specific types of expectancies about alcohol. Brown, Creamer, and Stetson (1987) found that adolescent COAs had significantly stronger expectancies that alcohol enhances cognitive and motor performance than did nonCOAs. Although no differences were found on six other subscales, this relation was replicated by Mann et al. (1987). More recently, we (Sher et al. in press) found that COAs had more positive expectancies for reinforcement from alcohol on three of four subscales (tension reduction, social lubrication, and performance enhancement) on an alcohol expectancy inventory of our own construction. The performance enhancement subscale is similar to the "enhances cognitive and motor functioning" subscale on the AEQ-A and the magnitude of COA/nonCOA differences was found to increase when subjects with any parental comorbidity were excluded from the sample.

However, four recent studies (Kaplan, Hesselbrock, O'Connor, and De-Palma 1988; Nagoshi and Wilson 1987; O'Malley and Maisto 1985; Schuckit 1984a) failed to find differences between young adult male COAs and nonCOAs using different measures of alcohol expectancies. Additionally, a recent study comparing COAs and nonCOAs on their reasons for drinking and not drinking (Hesselbrock, O'Brien, Weinstein, and Carter-Menendez 1987) failed to show any group differences. Consequently, the results on the differences in expectancies between COAs and nonCOAs are mixed. However, results from three independent samples demonstrating that expectancies for improved cognitive and motor functioning distinguish COAs from nonCOAs suggest that the finding may be reliable but rather specific in adolescent samples. Furthermore, the findings from the Sher et al. (in press) study employing college freshmen, using a different questionnaire, suggest that measurement issues may play an important role in demonstrating these differences in expectancies more generally.

Additional analyses by Mann et al. (1987) indicate that the strength of the relations between alcohol expectancies and alcohol involvement vary as a function of both family history of alcoholism and presumed prealcoholic traits. Much of the research conducted using a cross-sectional high-risk design simply attempts to demonstrate between-group mean differences. The Mann et al. (1987) data, although of interest in their own right, suggest the utility, for pursuing etiological leads, of contrasting the patterns of correlations among theoretically related variables in high- and low-risk groups.

We have recently shown, cross-sectionally, that a "causal" model linking family history of alcoholism, behavioral undercontrol, positive alcohol expectancies, and alcohol involvement is consistent with the hypothesis that the link between paternal alcoholism, behavioral undercontrol, and alcohol involvement is partially mediated by alcohol expectancies (Sher and Walitzer 1989). This analysis suggests that we can meaningfully integrate multiple risk variables at varying levels of psychobiological significance in models attempting to describe potentially critical, mediational linkages (see fig. 6.1).

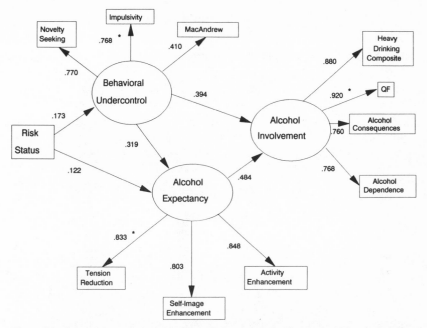

Figure 6.1. Structural equation model of the relation among family history (risk status), behavioral undercontrol, alcohol expectancy, and alcohol involvement in a sample of college freshmen. Note that the relation between family history and alcohol involvement appears to be completely accounted for by behavioral undercontrol and alcohol expectancy (i.e., the direct path from risk status to alcohol involvement is nonsignificant) and that part of the effect of behavioral undercontrol is mediated by alcohol expectancy.

Further research on the relation between family history of alcoholism and alcohol expectancies should be encouraged. Additional replication of the reported findings is needed as is detailed study of the factors leading to the development of specific alcohol expectancies such as enhanced cognitive and motor performance expectancies in high-risk and low-risk groups.

Future studies of the development of alcohol expectancies ought to begin in early childhood, since recent work (Greenberg, Zucker, and Noll 1985) indicates that even preschoolers have a surprising level of knowledge concerning alcohol and alcohol effects and that this knowledge is related to parents' drinking patterns. Should these recent positive findings prove replicable, interventions targeted at altering expectancies would appear to be a viable direction to take in prevention research with COAs. Certainly, on a priori grounds, alcohol expectancies should be subject to the same basic principles of change as other cognitive constructs such as attitudes. Although it is not known currently if firmly established alcohol expectancies are amenable to direct modification, researchers are beginning to explore this issue (Goldman 1989; Marlatt 1987).

Academic/School Achievement

There is consistent evidence that COAs evidence impaired academic achievement. Studies using standardized measures of academic functioning such as the Peabody Individual Achievement Test (PIAT) and the Wide Range Achievement Test (WRAT) (Bennett et al. 1988b; Ervin, Little, Streissguth, and Beck 1984; Hegedus, Alterman, and Tarter 1984; Marcus 1986) generally indicate impaired performance by COAs relative to nonCOAs (although Johnson and Rolf [1988] failed to observe COA/nonCOA differences on the WRAT in a sample of children 6–18 years of age). Examination of the school records of COAs and nonCOAs also reveals that COAs have greater academic difficulties, such as having to repeat a grade, failure to graduate from high school, and referral to a school psychologist (Knop et al. 1985; Miller and Jang 1977; Tarter, Jacob, and Bremer 1989). Childhood academic problems appear to be related to both paternal and maternal alcoholism.

The research is unclear as yet regarding the reasons behind the greater academic difficulties among COAs. Presumably, their impaired academic achievement could be attributable to underlying learning deficits, psychological maladjustment (e.g., conduct disorder), motivational problems, or a hellish homelife. (In the case of maternal alcoholism, fetal alcohol effects also need to be considered.) Hegedus, Alterman et al. (1984) examined the correlates of COAs' performance on achievement tests and found that measures of cognitive impairment related more consistently to academic underachievement than did family environment variables or measures of psychopathology. Methodological limitations of this study, however, make it difficult to place a high degree of confidence in these findings. Further research is required to describe the nature of the educational problems that COAs encounter and to determine the factors that may be causally involved.

Cognitive/Neuropsychological Functioning

Eighty-five years ago, MacNicholl (1905) reported a shocking relation between cognitive ability and drinking in parent and grandparent generations. Reporting on a sample of several thousand school children, MacNicholl (1905) claimed that 77 percent of schoolchildren with drinking (not necessarily alcoholic) parents or grandparents were "dullards" compared to 4 percent of children with no "hereditary alcoholic taint" (p. 117). A few years later, Elderton and Pearson (1910) in a study examining the intelligence of offspring of parents with differing drinking histories were unable to show any consistent relation between parental alcohol consumption and offspring intellectual competence. The noted Cambridge economist J. M. Keynes (1910–11) criticized the Elderton and Pearson study on methodological issues similar to those discussed in chapter 4 (failure to consider fetal alcohol effects, sampling, ascertainment of alcohol involvement, measurement of key variables) and concluded that "there is no evidence which justifies us in holding any decided opinion" (p. 344) concerning the role of parental alcohol consumption on children. Although the early studies are weak by modern standards, particularly in the ascertainment of parental drinking and offspring cognitive ability, they illustrate that conflicting reports on the extent of cognitive deficits in offspring of alcoholics have characterized the field since its beginning and critics have long pointed to methodological issues which compromise clear interpretation of data.

In this section we review a number of studies investigating cognitive and neuropsychological functioning in offspring of alcoholics. In order to organize these findings, studies using conceptually similar variables are grouped together in subsections. However, it is acknowledged that there are a number of alternative ways these data could be aggregated to yield different organizational structures. The present organization was based on a scheme that minimizes inferences concerning the function and localization of abilities sampled by various measures.

Sensorimotor Performance

(a) *Body sway.* Interest in the relation between body sway and family history of alcoholism stems from Lipscomb, Carpenter, and Nathan's (1979) observation (in two separate studies) that young adult male relatives of alcoholics swayed more when sober, especially when they had their eyes closed. There have now been several replications of this effect (Hegedus, Tarter, Hill, Jacob, and Winsten 1984; Hill, Armstrong, Steinhauer, Baughman, and Zubin 1987; Lester and Carpenter 1985; Tarter et al. 1989) as well as several negative findings (Behar et al. 1983; Nagoshi and Wilson 1987; O'Malley and Maisto 1985; Schuckit 1985b). The reasons for the contradictory findings are unclear but may be due to procedural differences among laboratories, sampling differences, etc. With the exception of the Behar et al. (1983) study, the negative findings were derived from studies using: (1) drinking-age subjects who were screened to eliminate abstainers and subjects with drinking problems, and (2) nonCOAs matched to COAs on drinking pattern. As discussed in chapter 5, each of these design features could serve to minimize COA/nonCOA differences. Consequently it is possible that the positive findings result from uncontrolled confounding factors associated with a family history of alcoholism. Alternatively, it is possible that the screening and matching procedures employed in the studies involving alcohol consumption eliminated meaningful between-group differences (e.g., truly vulnerable subjects were screened out of the high-risk group).

In summary, available data suggest that COAs evidence increased body sway relative to nonCOAs, but this finding is not robust across alternative sampling and matching strategies. Assuming that increased body sway is a marker of risk, the meaning of this finding is unclear. Presumably increased body sway indicates some form of neurological dysfunction, but from this finding alone it is difficult to implicate a specific neurological deficit or to speculate on how this deficit might be etiologically linked to drinking problems. Nevertheless, body sway appears to be a potentially valuable measure to include in future research studies.

(b) *Other sensorimotor tests.* A number of studies have examined the performance of COAs and nonCOAs on tasks measuring perceptual-motor functioning. The range of abilities sampled in these investigations is quite broad, encompassing tests primarily designed to measure motor speed (e.g., reaction time and performance on the Digit Symbol test from the WAIS) to complex perceptual-motor integration (e.g., the Tactual Performance Test of the Halstead-Reitan Neuropsychological Test Battery). Two studies employing a battery of measures of perceptual-motor performance (Tarter et al. 1984; Workman-Daniels & Hesselbrock 1987) failed to find significant differences between COAs and nonCOAs, while one study (Schaeffer, Parsons, and Yohman 1984) reported marginally poorer performances among COAs. Examination of specific tests of perceptual-motor performance including the Digit Symbol Test of the WAIS and the analogous Coding Test of the WISC-R (Drejer et al. 1985; Ervin et al. 1984; Workman-Daniels & Hesselbrock 1987; Schaeffer et al. 1984) and the Tactual Performance Test of the Halstead-Reitan (Hesselbrock, Hesselbrock, and Stabenau 1985a; Tarter et al. 1989; Workman-Daniels and Hesselbrock 1987) fails to show consistent group differences on any of these tests. A possible exception to these findings is Tarter et al.'s (1989) report that COAs performed worse on the Symbol Digit Modalities Test. Only the data reported by Schaeffer et al. (1984) are consistent with the notion that COAs are characterized by deficits in perceptual-motor functioning. Consequently, although somewhat limited, the available data suggest that COAs are not significantly impaired in this domain.

Verbal Ability

Several studies utilizing the Wechsler Adult Intelligence Scale (WAIS) have demonstrated significantly lower verbal ability in COAs relative to nonCOAs (Drejer et al. 1985; Ervin et al. 1984; Gabrielli and Mednick 1983; Sher et al. 1990). Even in studies reporting negative findings (Hesselbrock et al. 1985a; Johnson and Rolf 1988; Tarter et al. 1984; Workman-Daniels and Hesselbrock 1987), COAs still tended to perform worse than nonCOAs. Across seven studies that employed the WAIS, COAs performed approximately .5 standard deviations lower than did nonCOAs. When alternative measures of verbal ability are used, researchers still find decreased performance among COAs (Knop et al. 1985; Nagoshi and Wilson 1987; Tarter et al. 1984). Although some negative findings have been reported (Schaeffer et al. 1984), the data are strongly consistent across studies and show that COAs have poorer verbal ability than nonCOAs. However, despite their lower mean scores, COAs perform well within normal limits and their deficit in verbal ability is only a relative one.

Visuospatial Ability

Although the evidence is far less consistent than for verbal ability, there are some data suggesting that COAs show impaired spatial abilities. Several studies have compared the performance of COAs and nonCOAs on the Trail Making Test of the Halstead-Reitan Neuropsychological Battery (Hesselbrock et al. 1985a; Schaeffer et al. 1984; Schuckit, Butters, Lyn, and Irwin 1987a; Sher et al. in press; Tarter et al. 1984, 1989; Workman-Daniels and Hesselbrock 1987). The studies reported by Schaeffer et al. (1984) and Tarter et al. (1984) suggest that COAs exhibit impaired performance on these tasks, while the studies by Hesselbrock and his colleagues, Schuckit et al. (1987a), and Tarter et al. (1989) fail to show group differences. The studies reviewed above concerning *field dependence* are also potentially relevant here and show a similar, mixed picture. There is some evidence that COAs perform worse than nonCOAs on Block Design (see section on Abstraction/Conceptual Reasoning below), and two studies (Drejer et al. 1985; Tarter et al. 1989) found that COAs perform relatively poorly on the Porteus Maze test. A recent study by Alterman, Bridges, and Tarter (1986b), however, failed to find any differences between COAs and nonCOAs in a small sample of college students on mirror tracing or on the Maze Test of the Revised Beta Examination. Although limited, the positive findings reported to date suggest that further research in this area is warranted.

Learning and Memory

Several studies have examined learning and memory performance in COA and nonCOA groups on a variety of tasks (Drejer et al. 1985; Schaeffer et al. 1984; Schandler, Brannock, Cohen, Antick, and Caine 1988; Schuckit et al. 1987; Sher et al. in press; Tarter et al. 1984, 1989; Whipple et al. 1988; Workman-Daniels and Hesselbrock 1987). In general, these studies indicate that COAs do not have impaired learning/memory ability. However, Tarter et al. (1984), using the Logical Memory subtest of the Wechsler Memory Scale, and Whipple et al. (1988), using the Rey Auditory Verbal Learning Test, did find impaired performance among COAs. Also, Schandler et al. (1988), using a visuospatial paired-associate learning task showed learning deficits in a sample of elementary school COAs. Although limited, available data suggest that deficits in learning and memory are not pronounced among COAs, but the few positive findings reported to date suggest that further study in this area may be warranted.

Abstraction/Conceptual Reasoning

There are data on a variety of tasks which assess complex abstraction and conceptual reasoning in COAs and nonCOAs. Because three tasks (Halstead's Category Test and the Block Design and Similarities tests of the WAIS and WISC-R) have been used in multiple studies, our discussion will focus on the results of these three tests. It should be noted that several basic abilities underlie each of these tasks and none of them can be considered a pure measure of abstraction. For example, the nonverbal measures (Block Design and the Category Test) require conceptual reasoning, problem-solving skills, and other processes (e.g., visual analysis skills). In addition, each has relatively unique sources of additional variance (manual dexterity and motor speed for Block Design; memory ability for the Category Test).

To date, seven studies have examined the performance of COAs and nonCOAs on Halstead's Category Test (Drejer et al. 1985; Hesselbrock et al. 1985a; Hill, Steinhauer, Park, and Zubin 1990; Schaeffer et al. 1984; Schuckit et al. 1987; Sher et al. in press; Workman-Daniels and Hesselbrock 1987). COAs performed significantly worse than nonCOAs in two studies (Drejer et al. 1985; Schaeffer et al. 1984). In a third study (Workman-Daniels and Hesselbrock 1987), examination of the data indicates a relatively large effect size (approximately .55 standard deviations) despite the fact the difference was not significantly different. Taken together, the data suggest that COAs do evidence impaired performance on the Category Test relative to nonCOAs, but that the magnitude of these differences is relatively small and less likely to be found in college-student samples (Schuckit et al. 1987; Sher et al. in press).

Seven studies (Drejer et al. 1985; Ervin et al. 1984; Gabrielli and Mednick 1983; Schaeffer et al. 1984; Tarter et al. 1984; Whipple et al. 1988; Workman-Daniels and Hesselbrock 1987) have investigated differences between COAs and nonCOAs on WISC-R and WAIS Block Design. In each study, mean levels of performance were lower among COAs than nonCOAs. However, between-group differences reached significance in only two of them (Schaeffer et al. 1984; Whipple et al. 1988). Across the six studies in which sufficient data were presented to permit analysis of effect sizes, the mean effect size for studies using Block Design was .40 standard deviations. The findings of generally poor performance on Block Design and the Category Test is also consistent with the results of two studies (Nagoshi and Wilson 1987; Tarter et al. 1989) that reported impaired performance on another nonverbal measure of reasoning (Raven's Progressive Matrices).

Finally, COAs performed significantly worse than nonCOAs on the Similarities test in three studies (Ervin et al. 1984; Gabrielli and Mednick 1983; Sher et al. in press) and nonsignificantly so in another (Tarter et al. 1984). Paradoxically, the strongest effect was found in the Tarter et al. (1984) study, which illustrates how the presence or absence of "significant" findings in this area can be a function of sample size rather than "actual" between-group differences. The average effect size across these studies was .54 standard deviations.

In summary, despite a number of important differences among samples (including age of sample, ascertainment strategy, etc.), existing data suggest that COAs are impaired relative to nonCOAs on both verbal (Similarities) and nonverbal (Block Design and the Category Test) indices of abstraction/conceptual reasoning.

Emotional Processing

Baribeau, Braun, and Dube (1986) recently compared COAs and nonCOAs on a nonverbal (the Facial Expression Test [FET]) and a verbal (the Verbal-Contextual Test [VCT]) test of emotional processing. In these tasks the subject must correctly identify the emotions represented by visually presented stimuli (faces on the FET) or aurally presented stimuli (statements depicting common emotion-evoking situations on the VCT). No significant between group differences emerged.

Available data suggest that there are cognitive differences between COAs and nonCOAs, most notably deficits in verbal ability and abstraction/conceptual reasoning for COAs. In contrast, no reliable pattern of findings has yet been reported for measures of spatial ability, learning and memory, or perceptual-motor functioning (with the possible exception of body sway). Given the limited data currently available, no findings can yet be considered definitive, and it is certainly conceivable that future research might uncover additional deficits.

The etiological significance, if any, of impaired cognitive performance is presently unclear, as there are few studies examining the long-term correlates of cognitive deficits among COAs. In one of the few studies examining this issue, Werner (1986) found that pediatricians' ratings of COAs' intellectual development at age 2 predicted adjustment problems at age 18. If we assume that cognitive dysfunction does represent a potential indicator of vulnerability, several hypotheses could be put forth relating cognitive ability to later dysfunction. For example, impaired verbal ability and problem-solving ability may contribute to school failure and consequent loss of self-esteem or adoption of a deviant role. The findings of impaired educational achievement among COAs are consistent with this notion. A second hypothesis is that these cognitive impairments may lead to reduced coping abilities with consequent use of alcohol as a coping strategy. A third possibility is that alcohol consumption subjectively improves cognitive performance in some COAs and is thus reinforcing. This is supported by the results of Brown et al. (1987), Chassin et al. (1988), and Sher et al. (in press), who found that adolescent COAs tend to believe that alcohol improves cognitive and motor functioning. It is also possible that these deficits are epiphenomena and may only serve as a marker of a true etiological factor.

Similarly, the meaning of increased body sway among COAs is unclear, except perhaps to suggest that some form of neurological impairment is present. To date, no compelling explication of the possible etiological relevance of this finding has been proposed. Although increased body sway may ultimately prove useful as a potential marker of risk, its significance is currently obscure.

Summary

Available data suggest that COAs can be distinguished from controls on variables sampling a number of ostensibly disparate domains (personality, alcohol expectancies, and neuropsychological performance). In general, the genetic and environmental contributions to these differences have not been assessed, nor have the interrelationships of these variables. The recent work concerning the relationship between behavioral undercontrol and expectancies for reinforcement from alcohol (Goldman 1989; Sher et al. 1989) indicate that current investigators are beginning to address this issue. In addition, the specificity of these differences to alcoholism as opposed to parental psychopathology in general has not been addressed systematically (although see Tarter et al. 1989). Similarly, the relation of these deficits to subtypes of parental alcoholism has been largely unexplored.

7 Biological Characteristics

In this chapter, studies comparing COAs and nonCOAs on a number of biological variables are reviewed. As was true in the preceding chapter, the majority of these studies attempt to identify variables that might serve as markers or mediators of risk for alcoholism. Although it is clear that many if not all of the "psychological" variables reviewed in the preceding chapter have, at least, a biological basis or component (e.g., personality, cognitive functioning), what I have previously termed "psychological characteristics" are based on data derived from observations of overt behavior and/or self-reported characteristics. In contrast, the studies reviewed in this chapter are based on research strategies that generally involve direct measurement of biological characteristics and processes such as assays of body tissue or electrophysiological recordings of nervous system activity or other somatic processes. However, some of these "biological" variables (e.g., autonomic reactivity, event-related potentials) are closely coupled to psychological phenomena and thus the distinction between biological and psychological variables is often imprecise. Thus, my distinction between biological and psychological variables should not be viewed as representing a mind/body dualism but rather as a convenient strategy for classifying studies. Research relying upon the direct assessment of physiological and biochemical processes or states is reviewed in this chapter even if the interpretation of these studies directly implicates psychological variables. Although some of the studies reviewed below involved ethanol administration as part of the experimental protocols, data concerning responses to alcohol challenges are not presented in this chapter. *Thus all the findings reviewed below refer to characteristics of COAs when sober.* Data from studies comparing COAs and nonCOAs when intoxicated are reviewed in chapter 8.

Neurophysiological Characteristics

Electroencephalographic (EEG) recording involves the detection of brain electrical activity, usually, from noninvasive electrodes placed on the subject's scalp. The voltages detected by the electrodes are very small and must be greatly amplified in order to be studied. When amplified and displayed on an oscilloscope, computer display, or chart recorder, the EEG tracing appears as a series of oscillating lines which can be described in terms of the frequency and amplitude of the various waveforms making up each tracing. The pattern of electrical activity detected has been related to neuronal activity, more specifically synaptic and dendritic potentials (and not the summation of neuronal action potentials; Elul 1972).

Spontaneous EEG refers to the fluctuating pattern of voltages that are observed over time without reference to discrete sensory stimulation and cognitive challenges. In contrast, event related potentials (ERPs) are discrete waveforms that are elicited by direct sensory stimulation of the subject (e.g., a brief flash of light, an auditory click) or by engagement in a cognitive task (e.g., having the subject make a judgment about the properties of a stimulus). Because these ERPs can be difficult to discern against the "noisy" background of spontaneous EEG, most typically they are averaged over many trials so that the spontaneous EEG, which is random with respect to the ERP, is canceled out. With averaging over a sufficient number of trials, a specific waveform that represents the subject's response to sensory stimulation and/or a cognitive challenge is generated. This waveform can be analyzed in a number of ways but usually involves measurement of both the latency and amplitude of individual ERP components (characteristic peaks and troughs). The effects of signal averaging is graphically displayed in Figure 7.1, which illustrates the variability of single-trial ERPs and the improvement in the resolution of the ERP as more trials are averaged. Figure 7.2 illustrates how the latency and amplitude of specific ERP components can be measured.

Some authors make a distinction between evoked potentials or responses (EPs and ERs) and ERPs, with the former referring to waveforms of short latencies and associated with early sensory processing and the latter referring to waveforms of longer latencies and associated with tasks involving higher levels of information processing. For our purposes, however, all EEG waveforms that are time-locked to specific environmental challenges and averaged over multiple trials will be referred to as ERPs.

Spontaneous Electroencephalographic (EEG) Activity

In general, gross abnormalities in spontaneous EEG among alcoholics appear to be no more common than in the general population, although some studies suggest

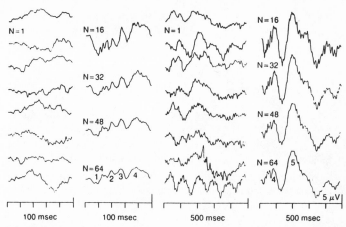

Figure 7.1. Illustration of the effects of signal averaging. The first and third columns represent EEG responses to a single stimulus, the second and fourth columns represent averaged responses to 16, 32, 48, and 64 repetitions. Reprinted from Hassett (1978) with permission of the author and W. H. Freeman and Company.

abstinent alcoholics may show "a generalized reduction in EEG alpha activity and increases in the fast frequencies" (cf. Ehlers and Schuckit, in press).

Gabrielli et al. (1982) found that 11–13-year-old boy (but not girl) COAs had significantly higher percentages of fast EEG activity (only >18 Hz) than nonCOA controls. The robustness of this finding is unclear since other reports by the same research team (Pollock et al. 1983, 1984) indicate that subjects from the same birth cohort at ages 19–21 years failed to demonstrate the increased fast-activity effect. A more recent study by Ehlers and Schuckit (1990) also failed to find differences between young adult male COAs and nonCOAs on fast EEG activity (12–20 Hz) when sober. Although it is possible that the excess of fast EEG activity among boy COAs observed by Gabrielli et al. (1982) is not a Type 1 error (perhaps representing a developmentally limited effect), it is difficult to place a high degree of confidence in this finding at present.

Recently Ehlers and Schuckit (in press) reported that young adult male COAs showed more power in the fast alpha frequency range (9–12 Hz) than nonCOAs when sober. This effect has yet to be replicated. A recent study by Kaplan et al. (1988) failed to find resting EEG differences between male COAs and nonCOAs in young adulthood when sober. Although this latter study did not report findings separately for various frequency ranges, the general lack of an association between family history and EEG power spectral-density distributions suggests inconsistency with the positive findings reported by Gabrielli et al. (1982) and Ehlers and Schuckit (in press). Although it is certainly possible that spontaneous EEG activity varies as a

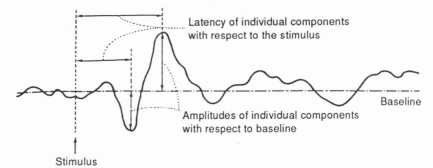

Figure 7.2. Illustration of the quantification of averaged ERP responses. Reprinted from Stern, Ray, and Davis (1980) with permission of the authors and Oxford University Press.

function of family history of alcoholism, at present there is a clear lack of replicable findings.

Event-Related Potentials (ERPs)

To date, studies examining the early ERP components associated with direct sensory stimulation (e.g., trains of auditory clicks, visual presentation of a continually reversing checkerboard pattern) fail to distinguish COAs from nonCOAs (Begleiter, Porjesz, and Bihari 1987; Neville and Schmidt 1985; Pollock et al. 1988a). This generalization might be somewhat qualified by Pollock et al.'s (1988a) recent finding that differences in the symmetry of the ERP recorded over right and left hemispheres differ between young adult male COAs and nonCOAs *when only right-handed subjects are considered.* Given the post-hoc nature of these latter findings concerning handedness and the lack of replication, at present there is little evidence to suggest that COAs and nonCOAs differ in the ERPs to simple sensory stimulation.

In contrast, studies examining ERPs elicited by tasks having a greater cognitive component have yielded some relatively provocative, positive findings. COAs do appear to differ from nonCOAs on ERPs elicited by several cognitive tasks (Begleiter, Porjesz, Bihari, and Kissin 1984; Begleiter, Porjesz, Rawlings, and Eckardt 1987; Elmasian, Neville, Woods, Schuckit, and Bloom 1982; O'Connor, Hesselbrock, and Tasman 1986; O'Connor, Hesselbrock, Tasman, and DePalma 1987; Schmidt and Neville 1985; Whipple et al. 1988). Male COAs (ranging in age from late childhood to young adulthood) have been shown to have reduced P3 (a positive ERP wave occurring approximately 300 msec after stimulus onset) or other late positive component of the ERP elicited by a visuospatial judgment task involving mental rotation (Begleiter et al. 1984; O'Connor et al. 1986, 1987), a visually presented continuous performance task (Whipple et al. 1988), a visual tracking task (O'Connor et al. 1987), and by auditory tasks involving tone discriminations

(Elmasian et al. 1982; Begleiter et al. 1987). These studies using (for the most part) differing procedures indicate that the finding of attenuated P3 among male COAs is neither age-, nor task-, nor modality-specific, nor is it dependent upon the type of data reduction technique. Neville and Schmidt's (1985) finding that young adult male COAs have a reduced negative ERP component (N430) in a language processing task (determining if two consecutively presented single letters rhyme) and findings reported by Patterson, Williams, McLean, Smith, and Schaeffer (1987) showing attenuated N1 components on an auditory processing task suggest that a wide range of tasks are capable of eliciting ERP differences between high-risk and low-risk subjects.

Despite these generally consistent findings, a few studies employing auditory discrimination tasks in male (Polich and Bloom 1988; Schuckit, Gold, Croot, Finn, and Polich 1988a) and mixed sex (Polich, Burns, and Bloom 1988) samples of college students failed to show evidence of P3 amplitude or latency differences between COAs and nonCOAs. This same group also failed to find P3 amplitude or latency differences between male COA and nonCOA college students on a visual discrimination task (Polich, Haier, Buchsbaum, and Bloom 1988). It is difficult to determine the reasons for these failures to replicate. However, it should be noted that these investigators employed small samples, college students, and relatively nonchallenging tasks. Any or all of these factors could plausibly be related to these failures to replicate.

Although not strictly a study of children of alcoholics, a recent study of adult (mean age of 34) men and their parents (Hill et al. 1990; Steinhauer, Hill, and Zubin 1987) found that it was the *latency* rather than the amplitude of P3 that distinguished alcoholic probands and their alcoholic siblings from their nonalcoholic siblings. Unaffected siblings tended to have shorter latencies than their affected siblings. Should this finding prove replicable, it suggests that decreased latency (perhaps indicating greater "cognitive capacity") might index a protective factor. However, the results of this study are difficult to interpret because there did not appear to be any straightforward relation between parental alcoholism and offspring P3, and because the P3 of alcoholic siblings appeared to be quite similar to the P3 of siblings from nonalcoholic families. Given the extent of replication of the previous findings suggesting the importance of P3 amplitude, not latency, as a correlate of risk (although see Elmasian et al. 1982), brief consideration of Hill and colleagues' findings is indicated. Subjects in that study were older on average than those in the previously cited studies, and presumably the reported findings could relate to either maturational differences in the samples or to the effects of more extensive histories of alcohol consumption. The negative finding regarding amplitude may also represent a Type 2 error.

On balance, it does appear that P3 and other late ERP components to relatively difficult cognitive challenges distinguishes COAs from nonCOAs and that this effect appears to be relatively robust across laboratories and experimental paradigms. Although, negative findings have been reported, most of these failures to replicate involve relatively small sample sizes, older subjects, subjects in higher educational settings, or relatively easy cognitive challenges. However, the meaning of P3 deficits is not yet clear. The findings that attenuated P3 has been related to decreased attentional capacity and attention deficit-hyperactivity disorder (ADHD) (cf. Zahn 1986), are consistent with family and longitudinal data suggesting a link between ADHD and alcoholism (cf. Tarter 1988). However, attenuated P3 components have been found in seemingly unrelated conditions, most notably schizophrenia, and may characterize unaffected relatives of schizophrenics (cf. Pritchard 1986; Zahn 1986). Also given the high comorbidity between alcoholism and antisocial personality disorder (see chapter 1) and the postulated common diathesis (Cloninger 1987a; Gorenstein and Newman 1980), it is somewhat surprising that psychopathic individuals have been shown to have enhanced P3 in certain experimental paradigms (Raine and Venables 1987, 1988). Given that attenuated P3 appears to characterize conditions unrelated to alcoholism, and that related conditions might show increased P3, the specificity of attenuated P3 and its relation to alcohol-related comorbidity needs to be better specified. Finally, differences between COAs and nonCOAs on P3 have been found from studies employing both auditory and visual modalities, possibly suggesting a single underlying deficit. However, auditory and visual P3s appear to have different generators, arguing against the notion that the P3 wave represents a unitary phenomenon (Johnson 1989a, 1989b). Nevertheless, the findings on P3 to date are intriguing and warrant clarification of the specificity and meaning of P3 deficits.

In summary, the neurophysiological data suggest that COAs demonstrate reduced amplitude in the P3 component of the ERP elicited by a variety of cognitive tasks. In contrast, analysis of the frequency spectra of the resting EEG has not been shown to reliably discriminate COAs and nonCOAs, nor have early and middle ERP components to sensory stimulation been shown to discriminate these groups. Although currently employed procedures for generating and reducing ERPs have been relatively successful in distinguishing COAs from controls, the parameters governing the conditions likely to maximize COA/nonCOA differences have yet to be clearly defined. Development of a protocol that appears to discriminate high- and low-risk groups most efficiently would facilitate further research on this promising lead.

The finding of reduced P3 may raise more questions than it answers. Pragmatically, reduced P3 might prove useful as a marker of vulnerability and might facilitate research and intervention; theoretically, the significance of reduced P3 is unclear. Although cognitive processes (stimulus evaluation, attentional resources, certain memory processes, etc.) may be indexed by P3, and generators of P3 are thought to have fairly localized generators in the CNS (e.g., in the hippocampal region), the etiological significance of this finding is currently obscure (although see chapter 9). The problems of attempting to explain the significance of the P3 findings are similar to those of relating the neuropsychological evidence described in chapter 6, and, as noted above, available data suggest that attenuated P3 and other late ERP components may reflect a generalized deficit common to a number of clinically distinct disorders.

Autonomic and Electromyographic (EMG) Characteristics

Measures of autonomic activity can, in certain paradigms, be useful for assessing internal states such as attention, stress, and general "arousal." Because of this, a number of studies have employed autonomic measures in examining possible differences between COAs and nonCOAs on basic processes related to motivation and emotion. Although not an autonomic measure, EMG activity is also often used to infer similar internal states, and studies using EMG measures are also reviewed in this section.

Basal Autonomic and EMG Levels

Existing data fail to indicate reliable COA/nonCOA differences in resting heart rate, finger pulse amplitude, skin conductance level, and frontalis EMG activity (Finn and Pihl 1987; Finn, Zeitouni, and Pihl 1990; Levenson, Oyama, and Meek 1987; Newlin 1985; Schuckit, Engstrom, Alpert, and Duby 1981; Walitzer and Sher 1990). Although these null findings are of little substantive interest in their own right, they are methodologically important in that they suggest that any differences found in reactivity to environmental stimulation (discussed below) are not confounded with "initial values effects" (i.e., the finding that changes in response to a stimulus are often related to baseline values).

Reactivity to Nonaversive Stimulation

Recently, Finn, Zeitouni, and Pihl (1990) found that male COAs with multigenerational family histories of alcoholism showed larger skin conductance responses and slower habituation rates to a series of nonaversive tones than control nonCOAs. Similarly, Walitzer and Sher (1990) found that male COAs showed greater reactivity to beverage cues (exposure to beer and unflavored seltzer) than nonCOAs on measures of skin temperature and frontalis electromyographic (EMG) activity (although not on measures of heart rate or skin conductance). These data suggest that COAs may be overreactive to a range of nonaversive stimuli. However, the limited number of studies in this area suggests caution in drawing any firm conclusions at present.

Reactivity to Aversive Stimulation

Data are mixed concerning the extent that COAs and nonCOAs differ in their responses to aversive stimulation (e.g., anticipation of painful electric shocks and making a speech). Studies by Finn and Pihl (1987) and their colleagues (Finn et al. 1990) suggest that male COAs with a multigenerational family history of alcoholism show increased reactivity to anticipated electric shock, while Levenson et al. (1987) failed to find differences between male and female COAs and nonCOAs in reactivity to a shock stressor and to a speech stressor. These seeming inconsistencies might be attributable to heterogeneity of subtypes of alcoholism. Studies by Finn and Pihl (1987, 1988) indicate that only subjects with multigenerational family histories of alcoholism appear to show increased stress reactivity, while subjects with alcoholic fathers but not alcoholic grandfathers fail to show this effect. Pedigree information on the COAs studied by Levenson et al. (1987) is not reported, but it is unlikely that the majority of subjects in that study would show alcoholism in multiple generations. Consequently, it appears reasonable to conclude that only a subset of COAs, those characterized by family pedigrees marked by a high degree of intergenerational transmission, show this hyperreactivity to aversive stimulation. Such cardiovascular hyperreactivity is potentially etiologically significant if it relates to subjective distress and possible motivation to use alcohol for stress relief.

To sum up, existing data suggest that COAs, especially COAs with a multigenerational history of paternal alcoholism, are more reactive to both non-aversive and aversive stimulation. Recently, Pihl, Peterson, and Finn (1990b) interpreted this pattern to suggest that SOMAs (sons of male alcoholics) "hyperreact to stimuli that might be considered intrinsically motivating" and contrasted this pattern with the data from the ERP studies (reviewed earlier), suggesting that SOMAs "hyporeact during situations that require the allocation of directed voluntary attention" (p. 296). Although these speculations are interesting, further research is needed to evaluate whether the sustained deployment of attention is the critical factor in determining stress reactivity in SOMAs or COAs more generally.

Biochemical Characteristics

Because the amount and activity of a number of important biochemical substances (e.g., enzymes related to neurotransmitter activity) are known to be under a high degree of genetic control, a likely place to look for mediators of genetic risk is in the broad domain of biochemical characteristics. Not surprisingly, substances related to neurotransmitter systems which are known to be important in the regulation of mood and behavior (e.g., the catecholamines and serotonin) have received the most attention to date. However, the empirical data base in this area is generally limited. Studies examining possible biochemical differences between COAs and nonCOAs in the metabolism of alcohol are reviewed in chapter 8.

Enzymes Related to Neurotransmitter Metabolism

Monoamine oxidase (MAO) is an important enzyme in the catabolism (breakdown) of the catecholamines (dopamine and norepinephrine) and serotonin (e.g., Cooper, Bloom, and Roth 1982). Because these neurotransmitters are thought to play a central role in regulating mood and behavior, MAO activity has often been studied for its potential relevance for understanding psychopathology in general and alcoholism in particular. In most studies, the human blood platelet is the source of MAO. Although two forms of MAO have been identified in the human brain (MAO-A and MAO-B), only MAO-B is found in blood platelets. Furthermore, although platelet MAO is usually assumed to be an index of brain MAO activity, available data have yet to demonstrate a significant correlation between brain and platelet MAO activity (Major, Hawley, Saini, Garrick, and Murphy 1985; Young, Laws, Sharbrough, and Winshilboum 1986). However, von Knorring and his colleagues (von Knorring, Oreland, Haggendal, Magnusson, Almay, and Johansson 1986) have reported a significant correlation between platelet MAO activity and cerebrospinal fluid (CSF) concentrations of serotonin's major metabolite (5-hydroxyindole acetic acid; 5-HIAA) in a sample of chronic pain patients. This suggests that platelet MAO activity is related to central serotinergic mechanisms.

Many studies have found low levels of platelet MAO activity among alcoholics (Brown 1977; Gottfries, Oreland, Wiberg, and Winblad 1975; Major, Goyer, and Murphy 1981; Major and Murphy 1978; Sullivan, Stanfield, Maltbie, Hammett, and Cavenar 1978; Takahashi, Tani, and Yamane 1976; Wiberg, Gottfries, and Oreland 1977). However, it is not clear whether these low MAO levels precede or result from excessive alcohol consumption. Existing data demonstrate that MAO activity levels of alcoholics are low and that there are transient increases in these levels during alcohol withdrawal; data are mixed, however, on the extent to which platelet MAO activity in alcoholics returns to its former low levels after prolonged abstinence (Brown 1977; Giller and Hall 1983; Major et al. 1981; Sullivan et al. 1978; Takahashi et al. 1976). Certainly, lower levels of platelet MAO activity do not appear to be a straightforward short-term effect of alcohol consumption; acute alcohol intoxication does not appear to alter platelet MAO activity in young, nonalcoholic men (Schuckit, Shaskan, Duby, Vega, and Moss 1982). However, recent data indicate that platelets from alcoholics show more pronounced ethanol-related inhibition of

MAO activity than platelets from nonalcoholics, suggesting either an innate or acquired sensitivity of MAO activity to ethanol among alcoholics (Tabakoff et al. 1988).

Several studies have demonstrated an association between family history of alcoholism and low platelet MAO activity and suggest that low platelet MAO activity may serve as a biological marker of risk. Alexopoulos, Lieberman, and Frances (1983) found that first-degree relatives of alcoholics had lower MAO levels than control subjects, and that this difference persisted even when first-degree relatives with a history of excessive alcohol involvement were excluded. Puchall, Coursey, Buchsbaum, and Murphy (1980) found that parents of low MAO subjects reported more symptoms of alcoholism than did parents of high MAO subjects. Sullivan, Cavenar, Maltbie, Lister, and Zung (1979) found that alcoholics with low MAO activity had more first-degree alcoholic relatives than alcoholics with high MAO activity. In seeming contradiction to these findings, Schuckit et al. (1982) failed to find a relation between family history of alcoholism and MAO activity in their study of young, male first-degree relatives of alcoholics. Findings from our own laboratory (Sher, Bylund, Hartmann, Walitzer, and Ray-Prenger 1987) suggests that there are not significant differences between COAs and nonCOAs in platelet MAO activity.

In summary, although generally supportive of the hypothesis that low MAO activity may represent a predisposition to alcoholism, the family history data are inconclusive and somewhat contradictory. Recent work by von Knorring and his colleagues (von Knorring, Bohman, von Knorring, and Oreland 1985; von Knorring, Oreland, and von Knorring 1987) suggests that low MAO activity may characterize only one form of alcoholism (the Type 2 alcoholism identified in the Stockholm Adoption Study), and perhaps the conflicting results stem from the failure to distinguish the type of alcoholism exhibited by parents in the reported samples. The hypothesis that low MAO activity might be related to Type 2 alcoholism is also consistent with the findings that low platelet MAO activity is associated with behavioral undercontrol traits such as sensation seeking and impulsivity (Fowler, von Knorring, and Oreland 1980; Murphy et al. 1977; Perris et al. 1980; Schooler, Zahn, Murphy, and Buchsbaum 1978). Also, to the extent that MAO activity may index central serotonin activity (von Knorring et al. 1986), the findings on platelet MAO activity become consistent with a roughly parallel literature relating low central serotonin activity to impulsivity, aggression, and early-onset alcoholism (Ballenger, Goodwin, Major, and Brown 1979; Buydens-Branchey, Branchey, Noumair, and Lieber 1989). It is also worth noting that rats bred for alcohol preference (Li et al. 1981) have low levels of brain serotonin (Murphy, McBride, Lumeng, & Li 1982, 1987), and that drugs that increase serotinergic neurotransmission decrease ethanol consumption (Murphy, McBride, Lumeng, and Li 1988; Murphy, Waller, Gatto, McBride, Lumeng, and Li 1985).

Although the data are somewhat mixed and the biological significance of platelet MAO activity is not definitively resolved, further research on the relation between platelet MAO activity and family history of alcoholism is clearly warranted. Platelet MAO activity appears to be related to both clinical alcoholism and family history of alcoholism, putative prealcoholic personality characteristics, and possibly central serotonin mechanisms. The extent to which careful subtyping of family history of alcoholism will result in more clear-cut findings for COAs awaits further study.

Dopamine-Beta-Hydroxylase (DBH)

This is an enzyme that catalyzes the conversion of dopamine to norepinephrine and consequently has been viewed as an index of noradrenergic functioning. Schuckit, O'Connor, Duby, Vega, and Moss (1981) compared plasma DBH activity levels between young, adult men with and without a family history of alcoholism and failed to find any between-group differences.

Transketolase

Mukherjee et al. (1987) recently reported that alcoholic fathers and their male children (ages 8–15) show an abnormality in the kinetics of a thiamine-dependent enzyme, transketolase, relative to control fathers and children. In a small pedigree study reported by these authors, the abnormality appeared to be transmitted via an autosomal recessive trait. Should the association with a family history of alcoholism prove replicable, this abnormality might prove to be a useful marker of alcoholism vulnerability.

Endocrine Hormones

Existing data fail to reveal differences between COAs and nonCOAs on basal plasma adrenocorticotropic trophic hormone (ACTH) levels (Schuckit, Risch, and Gold 1988b), basal prolactin levels (Moss, Guthrie, and Linnoila 1986; Moss, Yao, and Maddock 1989; Schuckit, Gold, and Risch 1987a; Schuckit, Parker, and Rossman 1983), basal plasma cortisol levels (Behar et al. 1983; Schuckit 1984b; Schuckit, Gold, and Risch 1987b), basal plasma triiodothyronine (T3) (Moss et al. 1986), basal plasma growth hormone (Moss et al. 1986) and basal plasma norepinephrine (Behar et al. 1983). Findings with respect to epinephrine are mixed; Swartz, Drews, and Cadoret (1987) report reduced urinary epinephrine among COAs compared to nonCOAs during rest and in response to a mental challenge in young adult male adoptees (with and without alcoholic biological fathers), and Behar et al. (1983) fail to find differences in plasma epinephrine among preadolescent and adolescent boy COAs and controls. Pending replication of the Swartz et al. (1987) findings, these data do not suggest that prolactin, ACTH, or adrenal hormones differentiate COAs from nonCOAs.

Moss et al. (1986) did find increased basal plasma thyrotropin in boy COAs but not girl COAs relative to controls, and these differences were increased following thyrotropin-releasing hormone (TRH) infusion. The results concerning thyrotropin are intriguing, as they appear to be male-limited and thus potentially related to a vulnerability specific to males. Should this effect prove replicable, the underlying cause of this dysfunction and its physiological and behavioral consequences should be explored. However, on balance, the data have yet to show replicable differences between COAs and nonCOAs on levels of endocrine hormones.

In sum, the available data generally fail to indicate consistent biochemical differences between COAs and nonCOAs although this situation may change as further data accumulate. The most promising line of research to date involves the study of platelet MAO activity which earlier research has linked both to alcoholism and to personality traits thought to be predisposing to later alcoholism. Although several negative findings have been reported with platelet MAO activity, the observation that platelet MAO activity may characterize only a subtype of alcoholism suggests that consideration of genetic heterogeneity may help delineate specific differences.

Summary

The review of research examining possible biological differences between sober COAs and nonCOAs yields several potentially important results. The most replicable of these findings concerns the attenuated late component (especially P3) of the ERP to challenging cognitive tasks which has been found by several independent laboratories employing different procedures. Although it seems unlikely that this deficit is unique to COAs and may characterize individuals at risk for a number of negative behavioral outcomes, the neurophysiologic data implicate that processes indexed by P3 and related waveforms may be etiologically important in the development of alcoholism. Similarly, the autonomic hyperreactivity reported by Finn, Pihl and their colleagues seems unlikely to be specific to COAs but nevertheless might represent an etiologically important pathway. The precise significance of these aberrations in responding to different types of environmental challenges has yet to be determined (although see Pihl, Peterson, and Finn 1990a, and chapter 9). It is important to point out that the major psychophysiological differences between COAs and nonCOAs (observed on ERPs and measures of autonomic reactivity) are observed when the organism is stimulated in some way (listening to tones, anticipating electric shocks, solving a perceptual discrimination task) and studies examining basal levels of various measures typically fail to differentiate subjects.

In the biochemical domain, platelet MAO activity may represent a variable that does distinguish COAs and nonCOAs. The potential etiological relevance of platelet MAO activity is great in that it has been: (1) associated with clinical alcoholism, (2) linked to other biochemical variables (serotonin) that appear to be associated with the development of alcoholism, and (3) correlated with presumed prealcoholic traits (aggression and impulsivity).

However, the variables that have been most consistently related to a family history of alcoholism (autonomic hyperreactivity, attenuation of late ERP components, and low platelet MAO activity) are unlikely to be specific to alcoholism and may be correlated with a range of maladaptive behavioral outcomes. This suggests that the biological basis of risk for alcoholism is shared with other conditions (possibly antisocial personality and schizophrenia). Certainly, this may ultimately prove to be the case (and would be viewed as consistent with studies of alcohol-related comorbidity). However, this notion does not appear to be consistent with the adoption study data or genetic theories that postulate that there is a form of alcoholism with its own specific etiology.

8 Responses to Alcohol

An important area of research concerns possible differences in ethanol effects between subjects with and without a family history of alcoholism. Given that alcohol consumption is a necessary condition for the development of alcoholism, the notion that COAs might respond differently to alcohol than non-COAs appears to be a reasonable working hypothesis. Three broad major alternative hypotheses concerning the relation between family history of alcoholism and alcohol effects can be proposed: (1) COAs are *especially sensitive to reinforcing alcohol effects* and are therefore more likely to drink frequently or in greater quantity because alcohol is particularly rewarding. (2) COAs are *especially insensitive to punishing alcohol effects* (nausea and discomfort, hangovers) and are therefore not likely to limit their alcohol involvement because of aversive side effects. (3) COAs are *especially insensitive to reinforcing alcohol effects* and are therefore more likely to develop drinking problems because they must drink in greater quantity to achieve desired alcohol effects.

It needs to be stressed at the outset that, for ethical reasons, it is desirable to exclude abstainers and naive drinkers from alcohol consumption studies. Therefore in most studies, it is not possible to attribute differences in ethanol sensitivity to initial sensitivity or acquired changes in sensitivity (sensitization or tolerance). Furthermore, there are a number of important methodological issues surrounding alcohol administration studies (see chapter 5) which need to be considered when evaluating the results of studies contrasting COAs and nonCOAs in their responses to alcohol.

Ethanol Absorption, Elimination, and Metabolism

Before we survey the literature on the subjective, behavioral, and physiological effects of alcohol in COAs, it is important to review first the evidence concerning ethanol absorption and metabolism. Existing data suggest that COAs do not differ from controls in either the peak blood-alcohol level reached after a given dose or in the rate of elimination (Behar et al. 1983; Ehlers and Schuckit 1990; Moss et al. 1989; Nagoshi and Wilson 1987; O'Malley and Maisto 1985; Savoie, Emory, and Moody-Thomas 1988; Schuckit 1981; Utne, Hansen, Winkler and Schulsinger 1977; and virtually all the ethanol consumption studies cited in the pages that follow). These findings suggest that differences between COAs and controls in response to a challenge dose of alcohol are not likely to be mediated by differences in blood alcohol concentration (BAC).

The evidence concerning possible differences between COAs and nonCOAs in acetaldehyde (the immediate metabolite of ethanol) are more contradictory. Schuckit and Rayses (1979) reported that young, adult male social drinkers with first-degree alcoholic relatives had higher blood acetaldehyde levels than controls following a .5 ml/kg dose of ethanol. However, in a subsequent study using a similar sample and a moderately higher dose of ethanol (.75 ml/kg), between-group differences in blood acetaldehyde levels were not reported (Schuckit and Duby 1982). Although high-risk subjects were reported to exhibit greater flushing (as determined by observer ratings and ear-pulse amplitude changes), appropriate statistical analyses were not provided. Even if the flushing findings are reliable, they are at best a weak proxy for direct assessment of acetaldehyde levels. In a study with 8–15-year-old boy COAs and controls (Behar et al. 1983), no differences in either blood or breath acetaldehyde levels were noted following a .5 ml/kg dose of ethanol. Although differences in acetaldehyde metabolism between COAs and nonCOAs would appear to have great etiological relevance, currently available data are insufficient to establish such differences. Consequently, attempts to replicate the Schuckit and Rayses (1979) finding would be extremely valuable.

Subjective Intoxication

A number of recent studies have compared high-risk and low-risk groups on subjective responses (perceived intoxication, mood, and perceived physical sensations) to alcohol. Before a discussion of alcohol's effect on subjective state in COAs and nonCOAs, it should be pointed out that the general literature of alcohol's effect on subjective state (especially mood) demonstrates that a number of variables (the prior state of the drinker, contextual factors including drinking environment and the presence of other drinkers) can moderate alcohol effects (cf. Freed 1978; Sher 1985b). However, the work on family history of alcoholism has tended to study alcohol effects in relatively sterile laboratory environments which may limit the range of subjective effects that can be observed.

To date, the published findings on subjective effects of alcohol in high-risk and low-risk subjects have yielded contradictory findings. At least five separate studies (Moss et al. 1989; O'Malley and Maisto 1985; Pollock, Teasdale, Gabrielli, and Knop 1986; Schuckit 1980a; Schuckit 1984a) have demonstrated that COAs show less subjective intoxication than nonCOAs after alcohol consumption. However, this decreased sensitivity was limited to the descending limb of the BAC curve in at least one study (Moss et al. 1989) and is typically observed at least an hour following alcohol consumption. At least one study found no differences in reports of intoxication between COAs and nonCOAs (Vogel-Sprott and Chipperfield 1987). Furthermore, several recent studies (de Wit and McCracken 1990; Kaplan et al. 1988; Nagoshi and Wilson 1987; Sher, Walitzer, Bylund, and Hartmann 1989) found that high-risk subjects report greater intoxication or other sensations of drug effects than low-risk subjects and appear to contradict the previous set of findings. It is difficult to reconcile these differences at present, but perhaps methodological differences among studies (alcohol consumption protocols, experimental tasks engaged in) may have led to the divergent findings.

One methodological difference that may prove to be critical in determining the directionality of COA/nonCOA differences on subjective intoxication is the limb of the BAC curve. De Wit and McCracken (1990) found that males with a family history of alcoholism (primarily COAs) showed increased reports of feeling drugged and "high" than males without a family history, but only during the ascending limb of the BAC curve (when blood alcohol levels are increasing). Moss et al. (1989) found male COAs reported decreased levels of intoxication, but only during the descending limb of the BAC curve. This general pattern, increased sensitivity on the ascending limb and decreased sensitivity on the descending limb, may prove to be a general pattern of findings across a number of studies of alcohol effects on COAs (Newlin and Thomson 1990) and will be discussed at the conclusion of this chapter and again in chapter 9.

Kaplan et al. (1988) suggest that the increased intoxication reports may be more related to alcohol cues than the actual pharmacological effect of alcohol, since the significant intoxication ratings occurred soon after beverage consumption. The possibility that high-risk subjects might be especially prone to placebo effects is supported by a recent study by Newlin (1985) who found that high-risk subjects tended ($p < .06$) to report greater intoxication following a placebo than low-risk subjects. Although other data appear inconsistent with this placebo-responding hypothesis (de Wit and McCracken 1990; Moss et al. 1989), differences between COAs and nonCOAs in placebo responding appears to warrant further research. The possibility that a family history of alcoholism is associated with greater placebo responding also deserves further study.

Observer Impressions of Intoxication

At least three studies used observer ratings of subject intoxication to compare high-risk and low-risk subjects. While Pollock et al. (1986) and de Wit and

McCracken (1990) failed to find differences, Nagoshi and Wilson (1987) found high-risk subjects were rated as more impaired than low-risk subjects, a result supporting the validity of their findings based on self-rated or subjective intoxication. The reliability of the rater judgments was not described in any of the reports. At present, there are insufficient data to establish whether high-risk or low-risk subjects *appear* more intoxicated after a given dose of alcohol. As a general note, it may be inappropriate to place too much confidence in observed differences in intoxication because such ratings are necessarily based only on what happens to be observed. Explicit analysis of overt behavior based upon performance tasks, content analysis of verbal behavior, objective analysis of social interaction, etc., would provide more objective and, one hopes, more interpretable evidence. Nevertheless, sensitive observers may be able to detect subtle and elusive effects of intoxication that more formalized assessment fails to detect. Thus, observer ratings are a potentially important method, but these rating dimensions should be clearly defined and observers should be trained to meet acceptable levels of interobserver reliability (which should always be reported).

Perceptual, Cognitive, and Cognitive-motor Functioning

A limitation of the research relying solely on subjective reports of intoxication is that it is not possible to determine whether differences in sensitivity are purely phenomenological or are based on relatively accurate reports of alcohol effects on cognition and behavior. Although "objective" ratings of intoxication are not so confounded, judgments of others intoxication can be highly imprecise and typically are not well operationalized. Objective, quantitative measurement of behavior holds the promise of confidently assessing the degree of alcohol's effects, as well as specifying the nature of the deficit more precisely.

Body Sway

There have now been several studies that examine differences in change in body sway following challenge doses of alcohol between individuals with and without a family history of alcoholism; results of these studies are mixed. Schuckit and his colleagues have reported that young adult males with a family history of alcoholism show less alcohol-induced body sway than family history negative controls (Schuckit and Gold 1988; Schuckit 1985b) and a comparable finding based on a sample of adult women has also been reported (Lex et al. 1988). However, the majority of studies reported to date fail to find COA/nonCOA differences on this variable (Behar et al. 1983; Lipscomb et al. 1979; Nagoshi and Wilson 1987; O'Malley and Maisto 1985). Consequently, the robustness of this effect is open to question. Furthermore, interpretation of any COA/nonCOA differences on body sway is problematic because it is not clear exactly what processes this variable is measuring beyond a global variable of intoxication.

Other Cognitive and Cognitive-motor Tasks

Several recent studies (Baribeau et al. 1986; Nagoshi and Wilson 1987; O'Malley and Maisto 1985; Pollock et al. 1986; Schuckit and Penn 1985; Wilson and Nagoshi 1988) have examined sensitivity to alcohol on a variety of perceptual, cognitive, and cognitive-motor tasks (e.g., Porteus maze tests, the Symbol Digit test, Grooved Pegboard, Rod and Frame test) among samples of young men with and without a family history of alcoholism. Despite numerous reports of nonsignificant differences on a wide variety of tasks (see Nagoshi and Wilson 1987), most of the significant findings suggest that COAs are more sensitive to the effects of alcohol across a variety of cognitive-motor tasks (O'Malley and Maisto 1985; Vogel-Sprott and Chipperfield 1987; Wilson and Nagoshi 1988), although findings of less sensitivity have been reported (Lex et al. 1988; Pollock et al. 1986). The potential importance of increased cognitive and behavioral impairment among COAs is unclear. However, in at least two studies where clear increased behavioral impairment in COAs was observed and subjective ratings of intoxication obtained, COAs did not report greater levels of perceived intoxication (O'Malley and Maisto 1985; Vogel-Sprott and Chipperfield 1987). This suggests that COAs might become impaired (both cognitively and behaviorally) more rapidly than non-COAs, but without insight into the extent of their impairment. Such a discrepancy between objective and subjective effects could conceivably lead an individual to more readily consume quantities of alcohol that have negative interpersonal and physical consequences.

Autonomic and Electromyographic Effects of Alcohol

Physiological recording of autonomic processes (e.g., the activity of the cardiovascular and eccrine systems) and muscle tension can provide useful data on information processing, motivational states, and affective states within certain experimental paradigms. These measures have been used widely in recent years by investigators hoping to characterize the presumed affective consequences of alcohol consumption. A major thrust of much of this work has been to test the so-called "tension reduction hypothesis" of alcohol use (Conger 1956) which posits that alcohol can reduce anxiety and other aversive states (is negatively reinforcing), and is consumed for tension-reducing effects. Evidence that certain individuals show marked stress-reducing effects of alcohol, has led to a search for individual-difference variables that relate to the magnitude of stress-response-dampening effects of alcohol (Sher and Levenson 1982). Family history of alcoholism appears to be one such individual difference (see below). Several reviews of the tension reduction literature have appeared in recent years (Cappell and Greeley 1987; Sher 1987b; Wilson 1988) and the interested reader is referred to these recent overviews. This section reviews the differential effects of alcohol on COAs and nonCOAs with resting to resting (baseline) levels, reactivity to simple nonaversive stimulation, and to stressful stimulation. It is only this last category (effects of alcohol on stress response) that directly addresses the tension-reducing effects of alcohol.

Resting Levels

Available data suggest that COAs show increased *heart rate,* relative to non-COAs, following a challenge dose of alcohol (Finn and Pihl 1987; Finn et al. 1990; Wilson and Nagoshi 1988). Although one study (Levenson et al. 1987) failed to find evidence for differential effects of alcohol on resting heart rate between COAs and nonCOAs, that study did not include predrinking baseline assessment of heart rate, and so may have had limited power to detect between group differences. The meaning of these effects on resting heart rate are unclear in that they might reflect a direct effect of alcohol on the cardiovasculature, reflect the effect of alcohol on central brain mechanisms controlling heart rate, or index an increased incentive value for alcohol (e.g., Fowles 1980). It should also be noted, that all of the studies showing significant COA/nonCOA differences were not placebo-controlled and so it is not possible to determine if the increased heart rate reflects the pharmacological effect of alcohol or placebo (anticipated) effects. However, Newlin's observation (1985) that COAs show a greater heart rate decrease to a placebo than nonCOAs, suggests that the observed heart rate increases are primarily pharmacological. Without further study, the significance of the heart rate findings is unclear, but the question of placebo reactivity clearly seems worthy of greater study. This is especially so given the relative ease of collecting heart rate data.

   With the exception of heart rate, there is little evidence of COAs and nonCOAs responding differently to alcohol on other autonomic measures such as finger *pulse amplitude, blood pressure,* and *electrodermal activity* (Finn and Pihl 1987; Finn et al. 1990; Levenson et al. 1987; Nagoshi and Wilson 1987; Schuckit and Duby 1982). Schuckit, Engstrom, Alpert, and Duby (1981) reported that high-risk subjects demonstrated decreased *frontalis muscle tension* following alcohol consumption relative to low-risk subjects, and that these differences were limited to periods when subjects were at rest. This finding was not replicated by Finn et al. (1990). Although the absence of replication and methodological weaknesses of the study (failure to include a placebo control, recording from only a single muscle group known to correlate poorly with other muscle groups) limits confidence in the results, the finding is potentially important, as it suggests that alcohol may be particularly reinforcing to COAs. Consequently, replication with methodological improvements of this finding would be valuable.

The Orienting Response

Finn et al. (1990) have demonstrated that alcohol dampened the magnitude of the electrodermal orienting response to simple tones in young, adult male COAs but not in nonCOAs. Comparable effects were seen in other measures of orienting (i.e., trials to extinction and half-recovery time). Because these COAs had been found to be hyperactive when sober, Finn et al. (1990) posited that alcohol served a "normalizing" function for these individuals. No other studies on orienting have been reported in the literature and so the robustness of this potentially important finding is unclear.

Stress Response

The ability of alcohol to dampen autonomic responses to discrete stressors has been of considerable interest since this effect is consistent with theories that alcohol can be tension-reducing and thus function as a reinforcer. Individual differences in this effect have been posited to represent a potential vulnerability to the development of drinking problems; that is, persons particularly vulnerable to alcohol's stress-response-dampening effects may be more likely to drink in greater quantity (Sher 1987). Numerous studies have been conducted to date examining the effect of alcohol on stress response, and decreased cardiovascular reactivity to alcohol has been a consistent finding (Sher 1987). Recently three studies (Finn and Pihl 1987; Finn et al. 1990; Levenson et al. 1987) found that COAs demonstrate more pronounced attenuation of the heart rate response to a stressor after alcohol consumption than nonCOAs. These findings are consistent with the notion that a family history of alcoholism is associated with a propensity to receive greater reinforcement from alcohol consumption.

In addition to providing interesting data that demonstrate the relation of family history of alcoholism to alcohol effects, each study provided some additional important findings germane to the larger question of differences in alcohol effects in high-risk and low-risk samples. Levenson et al. (1987) were among the first to include a relatively large number of female subjects in addition to a large number of male subjects in their high-risk study involving alcohol consumption. Of particular importance was the comparability of the major findings across genders.

An important feature of the Finn and Pihl (1987, 1988) studies is the distinction they make among risks groups on the basis of family pedigree.

These authors designated two at-risk groups; the first group with alcoholism in only one parent and little or no alcoholism in other family members, and the second group with paternal, bigenerational alcoholism. Only the bigenerational, paternal alcoholism risk group was found to demonstrate pronounced stress-response-dampening effects. This finding suggests the utility of defining risk groups on the basis of more extensive family pedigrees as a way to partition possible sources of etiologic heterogeneity. However, Levenson et al. (1987) have demonstrated analogous effects in subjects not subtyped, and across gender and so the necessity of delineating subtypes based on pedigree and gender as Finn, Pihl, and their colleagues have done is still an open question.

Yet another important difference among studies is the extent to which stress-response-dampening effects of alcohol are related to hyperactive stress responses when sober. Although Finn, Pihl, and their colleagues have reported that COAs are hyperactive when sober, this was not observed by Levenson et al. (1987). Perhaps these differences in findings are related to the use of a placebo control in the Levenson et al. (1987) study.

The findings of increased stress response dampening among high-risk subjects is of considerable interest, and further research should attempt to replicate these initial findings and investigate the biological mechanisms subserving these differences.

Effects of Alcohol on CNS Activity

To date, several studies using electroencephalographic measures of CNS activity have examined differences in responses of COAs and nonCOAs to alcohol. Although most of the subjective, behavioral, and autonomic measurements of alcohol effects reported in this chapter are probably attributable, at least in part, to alcohol's effect on the brain, use of neurophysiological measures holds the promise of providing direct measurement of alcohol's effect on various brain regions. Such direct assessment is potentially more sensitive to alcohol effects and could possibly uncover basic differences in COAs' and nonCOAs' ethanol sensitivity. Existing studies have examined the effects of alcohol on both spontaneous EEG and on event-related potentials. These studies are reviewed below.

Spontaneous EEG

Pollock et al. (1983) reported that, following consumption of a moderate dose of alcohol, young adult male COAs showed increased slow alpha energy (7.42–9.46 Hz), decreased fast alpha energy (9.46–12.10 Hz), and decreased mean alpha frequency relative to nonCOAs. In all of these comparisons, COAs were more affected by alcohol than nonCOAs, suggesting that

COAs are more sensitive to the effect of alcohol on the CNS than nonCOAs. In a secondary analysis of the data from this study, Pollock, Gabrielli, Mednick, and Goodwin (1988b) categorized the COAs into two groups: (1) those who showed a large decrease in mean alpha frequency following alcohol consumption (COA-A), and (2) those who showed a small decrease in mean alpha frequency following alcohol consumption (COA-B). Comparison among the resulting three groups (COA-A, COA-B, and nonCOAs) demonstrated somewhat differing patterns of self-reported subjective states between the two COA groups, although the differences are not that impressive. The potential importance of this study is that it illustrates a strategy for addressing the issue of heterogeneity of alcohol-reactivity among COAs.

Ehlers, Schuckit, and their colleagues (Ehlers and Schuckit 1988, 1990, in press; Ehlers, Wall, and Schuckit 1989) have reported a number of findings concerning the effect of alcohol on spontaneous EEG in a sample of young, adult male COAs and nonCOAs. Among their most noteworthy findings are: (a) COAs and nonCOAs do not differ in response to alcohol with respect to power in low frequency alpha range (7.5–9 Hz), (b) COAs show a less intense response to ethanol with respect to the stability and mean power of fast frequency alpha (9–12 Hz), and (c) COAs show a greater response to alcohol with respect to power in the beta activity range (12–20 Hz). The findings with respect to both low and high frequency alpha are at odds with Pollock et al. (1983) and, further, suggest that COAs are both *more sensitive* and *less sensitive* to alcohol's effect on EEG depending upon the EEG frequency band assessed. Furthermore, Kaplan et al. (1988) failed to find differences between COAs and nonCOAs in the effect of alcohol on EEG, but important methodological differences (such as quantification of the EEG data) could conceivably have led to the negative findings.

ERPs

At least three studies have examined differences in ERPs between COAs and nonCOAs following alcohol consumption (Elmasian et al. 1982; Pollock, Volavka, Goodwin, Gabrielli, Mednick, Knop, and Schulsinger 1988; Schuckit et al. 1988a). In a study of the P100 component to pattern-reversal visual-evoked responses, Pollock et al. (1988c) reported a significant interaction among family history, ''laterality'' (whether the recording electrode was over the left versus the right occipital lobe), and time relative to intoxication on latency of the P100 component. Examination of this interaction revealed that alcohol tended to increase interhemispheric differences in latency over time for COAs, and decrease interhemispheric latencies over time for nonCOAs. No effects on P100 amplitude were observed.

Elmasian et al. (1982) failed to find differential response to alcohol consumption on P3 amplitude and latency between young, adult male COAs and nonCOAs on an auditory discrimination task, although COA/nonCOA differences in P3 were observed under all dose conditions studied. However, it should be noted that this design included only five COAs in each of the three dose conditions employed and probably had extremely low power to detect between-group differences in alcohol effects. Schuckit et al. (1988a) reported that young, adult male COAs, relative to nonCOAs, evidenced faster recovery of alcohol-related increases in P3 latency to an auditory discrimination task following a high dose of alcohol. These differences were noted four hours after alcohol consumption.

At present, there is simply not enough research to permit even tentative conclusions about the importance of family history of alcoholism in alcohol's effect on electrophysiological aspects of CNS functioning. Research utilizing EEG and ERP measures of CNS activity should be encouraged because such measures are a potentially valuable, inexpensive, noninvasive approach to examining individual differences in alcohol's effect on the brain. Although several potentially interesting findings have been reported to date, none have been replicated and no clear generalizations can be made from the existing literature.

Biochemical Effects of Alcohol

Endocrine Hormones

Because of the role that a number of endocrine hormones play in modulating central neurotransmission and in modulating and affecting emotional states, several studies have examined the effect of alcohol on circulating hormone levels. Although Schuckit and his colleagues have reported a number of findings suggesting that COAs show reduced effects of alcohol on various hormones (especially during the descending limb of the BAC curve), none of these findings have been replicated by other laboratories and, thus, must be viewed as preliminary.

Schuckit and his colleagues (Schuckit et al. 1983; Schuckit et al. 1987a) have reported two investigations of the effect of alcohol on serum *prolactin* levels in young, adult males with and without a family history of alcoholism. The data tend to show that serum prolactin levels of family-history positive subjects are generally lower than those of family-history negative subjects approximately 2.5 hours after alcohol consumption. There are, however, a number of major inconsistencies across the two studies, and the data analytic strategy used in the better-controlled, later study (Schuckit et al. 1987a) is questionable. Furthermore, Moss et al. (1989) recently failed to find evidence of differential prolactin response to alcohol among a sample of young, adult male COAs and nonCOAs. Consequently, further replication is clearly needed of this potentially important effect. The effect is of considerable theoretical interest because alcohol's effect on prolactin levels might be viewed as a proxy for alcohol's effect on central dopaminergic systems (cf. Cloninger 1987a).

Schuckit and his colleagues (Schuckit 1984b; Schuckit et al. 1987b) have conducted two studies to examine the effect of alcohol on plasma *cortisol* level in male subjects with and without a family history of alcoholism. The findings generally suggest that family-history positive subjects show lower cortisol levels than family-history negative subjects following ethanol challenge. However, there are seeming inconsistencies across studies and questionable statistical analyses (for example, the failure to correct for inflated degrees of freedom associated with repeated-measure designs) in the better-controlled second study. Furthermore, Behar et al. (1983) failed to find evidence for differential effects of alcohol on cortisol levels in young male COAs and nonCOAs. Thus, while some evidence suggests that COAs show lower cortisol levels than nonCOAs after consuming alcohol, these findings need to be replicated.

Although the cause of these apparent differences in cortisol response to alcohol have generally not been addressed, several possible mechanisms can be considered, including direct effect of alcohol on the adrenals, effect of alcohol on the hypothalamic/pituitary axis, and a generalized stress response to the effects of alcohol. A recent study by Schuckit et al. (1988b) found that COAs show less of an *ACTH* response to alcohol than nonCOAs, suggesting that decreased cortisol release in COAs noted above might not be due to direct adrenal effects but to effects at the level of the pituitary or higher.

It should be emphasized that the differences in ACTH, prolactin, and cortisol response that Schuckit and his colleagues have observed occur more than an hour after alcohol consumption, at a time when blood alcohol levels are declining (i.e., during the descending limb of the blood alcohol curve). Consequently, these findings might be related to acute tolerance and not initial sensitivity.

A recent study by Swartz et al. (1987) examined differences in urinary *epinephrine* output in response to a challenge dose of ethanol (.5 ml/kg) between young adult male adoptees with and without a history of paternal alcoholism. Unfortunately, the data were not reported in a way that permits assessment of any ethanol X family history interaction effects. Behar et al. (1983) failed to find COA versus nonCOA differences in plasma epinephrine and norepinephrine responses to a .5 ml/kg ethanol dose.

Enzymes Related to Neurotransmitter Activity

Schuckit et al. (1982) failed to find alterations in *platelet MAO activity* following a moderate challenge dose of ethanol in either high-risk or low-risk subjects. This suggests that either large doses or chronic doses of alcohol may be necessary to alter platelet MAO activity. It is unlikely, however, that any differential effects of alcohol in high- and low-risk groups are mediated by differential MAO activity.

Schuckit et al. (1981) failed to find evidence of differential effects of alcohol on *DBH* activity in high-risk or low-risk subjects. An interesting finding in this study was that baseline DBH activity predicted peak subjective intoxication in the low-risk subjects but not in the high-risk subjects. However, the small samples involved limit confidence in this finding.

Differences between COAs and nonCOAs in Responses to Other Drugs

Because COAs are at high risk for the development of alcoholism, the previously cited studies in this chapter attempted to document COA/nonCOA differences in alcohol responses as a means for relating acute effects of a substance with abuse potential (alcohol) to a known risk for substance abuse (a family history of alcoholism). However, as described earlier, COAs may be at risk for other drug abuse (e.g., Cadoret et al. 1986). Consequently, a logical question to address is, "To what extent do COAs manifest differential sensitivity to other drugs of abuse?" Unfortunately, there are relatively few data on this question.

Recently, Ciraulo, Barnhill, Ciraulo, Greenblatt, and Shader (1989) reported the results of a pilot study of adult, male COAs which found that 75 percent of the COAs had a euphoric response to a 1 mg dose of alprazolam (a potent benzodiazepine) compared to only 17 percent of the nonCOAs. Although confidence in the study's findings is limited by several problems with the experimental design, the data are consistent with clinical data indicating that alcoholics are at high risk for benzodiazepine dependence (Ciraulo, Sands, and Shader 1988) and with the pharmacological data demonstrating that important effects of both benzodiazepines and alcohol are mediated by the GABA system (Ticku, and Kulkarni 1988). It should be noted that two recent reports of a study of benzodiazepine sensitivity (Monteiro, Schuckit, Hauger, Irwin, and Duthie 1990; Monteiro, Schuckit, and Irwin 1990) were apparently based on a sample of COAs and nonCOAs, unfortunately the data are not reported in a way that permits an evaluation of the extent to which Ciraulo et al.'s (1989) findings were replicated. Clearly, replication of this finding is needed as well as similar work examining COA/nonCOA differences in responses to a range of pharmacologically distinct substances.

Summary

The existing data, although incomplete, appear to point to two areas of consistency concerning the differential effects of alcohol on COAs and nonCOAs.

The first is that COAs are *less sensitive* to subjective intoxicating effects of alcohol. Although the robustness of this finding can be questioned, these data suggest that an insensitivity (either innate or acquired through early drinking experience) may lead COAs to drink in higher amounts to achieve intoxicating effects and consequently result in greater self-administered ethanol exposure. The second area of relative consistency appears contradictory to the first. That is, COAs appear *more sensitive* to a number of alcohol effects, especially the stress-response-dampening effect of alcohol. This finding suggests that alcohol consumption might be more reinforcing for COAs and that consequently, when under stress, they might be more prone to drink in greater frequency or in greater quantity. Although these effects might seem incompatible, alcohol is known to have widely varying effects and it is conceivable that the effects on subjective intoxication (in a nonstressed state) and autonomic stress response are relatively independent. The finding that certain drugs can block some effects of ethanol but not others (Weingartner, Rudorfer, Buchsbaum, & Linnoila 1983) indicates that differing effects of alcohol can be mediated by pharmacologically distinct mechanisms.

Newlin and Thomson (1990) have recently proposed that the seemingly contradictory literature on the direction of COA/nonCOA differences in alcohol effects can be resolved by considering the time course of intoxication. Limiting their review to the sons of male alcoholics, Newlin and Thomson (1990) argue that on the ascending limb of the blood alcohol curve (i.e., when blood alcohol levels are rising) COAs show larger effects of alcohol than nonCOAs. However, the situation is reversed on the descending limb of the blood alcohol curve where COAs show less sensitivity (i.e., greater acute tolerance). Acute tolerance refers to the development of tolerance within a drinking session. This pattern is illustrated in Figure 8.1. Newlin and Thomson (1990) propose that COAs are more sensitive to the slope of the blood alcohol curve than to the actual blood alcohol level, as if "the transition in state induced by the drug is more important than the state itself . . . (suggesting) a differentiator model of the psychobiological response to (alcohol)" (p. 339). Figure 8.2 hypothetically illustrates differences in COAs' and non-COAs' response to alcohol as a function of time since intoxication. If Newlin and Thomson (1990) are correct, this suggests that COAs might be doubly vulnerable to the effects of alcohol: (1) more sensitive to the reinforcing effects of alcohol, most noticeable during rising blood alcohol levels, and (2) less sensitive to the punishing effects of alcohol, most noticeable during decreasing blood alcohol levels. Although this theory is based on a considerable amount of data and appears quite reasonable, it needs to be stressed that there is relatively little evidence for this presumed pattern at the level of individual studies; Newlin and Thomson's analysis is based on isolated findings from numerous investigations. Newlin and Thomson's (1990) insightful analysis should encourage others to probe this model more carefully.

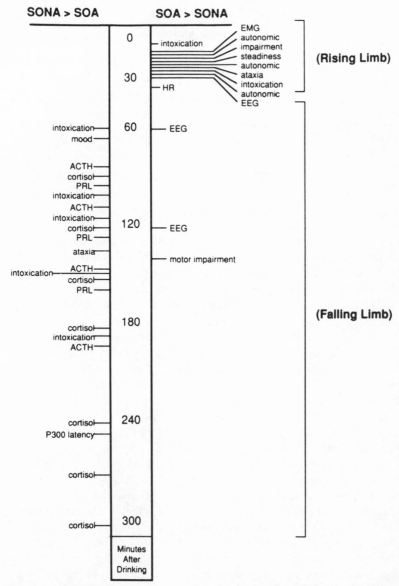

Figure 8.1. Illustration of the relation between time-since-drinking and differences in alcohol effects between male COAs and nonCOAs. COAs appear to be more sensitive to alcohol on the ascending limb of the BAC curve, and less sensitive on the descending limb. SOA = sons of male alcoholics. SONA = sons of nonalcoholics. Reprinted from Newlin and Thomson (1990) with permission of the authors and the American Psychological Association.

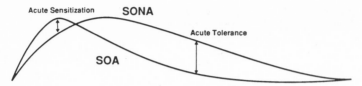

Figure 8.2. Schematic diagram of the differentiator model. Note greater acute sensitization during the ascending limb of the blood alcohol curve in sons of alcoholics (SOAs), and greater acute tolerance during the descending limb of the curve. Reprinted from Newlin and Thomson (1990) with permission of the authors and the American Psychological Association.

The work of Finn and Pihl (1987, 1988) dramatically demonstrates the utility of using more extensive pedigree data in subtyping COAs. Failure to take genetic heterogeneity into account may result in data that yield equivocal findings even when the dependent variables are truly etiologically relevant. Approaches that attempt to combine family history data with presumed phenotypic characteristics of risk (Levenson et al. 1987; Mann et al. 1987) may also help partition variance associated with genetic heterogeneity.

A number of potentially important results including the effects of ethanol on EEG and on neuroendocrine hormones need to be replicated before we can place any confidence in these findings.

In addition to considering genetic heterogeneity, future investigations of ethanol effects in COAs should employ larger samples to increase their statistical power and to permit appropriate multivariate analyses. Newlin's (1985) finding of greater placebo responsiveness among COAs suggests the utility of including nonplacebo controls as well as placebo controls in ethanol consumption studies. The wisdom of matching COAs and nonCOAs on drinking history and excluding problem drinkers also needs to be questioned. Such procedures can eliminate *meaningful* differences between groups (cf. Sher 1985a). Perhaps a useful alternative strategy is to oversample both COAs and nonCOAs and then apply exclusionary and matching criteria in post hoc analyses. Data could then be analyzed as a function of both liberal and restrictive sampling criteria. Finally, studies comparing COAs and nonCOAs in their responses to a range of psychoactive substances are needed to determine if differential sensitivity is specific to alcohol, to a narrow class of related substances (e.g., those that are cross-tolerant to alcohol, such as benzodiazepines and barbiturates), or to a wide range of drugs with abuse potential.

9   Models of Vulnerability

Although mediators of risk have yet to be conclusively identified, several researchers have recently proposed theories relating family history to the development of alcohol problems (e.g., Cloninger 1987a; Tarter, Alterman, and Edwards 1985; Zucker 1987). Although each of these theories will be briefly described, a detailed critique of each of these relatively complex theories will not be provided. Instead, the extent to which various "simple" mediational models are consistent with the empirical data reviewed in the preceding chapters will first be reviewed. By "simple" I mean that these models are meant only to describe possible *basic* mechanisms; psychobiologically, these processes might be quite complex. In the second part of this chapter, more complex models proposed by several recent theorists are discussed briefly. In the third part of this chapter, an overarching model that attempts to subsume most published models is proposed.

Simple Mediational Models

Table 9.1 provides an outline of three broad categories of simple mediational models. The first category, *models related to individual differences in pharmacological effects of alcohol,* addresses the general hypothesis that COAs react to alcohol in an abnormal way (e.g., are overly sensitive or tolerant) and that these abnormal reactions place them at risk for the development of alcoholism. The second category, *models related to individual differences in drinking motivation,* addresses the general hypothesis that COAs have psychological or psychobiological disturbances that provide excessive motivation (e.g., self-medication) for alcohol consumption. The third category, *other models,* contains additional possible simple models not readily subsumed under the first two categories. Additionally, the different proposed models are neither mutually exclusive nor exhaustive. It is worth noting that several years

Table 9.1 Simple Mediational Models

A. Models Related to Individual Differences in Pharmacological Effects of Alcohol
   —Sensitivity to reinforcing effects of alcohol
   —Initial insensitivity to reinforcing effects of alcohol
   —Insensitivity to adverse effects of alcohol
   —? Individual differences in alcohol expectancies
   —Proneness to tolerance development
   —Proneness to develop medical consequences of alcoholism
B. Models Related to Individual Differences in Drinking Motivation
   —Predisposition to experience negative mood states
   —Predisposition to seek out altered states of consciousness (sensation seeking)
   —Impulsivity
   —Impaired coping
   —? Alcohol expectancies
C. Other Models
   —Proneness to school failure & psychosocial sequelae
   —Exposure to alcohol

---

ago Schuckit (1980b) conducted a somewhat similar overview of the then-available research.

Models Related to Individual Differences in
Pharmacological Effects of Alcohol

The notion that COAs have an inherited predisposition to react to alcohol in an aberrant way is inherently appealing. Given that alcohol consumption is a necessary condition for the development of alcohol abuse and dependence and that COAs are at high risk for becoming alcoholic, the idea that there is something in the psychobiological makeup of the COA that makes alcohol particularly addicting for him/her would appear to be a very plausible working hypothesis. Numerous studies indicating fundamental differences in the way COAs and nonCOAs react to alcohol were reviewed in chapter 8, suggesting that this hypothesis holds great promise for helping us to understand the intergenerational transmission of alcoholism.

Before we review basic models relating individual differences in alcohol effects to risk for alcoholism, it should be emphasized that it does not appear that COAs and nonCOAs differ in their rates of alcohol absorption and elimination, nor have there been any replicated findings demonstrating COA/nonCOA differences in the rate or nature of alcohol metabolism. Thus, the COA/nonCOA differences in alcohol effects reported in the literature do not appear to be a simple function of differences in how alcohol is processed by the organism.

Sensitivity to reinforcing effects of alcohol. Studies demonstrating that COAs are more sensitive to the potentially reinforcing effects of alcohol (e.g., muscle relaxing, stress-dampening, electroencephalographic, and mood effects; Finn and Pihl 1987; Finn et al. 1990; Levenson et al. 1987; Nagoshi and Wilson 1987; Pollock et al. 1983; Savoie et al. 1988; Schuckit et al. 1981; Sher et al. in press) suggest that COAs may experience greater reinforcement from a given dose of alcohol. Heightened reinforcement value might lead to drinking in increased frequency and/or increased quantity. However, assessment of reinforcement value cannot be assumed on the basis of studying individual differences in alcohol effects alone. These effects must be related to individual differences in voluntary alcohol consumption. Only three published studies of which we are aware compared COAs and nonCOAs in voluntary drinking behavior under controlled, laboratory conditions (Chipperfield and Vogel-Sprott 1988; de Wit and McCracken 1990; Walitzer and Sher 1990). Only one of these studies (Chipperfield and Vogel-Sprott 1988) found clear evidence for increased alcohol consumption among COAs, but only when the subject drank in the presence of a heavy-drinking companion. This suggests that relatively sterile, neutral laboratory conditions may not be optimal for studying voluntary alcohol consumption, and that controlled investigations of drinking behavior in COAs may need to consider appropriate environmental conditions for observing drinking behavior (e.g., stress-inducing situations where opportunities for active coping are limited; cf. Sher 1987). Consequently, additional research is needed to determine whether COAs differ from nonCOAs on various operant tasks assessing voluntary alcohol consumption under appropriate environmental conditions.

Initial insensitivity to reinforcing effects of alcohol. An alternative model concerning reinforcement from alcohol is that vulnerability may be mediated by a relative perceptual insensitivity to the onset of the reinforcing effects of alcohol. Such a lack of self-awareness could lead to higher levels of alcohol consumption in order to achieve noticeable desired reinforcing effects. Over time, this increased consumption of alcohol could lead to a relatively rapid development of tolerance and other dependence phenomena. Research indicating that COAs appear to show less subjective intoxication following a challenge dose of ethanol (Moss et al. 1989; O'Malley and Maisto 1985; Pollock et al. 1986; Schuckit 1980a, 1984a) is certainly consistent with this model. Also, if Vogel-Sprott and Chipperfield's (1987) finding that COAs show little subjective awareness of their greater behavioral impairment proves replicable, this suggests that COAs may be more likely to drink to levels likely to lead to negative consequences.

Again, critical support for this model involves relating individual differences in alcohol effects to individual differences in alcohol-seeking behavior, and data on this last point are severely limited.

Insensitivity to adverse effects of alcohol.   Goodwin (1988) has suggested that susceptibility to alcoholism might be mediated by a lack of sensitivity to the adverse effects of alcohol. Such a lack of sensitivity would permit COAs to consume relatively large amounts of alcohol without recognizing punishing consequences. This is an intriguing hypothesis, but there is relatively little evidence directly supporting it. Newlin and Thomson's (1990) analysis of alcohol challenge studies with COAs points to two possible areas of support for this possibility. First, in their analysis of Schuckit's (1980a, 1984a) research on subjective intoxication, they find that the decreased sensitivity of COAs is relatively specific to adverse effects of alcohol. Second, their analysis concludes that COAs appear to be less affected by alcohol on the descending limb of the blood alcohol curve. Since the descending limb appears to be associated with more negative affective consequences of alcohol (e.g., Babor, Berglas, Mendelson, Ellingboe, and Miller 1983), this is generally consistent with Goodwin's (1988) hypothesis. Although we are not aware of studies directly relating acute, aversive effects of alcohol to ad lib drinking in COAs, this general hypothesis is consistent with the literature indicating that individuals who demonstrate a pronounced "flushing response" to alcohol (due to genetically determined variation in acetaldehyde metabolism) may be at relatively low risk for developing alcohol problems (Harada, Agarwal, and Goedde 1985; Harada, Agarwal, Goedde, and Ishikawa 1983; Harada, Agarwal, Goedde, Tagaki, and Ishikawa 1982).

Individual differences in alcohol expectancies.   The three preceding models posit that individual differences in alcohol effects are somehow translated into differences in drinking behavior. Presumably, this translation involves personal beliefs or expectancies surrounding anticipated consequences of alcohol consumption. COAs appear to have stronger expectancies for reinforcement from alcohol than nonCOAs (Brown et al. 1987; Mann et al. 1987; Sher et al. in press), and there seems to be a heritable basis for attitudes toward alcohol (Perry 1973). However, available research has yet to show a clear relationship between individual differences in the pharmacological effects of alcohol and individually held alcohol expectancies (e.g., Sher 1985b; Sher and Walitzer 1986). However, the work carried out to date has not yet assessed this issue systematically. Consequently, the extent to which COA/nonCOA differences in alcohol expectancies are attributable to individual differences in ethanol sensitivity is an open question. The notion that alcohol expectancies serve as a "simple" mediational model is described in the next section as well since the importance of this model does not necessarily rest on the reductionistic assumption that the expectancies are based on pharmacological processes.

Proneness to tolerance development. Although the notion that COAs are prone to rapid development of tolerance seems quite plausible, few studies directly address this point. Newlin and Thomson's (1990) review concludes that COAs show greater acute (i.e., within session) tolerance than nonCOAs. However, on autonomic measures, COAs have been found to show reverse tolerance (sensitization) to repeated administrations of alcohol over three sessions (Newlin and Aldrich 1986). Additional studies examining changes in ethanol sensitivity over time (both within and across sessions) are clearly needed to evaluate this model.

Proneness to develop medical consequences of alcoholism. There are strong reasons to suggest that genetic factors are responsible for susceptibility to a number of alcohol-related medical illnesses such as alcoholic liver disease (Saunders and Williams 1983) and Wernicke-Korsakoff syndrome (Nixon 1984). Although this is clearly an important avenue of research, this model concerns only the potential for physical morbidity given a personal history of excessive alcohol consumption. Thus although the model might help explain, in part, COAs' excess of alcohol abuse and dependence (since medical consequences constitutes a criterion for diagnosis), it does not necessarily address the issue of why COAs are more likely to drink in an excessive way, or to encounter social consequences.

Models Related to Individual Differences in Drinking Motivation

Irrespective of whether COAs respond to alcohol differently than nonCOAs, it is conceivable that COAs might be more internally motivated to use alcohol for any of a number of reasons. For example, if COAs were found to be more prone to dysphoria than nonCOAs, they might be expected to use alcohol more frequently for mood-enhancing effects ("self-medication"). Alternatively, if COAs' coping abilities were limited and they were less effective at controlling their stress reactions (either by direct action or self-regulation), they might be more motivated to use alcohol as a coping device. The next broad class of models covers several simple models of drinking motivation that are not clearly tied to individual differences in the pharmacological effects of alcohol.

Predisposition to experience negative mood states. Another model posits that COAs may be more prone to experience negative mood states and consequently may consume more alcohol for symptomatic relief ("self-medication"). Existing data show mixed support for this model. Studies comparing COAs and nonCOAs on Eysenck's Neuroticism scale yield contradictory findings, with some studies finding that COAs are more neurotic (Finn and Pihl 1987; Sher et al. in press) and at least one study showing no difference (Schuckit 1983). COAs have not been found to report high levels of trait anxiety (see chapter 6). However, as reviewed in chapter 3, reports of high levels of depression in COAs are common and one study found that COAs score high on a measure of "proneness to moderate depression" (Clair and Genest 1987).

The failure to consider heterogeneity of parental alcoholism may contribute to the mixed support for this model. If Cloninger's (1987a) theory of alcoholism subtypes is correct, then only offspring of Type 1 alcoholics would be expected to show high levels of negative mood states. Also, negative mood states might be more etiologically significant for alcoholism among women (Cloninger 1987a; Jones 1971). Although available data do not paint a clear picture, the notion that high rates of negative mood states serve as an important motivation for alcohol consumption among COAs must be considered a viable hypothesis.

Predisposition to seek out altered states of consciousness (sensation seeking). The finding that COAs are at high risk for other forms of substance use (Cadoret et al. 1986) suggests that drug-seeking behavior is not tied to the specific psychoactive effects of alcohol but may be more related to the changes in consciousness brought about by different substances. Sensation seeking is one trait that has been related to the use of a number of different substances, including alcohol (Zuckerman, Neary, and Brustman 1970). Studies by Alterman and his colleagues comparing COAs and nonCOAs on Zuckerman's Sensation Seeking Scale do not demonstrate that COAs are significantly higher on sensation seeking (Alterman et al. 1986a, 1989). However, as discussed earlier, the magnitude of COA/nonCOA differences on sensation seeking in the Alterman et al. (1989) study is approximately .5 standard deviations (a "medium" effect size). Additionally, we have found that young, adult COAs score higher on Cloninger's (1987c) measure of novelty seeking, a construct similar to, but not identical with, sensation seeking (Sher et al. in press). Finally, findings suggesting that both sensation seeking (Zuckerman, Buchsbaum, and Murphy 1980) and family history of alcoholism are related to low platelet MAO activity (see chapter 7) argue for continued evaluation of this model.

Also, according to Cloninger's (1987a) theory of alcoholism subtypes, only one type of alcoholism, Type 2, is posited to be associated with sensation-seeking-like traits. Potentially, more careful subtyping of parental alcoholism will result in more clear-cut findings regarding sensation seeking in COAs.

Impulsivity. Although far from conclusive, existing data suggest that COAs tend to be impulsive (see chapter 6). Impulsivity can be viewed as a mediator of vulnerability in that impulsive individuals can be assumed to have difficulty in inhibiting responses likely to lead to immediate reward but later punishment. That is, if drinking begins to become problematic, highly impulsive individuals can be posited to be less likely to develop effective inhibitory control of drinking.

More generally, impulsivity can be viewed as leading to impaired coping since successful coping is thought to require a relatively high degree of reflection and consideration of available behavioral options. Although the impulsivity model is attractive, the empirical data base is still relatively weak. Even if COAs are conclusively shown to be more impulsive than nonCOAs, the relation between impulsivity and the development of drinking problems will still need to be demonstrated.

Impaired coping. More generally, impaired coping can be seen as a potential model independent of impulsivity deficits. The deficits in intellectual problem solving noted earlier (pp. 86–92) might be generalizable to personal and social problem solving as well. Individuals with impaired problem solving may prefer alcohol use as a coping strategy in comparison to others who have greater problem-solving resources. This general notion is supported by experimental studies of stress-induced drinking (Sher 1987b), survey studies (Cooper, Russell, and George 1988), and clinical research (Marlatt and Gordon 1985). Although COAs do appear to have cognitive deficits (see chapter 6 and the ERP data reviewed in chapter 7), the relations among these deficits, coping abilities (e.g., social problem-solving), and the development of drinking remain largely unexplored.

Expectancies (once again). As discussed in chapter 6, alcohol expectancies have been demonstrated to be strong correlates of alcohol use and abuse, both cross-sectionally and prospectively. Furthermore, COAs have been shown to have stronger expectancies for reinforcement from alcohol, especially those expectancies concerning enhanced cognitive and motor functioning. As discussed above, it is possible that these expectancies are, in part, determined by genetic factors, possibly by individual differences in alcohol effects. However, it is also known that alcohol expectancies develop early in life, and prior to initiation of alcohol use. Although it is likely that these expectancies are altered by direct pharmacological experience with alcohol, important (nonbiological) social learning influences are presumed to have a major influence on expectancy development. Whatever the cause, enhanced expectancies for reinforcement from alcohol seem likely to play a significant role in mediating alcoholism risk (Sher et al. in press). In addition to a possible simple mediating role, recent evidence suggests that expectancies might serve an important moderational function. For example, it appears that positive expectancies for alcohol use potentiate the correlations between alcohol involvement and presumed vulnerability factors such as undercontrolled personality traits (Mann et al. 1987), coping styles (Cooper et al. 1988), and anxiety (Kushner 1990). Future research which integrates expectancies with other presumed vulnerability factors should help us better understand the role alcohol expectancies play in the transmission of alcoholism.

Other Models

At least two additional simple models can be posited which do not neatly fit into either of the two classes of models described above.

Proneness to school failure and its psychosocial sequelae. As discussed in chapters 3 and 6, COAs have a variety of childhood behavior problems, intellectual deficits, and are at high risk for school problems. One plausible model is that behavioral and cognitive deficits lead to school problems, social rejection, and consequent decreased self-esteem and/or the adoption of a deviant role. Although the sequencing of school failure, decreased self-esteem, and social deviancy is open to debate, developmental models of adolescent problem behavior point to causal chains similar to the one proposed here (Loeber 1990; Patterson, DeBaryshe, and Ramsey 1989). Either low self-esteem or deviant role may be seen as predisposing to heavier alcohol consumption. Evaluation of this model requires detailed prospective studies of COAs which are currently lacking.

Exposure to alcohol. As noted in chapter 2, exposure to parental drinking models can be viewed as a pathway toward developing drinking problems. The greatest difficulty facing this model is the evidence from the adoption studies which shows a lack of influence from being raised in an alcoholic home, in the absence of an alcoholic biologic background. Nevertheless, under certain circumstances modeling of an alcoholic parent's drinking behavior might prove to represent an important pathway to alcoholism. For example, McCord (1988) found intergenerational transmission of alcoholism was increased when the alcoholic was held in high esteem by his wife. Furthermore, it is clear that parental heavy drinking can lead to "aversive" transmission (Harburg et al. 1982).

Presumably, certain personality traits (e.g., sociability) might lead to greater involvement in social activities and exposure to drinking situations. One advantage of this type of "exposure" model is that it is potentially consistent with a genetic etiology mediated by personality traits (a type of gene-environment correlation). However, we are not aware of any data directly supporting this model and, as noted before, COAs have not been found to be characterized by extraversion (a construct closely associated with sociability). However, assortative pairing appears to be an important process in friendship formation with important implications for initiation in substance abuse (Kandel 1985). Presumably, assortative pairing can be caused, in part, by a number of genetically influenced personality characteristics.

To summarize, none of the simple models described above can be ruled out. Although there are varying degrees of support for each of these models, the etiological significance of each has yet to be firmly established. Nevertheless, these models have utility for evaluating the significance of accumulating data from diverse areas of inquiry and for generating research ideas.

It is likely that different models will have relevance for COAs characterized by different parental subtypes of alcoholism. Consequently, future research will need to incorporate controls for several possible sources of etiologic heterogeneity. This will require more extensive evaluation of parental and other familial psychopathology. Finally, it bears repeating that each of these models is undoubtedly overly simplistic and needs to be elaborated to encompass a broader array of psychosocial and physical influences over the lifespan.

Finally, assuming that the transmission of alcoholism is multifactorial and encompasses a relatively large number of genetic and environmental factors, it is possible that a number of these simple mediational mechanisms operate in conjunction with each other to confer risk to the individual. Consequently, more complex mediational models need to be considered.

More Complex Models

The absence of comprehensive data bases assessing the development and interrelationships of multiple mechanisms preclude any assessment of more detailed models. However, several more complex models have been proposed and will be briefly considered.

Newlin and Thomson's (1990) Model of Alcohol Effects

As discussed earlier (chapter 8 and above), Newlin and Thomson (1990) have proposed a model of alcohol effects (which they restrict to sons of male alcoholics— SOMAs) which posits: (1) greater sensitivity (i.e., acute sensitivity) to the reinforcing properties of alcohol on the ascending limb of the blood alcohol curve, (2) less sensitivity (i.e., acute tolerance) to the more punishing effects of alcohol on the descending limb of the blood alcohol curve, and (3) both of these processes (acute sensitivity and acute tolerance) increasing with repeated drinking experience. Although there is a reasonable amount of evidence consistent with the first two hypotheses, convincing demonstrations of both phenomena within a single drinking session are lacking. Also, the data in support of the third hypothesis are scant. Nevertheless, Newlin and Thomson's hypotheses are intriguing and hold promise for integrating the seemingly conflicting data on COAs and alcohol effects. The model, however, only addresses a limited range of mechanisms, those related to individual differences in alcohol effects. Consequently, it seems unlikely that it can provide a complete understanding of the intergenerational transmission of alcoholism.

Temperament Models

Recent models proposing that basic dimensions of temperament mediate the intergenerational transmission of alcoholism have been proposed by Cloninger (1987a) and Tarter (1988; Tarter et al. 1985). Although both theorists posit that genetically mediated temperamental traits underlie the transmission of alcoholism, the two theories differ in emphasis, specificity, and terminology.

Tarter et al. (1985) use Rowe and Plomin's (1977) six dimensions of temperament (activity, emotionality, sociability, attention span persistence, reaction to food, and soothability) to review the literature on the etiology of alcoholism and conclude that there is evidence to suggest that deviations on most of these temperamental dimensions (except sociability) contribute to alcoholism susceptibility. Tarter (1988) reaches a similar conclusion in a later review which focuses on emotionality, activity, and sociability (the traits that Buss and Plomin [1984] now see as the more basic dimensions of temperament). Tarter et al. (1985) speculate that these temperamental deviations are related to neurological dysfunction in the prefrontal cortex, limbic system, and midbrain. Evidence in support of the model is based on the data reviewed in chapters 3, 6, 7, and 8 that show a number of COA/nonCOA differences in psychopathology, personality characteristics, cognitive functioning, autonomic and CNS physiological abnormalities, and biochemical substances. In addition, data from a number of other areas of inquiry are cited (see Tarter et al. 1985; Tarter 1988). While the focus of the model is on temperament, other factors that might play an important moderating role (e.g., gender, environmental influences) are considered. There appears to be reasonable support for a number of the individual components of the model. However, overall support can be described as incomplete.

Cloninger's (1987a) model of the mediation of family history risk is also a temperament model. However, his theory differs from that of Tarter and his colleagues in several respects. First, although temperament is posited to underlie the major forms of alcoholism, separate temperamental underpinnings are proposed for alcoholism subtypes (Type 1 and Type 2). Second, the temperamental differences are related to the functioning of specific brain regions and associated neurotransmitters.

Basically, Cloninger (1987a, 1987b) proposes that there are three basic dimensions of temperament: (1) novelty seeking, (2) harm avoidance, and (3) reward maintenance. Each of these dimensions of temperament is thought to reflect fundamental motivations (behavioral activation, behavioral inhibition, and behavioral maintenance) which are defined, in part, by their relation to various environmental contingencies. An outline of these motivational/temperamental dimensions and associated variables is presented in Table 9.2. Each of these temperaments is thought to be moderately heritable, and largely independent of each other. Type 1 alcoholism (see chapter 1), is posited to be related to low levels of novelty seeking, and high levels of reward dependence

Table 9.2 An Outline of Cloninger's Theory of Temperament

Brain System (related temperament dimension)	Principal monoamine neuromodulator	Relevant stimuli	Behavioral response
Behavioral activation (novelty seeking)	Dopamine	Novelty Potential rewards or their conditioned signals Potential relief of: punishment or monotony or their conditioned signals	Exploratory pursuit Appetitive Approach Escape Active Avoidance
Behavioral inhibition (harm avoidance)	Serotonin	Conditioned signals for: punishment, novelty, or frustrative nonreward	Passive Avoidance Extinction
Behavioral maintenance (reward dependence)	Norepinephrine	Conditioned signals for reward or relief of punishment	Resistance to extinction

Source: Adapted from Cloninger (1987a). Reprinted with permission of the author and the American Association for the Advancement of Science.

and harm avoidance. In contrast, Type 2 alcoholism (see chapter 1) is posited to be related to high levels of novelty seeking, and low levels of reward dependence and harm avoidance. These configurations are thought to shape relatively distinct forms of alcoholism: (1) Type 1 with later onset, "loss of control" drinking, and greater affective disturbance, and (2) Type 2 with earlier onset, "inability to abstain" drinking, and more antisocial behavior. As discussed in chapter 1, although there is good reason to delineate subtypes based on more antisocial (Type 2) and neurotic (Type 1) characteristics, the extent to which these prototypes conform to other aspects of Cloninger's (1987a) theory has not been resolved. Several recent papers on the Type 1/Type 2 distinction raise questions about the theory and fail to confirm some of the predictions of the model. First, it is not clear whether Type 2 alcoholism should be considered a form of primary alcoholism or a complication of antisocial personality disorder (e.g., Irwin, Schuckit, and Smith 1990). Second, the clinical correlates of Type 1 and Type 2 alcoholism are not as distinct as the theory predicts (e.g., Irwin et al. 1990). Third, there is little evidence that the temperament of offsprings of Type 1 and Type 2 alcoholics differ as predicted by theory (Schuckit, Irwin, and Mahler 1990). Fourth, the neurochemical underpinnings of each temperament dimension described by Cloninger (1987a) remain controversial (see Cloninger 1988; Zuckerman 1988). Although the strongest evidence concerning the validity of the Type 1/Type 2 distinction is derived from the Swedish Adoption Study (Cloninger et al. 1981a), it needs to be underscored that detailed clinical and personality data were not available on that sample, and the basic findings await replication. It is clearly possible that the distinction between a more antisocial, early-onset form of alcoholism and a later-onset, more neurotic form is attributable to environmental factors affecting age of onset, not separate genetic factors underlying each of the two separate forms (Vaillant 1989).

Despite the limited support for the theory to date, it should be emphasized that there are methodologic limitations to the studies which fail to confirm key predictions, and much additional data are needed to more fully evaluate the model. Although early uncritical acceptance of the theory may have been unwarranted, abandonment of what appears to be a promising theory is premature. Whatever the ultimate fate of the model, it has already served an important function by challenging researchers to consider etiological heterogeneity from both methodological and theoretical standpoints.

Zucker's (1987) Developmental Model

Like Cloninger (1987a), Zucker (1987) proposes separate mediational pathways for different subtypes of alcoholism. These four subtypes are termed (1) antisocial alcoholism, (2) developmentally cumulative alcoholism, (3) developmentally limited alcoholism, and (4) negative affect alcoholism. Antisocial alcoholism is similar to Cloninger's Type 2 alcoholism and is presumed to affect primarily males, to have high heritability, and is associated with early onset and poor prognosis. Developmentally cumulative alcoholism is presumed to affect both males and females (but more so males), is associated with moderate levels of parental deviance and moderate heritability, and is thought to be a "cumulative extension" of problem drinking and behavior problems. Developmentally limited alcoholism is also seen as affecting males and females (but more so males), and is seen as being a relatively benign form of alcoholism that is associated with adolescent development issues and the influence of heavy-drinking peers but without substantial genetic influence. This form of alcoholism is thought to remit with the assumption of successful adult role-functioning. Finally, negative affect alcoholism is seen as a predominantly female affliction that is associated with drinking to cope with dysphoria and distressed interpersonal relationships, is thought to be related to a genetic predisposition to experience dysphoric states, and appears similar to Cloninger's Type 1 alcoholism. Although some authors might argue that antisocial alcoholism and negative affect alcoholism might be best conceptualized as complications of other primary psychological disorders (antisocial personality disorder and affective/anxiety disorders, respectively), Zucker makes a strong case for considering these four prototypes.

A particular strength of the model is the emphasis on nongenetic developmental and environmental influences, especially within the context of environmental challenges at each stage of development. In contrast to the other models reviewed in this section, Zucker's theory is not very explicit at the level of genetically determined biopsychological mechanisms. However, there appears to be reasonable support for the various presumed etiological correlates of the different subtypes. The relatively "macro" level of the model, however, restricts its explanatory power to relatively high-level constructs.

Pihl, Peterson, and Finn's (1990a, 1990b; Pihl 1990) Integrative Model

One of the most ambitious models of the mediation of risk among COAs proposed to date is implied in Pihl et al.'s (1990a) recent review of the literature on COA/non-COA differences and elaborated by Pihl et al. (1990b). Like Newlin and Thomson, Pihl and colleagues limit their speculations to intergenerational transmission of risk to SOMAs, addressing an alcoholism subtype similar to Cloninger's Type 2 alcoholism. In many respects, the theory is similar to that proposed by Tarter (1978, 1988; Tarter et al. 1985). However, Pihl and colleagues go somewhat further than these theorists in proposing a more comprehensive model which systematically links biochemical variables, localized brain functions, autonomic and neurophysiological activity, cognitive functioning, childhood behavior problems, and the reinforcing effects of alcohol. Briefly, their model posits that heritable factors influence brain areas (prefrontal cortex and the limbic system) thought to underlie basic cognitive processes such as stimulus classification and associated attentional processes. These basic cognitive deficits are thought to contribute to childhood behavior problems such as attention deficit hyperactivity disorder (ADHD) and conduct disorder, and possibly to school failure. These cognitive deficits are also thought to be reflected physiologically in hyporeactivity to stimuli requiring sustained attention and hyperreactivity to stimuli "whose motivational significance is inherent or involuntary" (Pihl et al. 1990b, p. 296). Alcohol intoxication is thought to play a "normalizing" function by attenuating these abnormal response tendencies, and to be reinforcing for that reason. Furthermore, they speculate deficits in serotonin functioning may be related to the underlying deficit.

It is difficult to evaluate the overall strength of the model that Pihl and colleagues propose. Certainly, all of the individual parts of the model have some degree of empirical support. Furthermore, there is a good deal of indirect support (and some direct support) for some of the linkages they propose. However, direct assessment of the model in all its complexity requires a data base far beyond what is currently available. Nevertheless, the model is clearly comprehensive and integrative and could serve an important heuristic function.

An Heuristic, Overarching Model

Considering the simple models described above and some of the proposed linkages described by the theorists in the preceding section, a broad, highly tentative model can be proposed. At present, the evidence for various components of the model range from very strong to nonexistent. However, where empirical support is weak or nonexistent, only theoretically plausible mechanisms and linkages are proposed.

The purpose of the model schematized in Figure 9.1 is to outline a number of possible simple and complex pathways that might mediate the effect of family history on offspring alcoholism, not to propose a comprehensive theory of alcoholism. It is anticipated that important variables and/or pathways are omitted, and that some of the hypothesized linkages might not hold up to empirical testing. Nevertheless, the model proposed is seen as providing an integrative framework for understanding the potential role of numerous variables at varying levels of psychobiological organization. Implicit in the model is that there are multiple, interrelated pathways with important genetic and environmental influences. However, determining the extent to which given variables reflect genetic versus environmental influences cannot be assumed on the basis of how ostensibly "environmental" the variable appears to be. That is, variables such as parenting behavior, life stress, and peer influence all appear to reflect environmental sources of variance but each might have important genetic determination (e.g., gene-environment covariation). It should be stressed at the outset that most of the variables in the model are complex and multidimensional. For example, family history of alcoholism is clearly heterogeneous (at least clinically) in terms of both course and comorbid psychopathology. There are clearly multiple dimensions of variables such as parenting, temperament/personality, and emotional distress. Nevertheless, for the sake of simplicity, it is of value to consider these broad, heterogeneous factors as conceptual entities. It should also be emphasized that all variables endogenous to the model have important influences beyond those specified. Variables as diverse as temperament, life stress, and alcohol expectancies are presumably affected by systematic influences not considered here. Finally, a number of possible moderating variables are also considered, and some variables serve as both mediators and moderators within the model.

Family history of alcoholism is conceptualized as reflecting the clinical phenomenon of alcoholism in the individual's biological relatives and subsumes heritable influences, the influence of parental alcohol consumption on germ cells and on the fetus, as well as the psychosocial effects of having an alcoholic parent.

Due to its complexity, the model outlined in Figure 9.1 defies simple description. In order to portray the model beyond this schematic, a brief description of a few of the indirect pathways (submodels) from family history

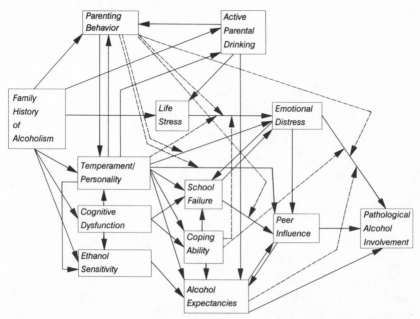

Figure 9.1 Comprehensive model of the relation between family history of alcoholism and pathological alcohol involvement in offspring. Note that most of the variables in the model are assumed to be heterogeneous (i.e., factorially complex). Mediating paths are indicated by solid lines, moderating paths are indicated by dashed lines.

of alcoholism to the offspring's pathological alcohol involvement will be provided. We term these submodels (1) *the enhanced reinforcement model,* (2) *the deviance-prone model,* and (3) *the negative affect model.* However, none of these submodels can be viewed as entirely independent, and the boundaries between one submodel and another are ultimately arbitrary. Consequently, each of the submodels will be delimited to several salient constructs for the purpose of illustration.

The Enhanced Reinforcement Submodel

In its most basic form, the enhanced reinforcement model (see Figure 9.2) posits that family history of alcoholism is causally related to increased reinforcement value from alcohol which in turn leads to an increased likelihood of developing alcohol problems and dependence. (Although this model is focused on reinforcement, decreased sensitivity on the descending limb of the BAC [e.g., Newlin and Thomson 1990] can easily be accommodated to the model.) The model posits a direct path from family history to ethanol sensitivity (perhaps due to direct effects of alcohol on brain centers related to reward). In addition, ethanol sensitivity is also posited to be related to cog-

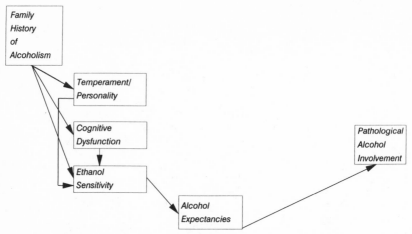

Figure 9.2 Schematic diagram of the enhanced reinforcement submodel. Note that most of the variables in the model are assumed to be heterogeneous (i.e., factorially complex).

nitive dysfunction (e.g., Pihl et al. 1990b) and temperament/personality (e.g., Levenson et al. 1987; Sher and Levenson 1982). It is further proposed that pharmacologically mediated individual differences in ethanol sensitivity are translated into increased expectancies of reinforcement from alcohol with sufficient drinking experience. These expectancies are, in turn, thought to be the proximal mediator of drinking behavior.

The Deviance-prone Submodel

In contrast to the enhanced reinforcement submodel, which focuses on individual differences in the pharmacological effects of alcohol, the key variables in the deviance-prone submodel (see Figure 9.3) are largely behavioral and the major explanatory concept is deficient socialization. Family history of alcoholism is posited to have direct effects on parenting behavior, temperament/personality, and cognitive dysfunction. A "difficult" temperament (Thomas and Chess 1977) in transaction (i.e., bidirectional causation; cf. Sameroff and Chandler 1974) with ineffective parental control (e.g., Dishion, Patterson, and Reid 1988) leads to unsocialized behavior resulting in poor academic adjustment and school failure. Associated cognitive deficits are also posited to contribute to school failure. School failure is posited to lead to association with deviant, substance-abusing peers, both directly and as an indirect effect mediated by low self-esteem (e.g., Kaplan 1975). (Increased emotional distress is assumed to be bidirectionally related to school failure.) In addition, a direct path from temperament/personality to peer influence is posited because it is assumed that more venturesome, sensation-seeking individuals are likely to seek out peers with similar traits. In this submodel, peer

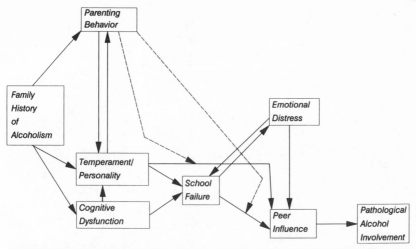

Figure 9.3 Schematic diagram of the deviance proneness submodel. Note that most of the variables in the model are assumed to be heterogeneous (i.e., factorially complex). Mediating paths are indicated by solid lines, moderating paths are indicated by dashed lines.

influence is viewed as the mediating mechanism most proximal to increased alcohol use.

In addition to the mediational pathways outlined above, moderating effects of parenting behavior on paths to peer influence are proposed. These moderating effects are viewed as representing the parents' success or failure at monitoring the child's peer relationships with deviant peers.

The Negative Affect Submodel

The negative affect submodel (see Figure 9.4) focuses on proneness to experiencing negative affective states, a high level of life stress, and the effectiveness of coping resources. (For reviews of stress and coping models of substance abuse, including alcoholism, see Shiffman and Wills 1985). Family history is posited to lead to temperamental characteristics that predispose the offspring to experience negative affective states such as anxiety and depression. Although it is clear that life stress is related to a family history of alcoholism (Brown 1989, Roosa et al. 1988), the model is not limited to stress directly related to a parent's drinking history. Also, the effects of stress related to parental alcoholism are not necessarily restricted to acute effects but can be viewed as having delayed effects as well. Life stress is posited to have direct effects on emotional distress which, in turn, is moderated by temperament. Certain temperamental types are presumed to be especially vulnerable to certain forms of life stress (e.g., personal loss, threats to autonomy). Coping ability is thought to be influenced in part by inherited temperamental

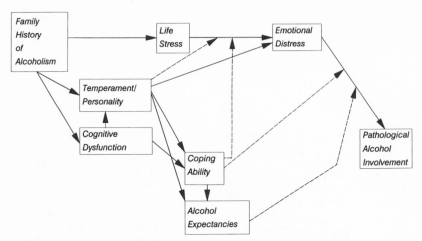

Figure 9.4 Schematic diagram of the negative affect submodel. Note that most of the variables in the model are assumed to be heterogeneous (i.e., factorially complex). Mediating paths are indicated by solid lines, moderating paths are indicated by dashed lines.

characteristics and cognitive abilities. In this model, coping is thought to play a moderating role by buffering both the relationship between life stress and emotional distress (by actively reducing the impact of the stress), and the relationship between emotional distress and pathological drinking. Although less central in this submodel, alcohol-related expectancies for relief from psychological distress are posited to be related to impaired coping ability (Cooper et al. 1988). In addition, these expectancies are posited to moderate the path from emotional distress to pathological drinking (Kushner 1990). Although this submodel emphasizes life stress and coping, a direct path from temperament/personality to emotional distress is also considered since some individuals may experience considerable affective disturbance in the absence of precipating stressors. This latter pathway might be more important for individuals with substantial family histories of affective and anxiety disorders.

Again, the overarching model summarized in Figure 9.1 is viewed only as a starting point, and, again, it is likely that key constructs and pathways are overlooked and have yet to be identified. Even more probable, the model is overidentified, and some constructs and pathways may not be necessary for a complete understanding of the intergenerational transmission of alcoholism. Nevertheless, this model is viewed as an important starting point for considering multiple, complex pathways and could serve as a guide for researchers wishing to integrate findings from a number of seemingly disparate domains.

Summary

Existing empirical research and theory have identified a number of plausible routes for the intergenerational transmission of alcoholism. Although a number of "simple" mediational pathways can be considered, it is likely that each of these pathways represents only a small part of the picture and that a comprehensive understanding of the effects of parental alcoholism must be considered in the context of a broad matrix of biopsychosocial influences. From this perspective, there is no simple cause of the increased risk of alcoholism for COAs, and to some this might appear discouraging. However, alcoholism in humans is a complex, multifactorial problem, and an adequate explanation must consider a host of potentially important influences. As stated eloquently by Robins, West, Ratcliff, and Herjanic (1979, p. 326) more than a decade ago: "Studies of the transmission of alcoholism from parent to child that do not examine the chain of pathologies through which that transmission takes place can produce an illusion of simplicity. Further, they may seem to conflict with studies that emphasize family and personality structure as predictors of alcoholism when no real conflict exists. . . . Parental alcoholism, family structure, and prealcoholic behavior patterns form a complex of closely interrelated patterns that are passed on together from generation to generation."

Despite the complexity of the model appearing in Figure 9.1, it should be noted that there might be a very limited number of final common pathways which could serve to make preventive efforts less complex. For example, expectancies of reinforcement from alcohol might prove to be a critical variable affecting most pathways, and interventions targeted at this variable might prove to have far-ranging preventive effects.

Several limitations of the models proposed deserve some mention. First, a developmental perspective is generally lacking. Although it is likely that some submodels (e.g., deviance proneness) might be more relevant to earlier onset problems while others (e.g., negative affect) are more relevant to later onset problems, a truly comprehensive model will incorporate different mediating mechanisms in the prospective context of developmentally specific life tasks and transitions. Also, although some moderating influences are considered in the model, this aspect of the model is relatively undeveloped. The general issue of moderation of risk is considered further in chapter 10.

10 Moderating Variables

Research comparing COAs with nonCOAs has generally attempted to identify variables that might *mediate* risk for alcoholism and other morbid outcomes. As discussed in chapter 4, another important focus of research on COAs attempts to identify factors that might *moderate* the influence of risk factors, variables that statistically interact with risk factors in predicting outcome. (Variables that exert only main effects in predicting outcome might be more clearly conceptualized as either mediating variables (see chapters 4 and 9) or independent risk factors.) As discussed in chapter 4, moderator variables can often be viewed as "protective factors," attenuating the morbid influence of parental pathology, or "exacerbating factors," amplifying family history effects. The distinction between "protective" and "exacerbating" effects is somewhat arbitrary and conceptually unimportant since these two terms represent opposite views of the same phenomenon. For example, if social class were found to interact with family history of alcoholism, we could equally say that high social class "protects" against the familial transmission or that lower social class "exacerbates" family history effects.

As discussed in chapter 4, a more refined notion of moderation is that of "moderated mediation." That is, the moderator interacts with an identified mediator of family history in predicting outcome. A graphic illustration of this is provided in Figure 9.1, which shows several variables that, in addition to serving as mediators, moderate the effects of specific mediators. For example, in Figure 9.1, parenting behavior is postulated to moderate the relation between temperament and emotional distress, school failure and peer influence, etc.

Despite the critical importance of moderating variables in understanding the intergenerational transmission of alcohol problems, relatively few data exist which clearly demonstrate moderating effects on parental alcoholism. In large part, this is because the studies have not been designed or analyzed appropriately to demonstrate moderation. A major interpretive problem facing several studies that purport to identify potential moderating effects is the failure to consider family history negative (or nonCOA) controls in the study design. Some studies have shown that *among COAs,* those high on a given variable are more likely to develop alcoholism while those low on the variable are less likely to develop alcoholism (Rogosch et al. 1990). For example, Werner's (1986) finding that temperamental differences in infancy predict outcome among COAs has been cited as indicating that temperament might serve as a moderator variable or "protective factor." However, it is equally plausible that temperament is a mediator of risk and that a "good" temperament connotes a lack of risk, not a buffering of risk. Alternatively, temperament could be viewed as an independent risk factor, unrelated to parental alcoholism but significantly associated with offspring alcoholism. Similarly, disrupted family rituals (Wolin et al. 1979, 1980; see chapter 2 and below) have been posited to be an important moderator of alcoholic outcomes among COAs. However, the failure to consider disrupted family rituals in nonCOA families makes it impossible to determine if disrupted family rituals are mediating or moderating the effects of family history, or serving as an independent risk factor. (Of course, the source of disruption of family rituals in nonalcoholic families would presumably be due to something other than parental alcoholism.) The failure to make this type of distinction limits our ability to conceptualize many of the emerging findings in COA research.

Potential Moderators

In this section we will review a number of variables that various authors have identified as potential moderators of outcome in COAs. Although a number of these findings are intriguing, it is probably safe to say that, to date, no moderators have been conclusively identified.

Social Class

Perhaps the clearest demonstration of a variable that moderates the effect of parental alcoholism was reported in the Swedish Adoption Study. Cloninger et al. (1981a) showed that postnatal milieu (largely social class) interacted with family history of alcoholism in determining the frequency and severity of alcoholism in Type 1 alcoholism. Although this finding is post hoc and needs to be replicated, the purported finding of a clear gene-environment interaction suggests that at least one form of alcoholism (Cloninger's Type 1) is subject to important environmental moderation. It should be noted, however, that at least one study (Nylander and Rydelius 1982) failed to find differences in lower and higher social class COAs (assessed when most COAs were in early to mid-adulthood).

Family Variables

As noted in chapter 2, Wolin and his colleagues (Wolin et al. 1979, 1980) have demonstrated that the disruption of family rituals such as celebrating holidays, taking vacations, etc. is a variable that distinguishes alcoholic families that do and do not transmit alcoholism to their offspring. Following up on this work, Bennett, Wolin, Reiss, and Teitelbaum (1987) replicated the basic finding (especially for male COAs of alcoholic fathers) that alcoholic families characterized by a lack of disruption tend to produce fewer alcoholic offspring. However, they went further and related intergenerational transmission to a number of variables in both the COA's family of origin and the nuclear family of the COA in adulthood. Family-of-origin variables that tended to decrease intergenerational transmission included the extent that the COA's family dinners were not disrupted in the family of origin, and a high level of deliberateness in family rituals in the nuclear family. Interestingly, these authors also examined a number of variables surrounding the COA's spouse and found that a high level of dinner rituals in the spouse's family of origin tended to reduce intergenerational transmission, while intergenerational transmission was increased if the COA married another COA. Taken together, these findings suggest that the preservation of family rituals both in the family of origin and the nuclear family of the COA in adulthood is an important predictor of whether alcoholism is transmitted from parent to offspring. However, this research does not adequately rule out third-variable explanations and questions concerning direction of causality, and so it is difficult to determine whether ritual preservation plays a causal role in "protecting" COAs or whether the relation is spurious. Also, the failure to examine the interaction of ritual preservation and family history of alcoholism in the reported analyses makes it difficult to attribute the findings to a moderating process. (A recent publication by this research group [Bennett et al. 1988a] examined the effect of deliberateness of family ritual on behavioral, cognitive, and emotional functioning of schoolage COAs and nonCOAs, but failed to jointly consider parental alcoholism and family ritual preservation.) Despite the methodological problems of the work by Wolin, Bennett, and their colleagues, their findings are provocative and indicate that family process is a potentially important area for continued investigation.

Other family variables that may have a moderating role is suggested by the work of McCord (1988). In a follow-up of men 45 to 53 years old who had participated in the Cambridge-Somerville study when preteens or adolescents, McCord attempted to identify variables that moderated the effect of paternal alcoholism. The major finding emerging from this study was a significant interaction between paternal alcoholism and the mothers' esteem for their husbands. Mothers who held their alcoholic spouses in high esteem were almost twice as likely to have alcoholic sons than mothers who did not hold their alcoholic spouses in high regard. Among subjects with nonalcoholic fathers, the rates for alcoholism were similar regardless of the mothers' level of esteem for their spouses. These data, which are compatible with a modeling (i.e., imitation) hypothesis of alcoholism transmission, suggest that modeling effects are not simply based on level of parental consumption but on how highly an alcoholic model is valued by key family members. McCord (1988) also argues that maternal control of the boy interacts with paternal alcoholism in predicting offspring alcoholism; however, the data she presents do not bear this out. (The interaction between father's alcoholism and maternal control is not statistically significant.) Given the lack of a correlation between maternal control and father's alcoholism in the sample, it appears that maternal control might best be considered an independent risk factor.

Werner (1986) identified a number of family variables that distinguished COAs who did and did not develop serious behavior problems by the age of 18 using a longitudinal sample of predominantly lower class children in Kauai, Hawaii, who had been assessed at regular intervals since birth. Again, this design does not unambiguously define moderators and it is unclear if the various findings should best be conceptualized as suggesting mediator, moderator, or independent risk factor effects. Nevertheless, the findings are of potential interest and will be briefly mentioned here. Werner's major finding was that COAs who developed serious problems were distinguished from COAs who did not on a number of variables related to the quality of the care-giving environment (e.g., amount of attention from primary care-givers, family conflict during infancy, birth of another sibling within the first two years of life). Although we cannot unambiguously attribute a moderator role to care-giving environment, Werner's findings suggest we can look at a number of family characteristics early in the life of the COA that presage significant problems by early adulthood.

The data on the possible moderating role of family variables described above (and also see chapter 2) suggest a number of interesting correlations between various aspects of the family and offspring adjustment. However, the nature of the findings reported to date limits our ability to interpret the meaning of these findings in an integrated model of the transmission of alcoholism and related problems among COAs.

Social Support

For the past fifteen years, social support has been viewed as a key variable in moderating the relation between life stress and a host of negative outcomes (Caplan 1981; Cohen and Wills 1985; Dean and Lin 1977; House and Kahn 1985). Given that growing up in an alcoholic home can be viewed as a major stressor with negative effects on COAs, it is logical that several researchers have investigated the nature and extent of social support in COAs. These data are somewhat difficult to evaluate because of the different measures employed by various investigators and the scarcity of reported findings. It does appear that COAs report less social support from their families than nonCOAs (Benson and Heller 1987; Holden, Brown, and Mott 1988), and this is consistent with Werner's (1986) finding on care-giving environment and the data reviewed in chapter 2 on family milieu. However, with respect to support from friends, COAs report levels that are equivalent (Benson and Heller 1987) or higher (Holden et al. 1988) than those reported by nonCOAs. Perhaps more relevant to the question of moderation, Clair and Genest (1986) reported that COAs and nonCOAs received comparable emotional support but COAs reported significantly less informational support from their social support networks than nonCOAs. Furthermore, informational support was found to correlate negatively with depression proneness and positively with self-esteem among COAs. This finding alone does not implicate either a main or a buffering effect for social support, although it suggests that social support may be an important variable to consider in predicting COA adjustment.

The larger literature on social support is consistent with both buffering and main effect roles across a large range of outcomes. Buffering roles are more likely when "the social support measures assess the perceived availability of interpersonal resources that are responsive to the needs elicited by stressful events" (Cohen and Wills 1985, p. 310). However, one study has shown that social support processes appear to differ greatly between offspring of parents with serious problems (either mental or physical) and children of normal parents (Hirsch and Reischl 1985). Consequently, generalizations from the general literature on social support to the population of COAs need to be made cautiously. Future research will need to consider social support variables in the context of variables beyond life stress, such as personality and preexisting disorder, since these other variables are empirically related to social support and need to be considered in an overall model if unique effects of social support are to be isolated (Monroe and Steiner 1986).

Personality Variables

Most of the literature on personality in COAs has focused on the presumed mediating effects of personality traits (e.g., Cloninger 1987a). However, personality traits could be hypothesized to serve a moderating role as well. For example, certain positive psychological characteristics could serve to "hold in check" genetically transmitted tendencies to alcoholism. Rogosch et al. (1990) recently demonstrated a significant correlation between parental alcoholism and dispositional self-awareness in predicting alcohol-related problems and alcohol consumption in a sample of adolescents. Among subjects high in self-awareness, no correlation between parental alcoholism and offspring drinking was observed. Low self-aware subjects, however, did show a correlation between parental alcoholism and their quantity-frequency of alcohol consumption and alcohol-related consequences. These findings suggest that high self-aware subjects are "protected" from the morbid effects of parental alcoholism. Chassin et al. (1988, p. 215) note that "high self-awareness is associated with conformity to explicit proscriptions against [norm-violating behavior] . . . [and thus] . . . highly self-aware adolescents may be more sensitive than their low self-aware peers to explicit legal proscriptions against alcohol use . . . or they may be more sensitive to implicit sanctions against drinking from family and peer norms." Although these findings are intriguing, limitations of the data set concerning ascertainment of family history argue for caution in generalizing these findings.

Rogosch et al. (1990) also reported that so-called prealcoholic personality traits (what we have termed "behavioral undercontrol" in chapter 6) also moderated the relation between parental alcoholism and adolescent alcohol involvement. This effect was not replicated by Walitzer (1990) and seems to conflict with a number of other findings suggesting a mediating role for this variable. Consequently, pending further replication, it is difficult to place a high degree of confidence in this finding.

Werner (1986) reported that 85 percent of COAs who failed to develop problems by age 18 were perceived as "cuddly and affectionate" during infancy, compared to only 42 percent of COAs who did develop behavioral problems by age 18. Although she interprets these findings as suggesting that a favorable temperament and/or a positive infant-care-giver relationship makes these children "resilient" to the stressful effects of growing up in an alcoholic home, the failure to document an interaction makes it difficult to distinguish resilience from vulnerability. The finding does point to early temperament traits and parent-child interaction as important predictors of outcome among COAs.

At present, relatively few data exist demonstrating personality moderators of risk for alcoholism. Investigations seeking to examine moderating effects are rare, however. The finding that high self-awareness may serve as a moderating factor is intriguing, and further research on personality traits that may serve a buffering role in COAs should be encouraged.

Cognitive/Intellectual Variables

Werner (1986) identified a number of intellectual deficits among the COAs who developed serious behavior problems by age 18, and these deficits were present throughout childhood and early adolescence. At two years of age, almost 16 percent of the COAs who were to develop problems were rated below normal in intellectual development by a pediatrician in comparison to 0 percent of the COAs who fared well. Standardized aptitude and achievement tests administered throughout grade- and high-school continued to demonstrate significant intellectual deficits, especially in the verbal domain. Although Werner's (1986) findings are dramatic, it is not clear if good intellectual ability buffers risk or indicates a lack of risk. Re-analysis of these data in the context of a nonCOA control group would help clarify this issue.

Coping

One way that intellectual competence or deficiency might play a moderating role is through its effect on coping. Coping can be generally thought of as "constantly changing cognitive and behavioral efforts to manage specific external and/or internal demands that are appraised as taxing or exceeding the resources of the person" (Lazarus and Folkman 1984, p. 141). In chapter 9 we considered that coping might serve both a mediating and a moderating role in the transmission of risk in COAs. Although the general importance of coping cannot be overstated, there are relatively few studies that address the role of coping in predicting outcomes among COAs at present, and so our ability to evaluate this important domain is limited. Before briefly considering the limited data available, it needs to be pointed out that distinguishing coping processes from outcome can be difficult because adjustment (what we usually consider an outcome) and coping are sometimes used almost interchangeably. Similarly, preexisting traits such as personality may relate intimately to coping processes and so there appears to be much conceptual overlap between the constructs of coping and other important variables. Only by considering coping measures in the matrix of other important variables, ideally in a longitudinal framework, can we begin to make critical conceptual distinctions. Also, our ability to assess coping is limited, and many assessment techniques are tied to self-reports of covert processes that are often automatic. Determining the validity of such reports can be particularly problematic.

Using the Ways of Coping Questionnaire (Folkman and Lazarus 1980), Clair and Genest (1986) found that, as a group, young adult COAs reported using more "emotion-focused" coping (coping efforts aimed at managing emotional distress) than a comparison group of nonCOAs, and particularly coping processes that relied on avoidance strategies. No between-group differences were found on "problem-focused" coping (coping efforts aimed at altering the distressing situation). When Clair and Genest (1986) examined the correlation between coping factors and "adjustment," they found that problem-focused coping, but not emotion-focused coping, was related to self-esteem and depression proneness. Although interaction effects were not evaluated, they also reported that none of the correlations between coping and adjustment were significant for the nonCOAs, suggesting that problem-focused coping may serve a moderator function. This is a potentially important finding that needs to be replicated. It certainly suggests that intervention efforts aimed at improving COAs' abilities to cope actively with their difficult situation are reasonable.

Summary

Research on variables that moderate the influence of family history of alcoholism on offspring adjustment and drinking problems is in its infancy. Much greater attention to variables that may moderate the expression of risk is necessary if we are to gain a fuller understanding of the effects of parental alcoholism on offspring and on intergenerational transmission of alcoholism in particular. At present, we can not make any strong statements concerning variables that appear to moderate the effects of parental alcoholism. The broad domains that previous research has addressed (social class, family interaction, social support, coping, and personality) appear to represent a set of promising variables. However, we need more data from well-designed and well-analyzed studies before we can confidently evaluate the role that purported moderators play in buffering risk.

Research focusing on moderator variables that might be amenable to direct modification holds promise for developing intervention programs for reducing morbidity among COAs. This research should go hand in hand with research on mediating variables so that moderation of specific mediational pathways can be assessed (moderated mediation) and the influence of multiple variables can be evaluated simultaneously (e.g., see Figure 9.1). This strategy is likely to provide more detailed information on the nature of risk and protective factors.

11 The Clinical Literature

WITH PHIL MOTHERSEAD

The major focus of this book has been on etiological processes related to alcoholism, specifically variables and processes that explain the intergenerational transmission of alcoholism. The majority of scholarly publication in this area has been generated by empirical researchers interested in COAs as an "at risk" population. Although the prevalence of a number of psychological problems in COAs has been noted to be high (see chapter 3), these problems have been described in terms of standard diagnostic systems (e.g., the DSM) or scores on various psychological tests. We have provided relatively little consideration of the burgeoning literature on COAs generated by clinical writers who have described a number of long-term, pathological effects of growing up in an alcoholic home and who have developed treatment programs specifically tailored for COAs.

In recent years there has been a dramatic increase in the awareness of the potential effects of parental alcoholism, with extensive coverage in the media. In the past few years, national magazines such as *Newsweek* (Leerhsen and Namuth 1988), *Time* (Desmond 1987), *People* (Chu 1988), and even *Girl Scout Leader* (Craven 1988) have featured cover stories on COAs. Autobiographies of famous COAs such as Kirk Douglas (1988) and Suzanne Sommers (1988) have been commercial successes, as have a number of self-help books for COAs (e.g., Beattie 1987; Black 1982; Cermak 1988; Woititz 1983). In addition, there has been a clear increase in publications tailored for clinical professionals such as books (Brown 1988; Vannicelli 1989) and journal articles (Beletis and Brown 1981; Brown and Beletis 1986; Cermak and Brown 1982; Hibbard 1987; Kern 1985). As described in the popular and clinical literature, being a COA or an adult child of an alcoholic (ACOA) implies a host of potential clinical problems with various authors recommending different approaches to treatment.

In this chapter, we review a number of the concepts discussed in the popular and clinical literature on COAs. However, some caveats are in order regarding the scope and focus of the chapter. First, the clinical literature on COAs and ACOAs is based primarily upon anecdotal, case history reports, with few empirical research findings. These types of data do not lend themselves to the same types of analysis utilized in empirical research, and thus cannot be evaluated as confidently as data subjected to statistical evaluation. Second, we will highlight the key features of a number of concepts and approaches without any attempt to exhaustively examine any one particular orientation. The goal is to briefly summarize recent literature and, we hope, to provide direction for further work in this area. The main topics reviewed include: (1) history of the ACOA movement, (2) the concept of codependency, (3) other purported characteristics and roles of COAs and ACOAs, (4) clinical developmental theory, (5) current therapeutic approaches, (6) education and prevention, and (7) social-psychological dimensions.

History of COA Movement

Although scholarly writing on the special problems of COAs go back to at least the turn of the century (MacNicholl 1905; Sullivan 1899), the current lay and clinical interest in COAs (what we term the COA movement) appears to have begun with the publication of Margaret Cork's (1969) book, *The Forgotten Children.* This book describes a group of 115 school-aged COAs with a variety of problems including low self-confidence, difficulty in making and keeping friends, and in expressing emotion (especially anger and resentment). Others in the field of alcoholism treatment had worked to shift the focus from the alcoholic to other family members (e.g., Jackson 1954). However, it was not until the "forgotten victims" were identified and described by Cork that the intense popular and clinical interest in the COA and ACOA began to take shape. During the 1970s, scholarly reviews of the early empirical literature on COAs (e.g., El-Guebaly and Offord 1977, 1979) pointed out the documented problems that offspring of alcoholic parents exhibit across the life span. Later, clinicians such as Black (1982) and Wegscheider (1981) began to describe characteristic roles adopted by ACOAs from their therapy caseloads. Woititz (1983) had studied low self-esteem in COAs and later came out with her influential text, *Adult Children of Alcoholics,* describing her clinical experiences with this population. During this period greater numbers of ACOAs apparently began to identify with the characteristics that were being applied to them by counselors, social workers, and other professionals. The popular press contributed to the COA movement with stories appearing in major periodicals (e.g., *Time, Newsweek* and *People*), news dailies and Sunday supplements, and the self-help books and autobiographies mentioned above. In addition to the mass media and trade books, several newsletters addressing COA/ACOA issues have evolved and are currently being published, including: *Alateen Talk* (Alateen's bimonthly newsletter), *Inside Al-Anon* (newsletter for both Alateen and Al-Anon groups), *COA Review* (international newsletter for COAs), and *NACA Network* (newsletter for the National Association for Children of Alcoholics). Today, in almost any sizable community, therapy groups for COAs and ACOAs are flourishing. Many of these same COAs and ACOAs appear to constitute a significant part of the caseload of a number of public and private mental health agencies.

The ACOA movement has now broadened in scope to encompass a variety of adults from dysfunctional families. The "Adult Children" movement conveys the message that you should confront your chaotic childhood and work through the pain that you have repressed (Blau 1990). Millions of adults can identify with painful childhood experiences and relate these experiences to their present unhappiness. Identifying one's self as an adult child thus begins the recovery process, a process that often becomes a "life style" (Kaminer 1990).

The recent trend of so-called "parent bashing," the blaming of one's parents for personal problems, appears to have become an obsession as well as good business in publishing circles (Blau 1990). Terms such as "unseen casualties" and "hidden tragedy" as well as "forgotten children," appear to add a strong emotional component to the COA movement. Stark (1987, p. 58) begins a recent article with the title "Forgotten Victims: Children of Alcoholics. Overshadowed by Family Turmoil, They Live in an Atmosphere of Anxiety, Guilt and Denial That Can Last a Lifetime." The enduring negative effects of having grown up in an alcoholic family now constitute the somewhat amorphous concept of the ACOA.

Despite the popular acceptance of much of the ACOA lore, the related broad concepts of ACOA, "adult children" and codependency, have begun to come under attack from some professionals (Kaminer 1990). At least two parodies of ACOA articles have recently appeared in professional journals: "Adult cousins of alcoholics" (Miller 1987), and "Adult pets of alcoholics: Another underserved population" (Weinberg and Schnapps 1987). A noted childhood expert has commented, "I have a feeling we're soon going to have special groups for third cousins of excessive sherry drinkers. . . . You don't know whether to laugh or cry over this stuff" (Robert Coles, cited in Kaminer 1990, p. 1). As we will see, the clinical literature on ACOAs and codependency contains many generalizations and unsubstantiated broad assumptions. However, rather than simply dismiss this literature, we will review and comment on the major clinical concepts in it. As with any area of inquiry in the social and behavioral sciences, the ultimate validity of the concepts put forth by a host of clinical writers will depend upon the extent they hold up to empirical scrutiny.

Codependency

Approximately ten years ago the concept of codependency emerged and was easily applied to COAs as well as spouses of alcoholics (Cermak 1984). Codependency evolved from the label "coalcoholism" which, in earlier literature, described spouses of alcoholics, usually women, who were excessive caretakers and overly dependent (Wegscheider 1981). The concept of codependency has now been applied to every possible type of addiction. Codependents are often considered "adult children" in that their dependency has masked their childlike self (Kaminer 1990). Self-help books providing ways to deal with this phenomenon have flooded the market. *Codependent No More* (Beattie 1987) emerged as a best seller (with more than a million copies sold), providing instruction to codependents on how to gain control of their lives. A follow-up book, *Beyond Codependency,* (Beattie 1989) focuses on recovery. Despite the enormous attention given to the concept of codependency, relatively little effort has been made, empirically or theoretically, to define the term. As Beattie (1989, p. 11) states, "In spite of the emergence of the word codependency, and so many people recovering from it, it is still jargon. No standard definition exists. We haven't agreed on whether codependency is a sickness, a condition, or a normal response to abnormal people. We still haven't agreed on whether it's hyphenated: codependency or co-dependency?" To date, no professionally agreed on diagnostic classification exists as to the categories of codependency or ACOA.

Cermak (1984, 1986) has called for the development of a diagnostic classification for codependency (Codependent Personality Disorder) combining personality disorder symptoms from the Diagnostic and Statistical Manual of Mental Disorders (DSM III; see Table 11.1). In Cermak's (1986, p. 42) words, "Codependency is a pattern of immature adaptive mechanisms that exists in alcoholics, many spouses of alcoholics, and many children of alcoholics." Many of the manifestations of codependency become overt after involvement in a committed relationship. This excessive dependence on another person eventually becomes pathological and influences all relationships (Wegscheider-Cruse 1985). As pointed out by Brown (1988), the term "codependence" is often applied to individuals who organize their lives around other people and/or things. Codependence is not viewed as necessarily negative or dysfunctional. The dysfunctional codependent position occurs when the individual is unable to regulate closeness and unable to develop an independent autonomous self.

Table 11.1 Diagnostic Criteria for Codependent Personality Disorder

---

A. Continued investment of self-esteem in the ability to control both oneself and others in the face of serious adverse consequences.
B. Assumption of responsibility for meeting others' needs to the exclusion of acknowledging one's own.
C. Anxiety and boundary distortions around intimacy and separation.
D. Enmeshment in relationships with personality disordered, chemically dependent, other codependent, and/or impulse disordered individuals.
E. Three or more of the following:
   1. Excessive reliance on denial
   2. Constriction of emotions (with or without dramatic outbursts)
   3. Depression
   4. Hypervigilance
   5. Compulsions
   6. Anxiety
   7. Substance abuse
   8. Has been (or is) the victim of recurrent physical or sexual abuse
   9. Stress-related medical illnesses
   10. Has remained in a primary relationship with an active substance abuser for at least two years without seeking outside help

---

Source: adapted from Cermak (1988) with permission of the author.

In summary, the term codependent has been used as a synonym for ACOA, but neither term is unambiguously defined. The observation that many members of alcoholic families may develop excessive dependence on others is important in determining more specific classification criteria for ACOAs. Cermak's (1986) work toward specifying diagnostic criteria of Codependent Personality Disorder is helpful, although some might argue that this is simply a Mixed Personality Disorder or a Dependent Personality Disorder for which criteria already exist (e.g., American Psychiatric Association 1980, 1987). Furthermore, a controversy exists as to whether ACOAs are suffering from a personality disorder (which implies deeply ingrained patterns of dysfunctional interpersonal traits) or from transient adjustment problems (which presumably are much easier to overcome). Although the need for a diagnostic category such as Codependent Personality Disorder has yet to be compellingly argued, Cermak's (1986) diagnostic criteria appear to be a step in the right direction. Simply being the offspring of an alcoholic is not, in and of itself, sufficient to warrant the diagnosis of codependency. "Diagnosis" should be based on operational criteria (however vague) referenced to the intra- and interpersonal functioning of the COA. This perspective appears more logical than that expressed by some (e.g., Black 1982), that simply being a COA implies significant psychological problems.

There has been virtually no empirical research examining the validity of the Codependent Personality Disorder construct. There are at least two questions that need to be addressed by future research. First, is the construct of codependency sufficiently distinct from other personality disorder diagnoses that a new diagnostic category is warranted? Second, do offspring of alcoholics (or other substance abusers) appear to meet codependency criteria more often than the general population or those in any of a variety of special populations (e.g., offspring of parents with physical disabilities or handicaps; see Brown 1988)?

Purported Characteristics and Roles of ACOAs

The characteristics that define the ACOA vary according to the particular author surveyed. The following may help to illustrate the extent of the diversity in the clinical literature. Woititz (1983, 1984) developed a list of 13 characteristics of ACOAs from some 500 observations observed in her clinical practice (see Table 11.2). According to Woititz (1984) the source of many of the ACOAs' problems (i.e., characteristics) is often a lack of information rather than an emotional imbalance. Characteristics of ACOAs are thought to result from family systems which are inconsistent, incongruent, and filled with double messages. For example, ACOAs are described as buying into a "myth of normalcy" in which they judge themselves very harshly due to their inability to live up to an ideal fantasy. The "guess at what is normal" characteristic results from perceptions being invalidated by parents and other significant others. ACOAs are described as feeling different from others and lonely, even in crowds, due to their excessive isolation in childhood (Woititz 1984).

Defensive mechanisms that ACOAs reportedly adopt include denial, all-or-none thinking, excessive control, avoidance of anger, self-blame, and assumption of responsibility for others (Brown 1988). A great deal of the clinical/theoretical ACOA literature reports that ACOAs have a tendency to be overcontrolling in relationships, avoidant of self-disclosure, lacking in trust, and exhibiting difficulty with intimacy (Black 1982; Brown 1988; Cermak 1986; Wood 1987). Black, Bucky and Wilder-Padilla (1986) surveyed a group of ACOAs and a group of adults raised in nonalcoholic homes as to their perceptions of interpersonal and family problems. The ACOAs reported difficulty with trust, intimacy, independence, expression of needs, and utilization of interpersonal resources (i.e., support systems). Cermak and Brown (1982) interviewed a small clinical sample of ACOAs and described them as having difficulty in relationships due to a lack of trust and an excessive need to be in control. The ACOAs in this sample tended to view their personal feelings in a negative way, evidently due to the association of affect with a lack of internal control. Vulnerability, especially in interpersonal situations, was lessened by overtly conveying an image of complete control.

Table 11.2 Putative Characteristics of Adult Children of Alcoholics

Woititz (1984)
1. Guess at what normal is
2. Have difficulty following a project through
3. Lie when it is just as easy to be truthful
4. Judge themselves without mercy
5. Have difficulty having fun
6. Take themselves very seriously
7. Have difficulty with intimate relationships
8. Overreact to changes over which they have no control
9. Constantly seek approval and affirmation
10. Feel different from other people
11. Are super-responsible or super-irresponsible
12. Are extremely loyal even when loyalty is undeserved
13. Impulsively lock themselves into a course of action without examining the consequences

Brown (1988)
1. Denial
2. Dichotomous all-or-none thinking
3. Overly controlling
4. Self-blame
5. Assumption of responsibility for others
6. Intense anger

Cermak (1984) & McKearn (1988)
1. Isolation and psychic numbing
2. Depression related to survivor guilt
3. Anxiety reactions
4. Sleep disturbances and nightmares
5. Intrusive thoughts
6. Deep-seated anger (rage)
7. Avoidance of feelings

Similarities between symptoms of family members of alcoholics and post-traumatic stress disorder (PTSD) clients have also been noted (Cermak 1984; McKearn 1988). The comparisons describe both ACOA and PTSD individuals as having been exposed to intense and prolonged stress, with neither having the opportunity for normal processing of the emotions they experienced (McKearn 1988). The common symptoms that are reported by both client groups include depression, isolation, rage, avoidance of feelings, survival guilt, anxiety reactions, sleep disturbances/nightmares and intrusive thoughts. Although overlap exists between symptoms, it remains unclear if both the ACOA and PTSD constructs constitute a single syndrome.

Role reversal and role conflict have been associated with the COAs' adaptation to their family environments (Booz-Allen and Hamilton Inc. 1974; Nardi 1981; Wilson and Orford 1978). The inconsistency of parental roles and the demands placed on the COA to anticipate and complement these roles, are believed to lead to confusion and conflict (Nardi 1981). In addition to general role reversal and role conflict, two clinicians (Black 1982; Wegscheider 1981) have identified specific roles that COAs identify with and perform into their adult lives (see Table 11.3). ACOAs have been described as overly rigid in their identification with their particular role, to the extent that they are unable to function outside of that role (Deutsch 1982). Black (1982) describes the progression of the various COA roles into adulthood and the particular problems that ensue. The patterned roles that begin in childhood are thought to persist into adulthood and result in depression, isolation, and loneliness. For example, adult "placaters" continue to give to others and to seek out takers, which results in their feeling apart from others and extremely lonely. "Adjusters" continue, into adulthood, avoiding positions in which they are expected to take control. They also suffer from having little sense of direction or power in their lives and often become isolated, lonely, and depressed. Wegscheider (1981) describes the "Hero" as the firstborn child who becomes locked into a triangle with the alcoholic parent at one corner and the enabling spouse at the other corner. This child is portrayed as taking on the impossible dream of making everything right within the family. The price that the adult "Hero" pays, according to Wegscheider (1981), is often intense anger, psychosomatic problems (stomach ulcers, migraines) and excessive perfectionism. The "Scapegoat," usually the second child according to Wegscheider, is left out of the family triangle and thus resorts to acting-out. Because the "Hero" has dominated the so called good and responsible characteristics, the "Scapegoat" chooses the bad, irresponsible traits (open rebellion, belligerence, promiscuity, etc.). Adult "Scapegoats" continue a pattern of antisocial behavior and often become chemically dependent (Wegscheider 1981). The "Lost Child," usually the third child according to Wegscheider, chooses to withdraw into his/her own world. "Lost Children" are depicted as blaming themselves for not fitting into the family. Their continuing seclusion prevents them from acquiring social skills, thereby perpetuating their loneliness. Adult "Lost Children" are described as obsessed with possessions and as binging on food and alcohol to compensate for their loneliness. Wegscheider (1981) portrays portrays the "Mascot," usually the youngest child, as obtaining attention and relief from anxiety by showing off and being funny. The adult "Mascot" is excessively fearful, manipulative, and unable to focus on tasks for any length of time.

COA roles are thought to be adaptive when first adopted in the alcoholic home environment, but ultimately prove to be maladaptive outside of this setting. As discussed in chapter 3, there is little evidence that these prototypic roles characterize COAs as a group, or that the putative characteristics of each role cluster together. Only one role, "Acting Out" (i.e., Problem Child or Scapegoat), has been shown to be more prevalent in COA populations (Rhodes 1984), and this observation is consistent with the data on conduct

Table 11.3 Purported Roles Adopted by Adult Children of Alcoholics

Black (1982)	
Problem Child	Gets into trouble with authorities
Responsible Child	Takes on the parental role and is in control
Family Pet	Uses humor to cope with the pain
Adjuster	Changes to fit whatever the demands of the situation are
Placater	Tries to please and comfort everyone
Wegscheider (1981)	
Hero	"Good child" who is the stable source of dependability
Scapegoat	Uses defiant and angry behavior to get attention
Lost Child	Has given up, is withdrawn and isolated
Mascot	Carefree, fun-loving, and uses clowning strategy

disorder reviewed in chapter 3. There is also scant evidence that the relationship between birth order and role type reported by some authors (Deutsch 1982; Wegscheider 1981) is valid.

In summary, the purported characteristics of ACOAs are quite numerous and varied. The work to date has been anecdotal and descriptive rather than empirical. The population of individuals who are described by the ACOA label may be more heterogeneous than implied by the popular literature. Clearly, not all COAs should be considered at risk for the development of psychopathology (Burk and Sher 1988; Heller et al. 1982; also see chapter 3). Furthermore, the negative characteristics that have been ascribed to COAs and ACOAs may be overstated, applicable to anyone growing up in a stressful environment, and possibly descriptive of a large portion of the general population. Although the popular literature has been beneficial in bringing the concerns of COAs and ACOAs to the attention of the public and professionals, the overall scientific and clinical utility of these generalizations remains open to further examination.

Social Developmental Theory

Developmental issues such as attachment and separation are also critical in influencing adult adjustment (Ainsworth, Blehar, Waters, and Wall 1978; Bowlby 1969) and may be important organizing principles when considering the key psychological processes characterizing the adjustment of COAs. Development involves progression through successive stages, and events may have significance depending on when they occur in the developmental sequence. In psychosocial theories of development, stages are defined in terms of critical psychosocial experiences. For example, types of interactions with parental figures, during early childhood and adolescence, may be important in the development of autonomy and independence. The manner in which each "psychosocial crisis" is managed prepares the way for ensuing challenges. In contrast to descriptive labels or diagnostic categories, the developmental approach provides a comprehensive model encompassing external and internal life stressors across the life span.

Developmental theories have been applied to both the etiology and manifestation of ACOA emotional and psychological problems (Ackerman 1983; Beletsis and Brown 1981; Brown 1988). The developmental concepts of attachment and separation may provide models for understanding the occurrence of dysfunctional behavior often attributed to ACOAs. For example, attachment theory emphasizes the affectional bond between child and caregiver as primary in the establishment of security (Bowlby 1980). Without this sense of security further developmental processes are delayed or distorted. Bowlby's theory assumes that, barring major discontinuities in life experience, quality of attachment is enduring throughout one's life. Three prototypic patterns of attachment have been identified by Ainsworth, Blehar, Waters, and Wall (1978): secure, insecure-avoidant, and insecure-ambivalent/resistant. Recently, Main and Solomon (1986) described a fourth pattern of attachment they termed insecure-disorganized/disoriented. In a recent study of infant attachment that used Ainsworth et al.'s (1978) "strange situation" procedure, maternal drinking patterns prior to pregnancy and during pregnancy were related to attachment patterns in one-year-olds, with "insecure patterns" associated with higher maternal alcohol use (O'Connor, Sigman, and Brill 1987). It is difficult to identify the specific factors underlying the observed association between heavy maternal alcohol consumption and insecure attachment. Presumably, the association could be attributable to fetal alcohol effects, inherited temperamental characteristics, or dysfunctional parent-care-giver interaction. Nevertheless, O'Connor et al.'s (1987) findings suggest the potential importance of studying early effects of parental alcoholism on offspring attachment behavior.

Attachment has been described as the earliest form of coping (Compas 1987), and early attachment experiences may greatly influence the development of competence in interpersonal situations. Brown (1988) maintains that ACOAs display cognitive schemas that distort and exacerbate anxiety but at the same time provide a sense of attachment and loyalty to the dysfunctional parent. This type of parental attachment could be described as "insecure" and could contribute to recurrent interpersonal problems. The extent of the "insecure attachment" (anxiety level, degree of perceived threat, conflict) between the COA and parental figures could serve to either mitigate or exacerbate later emotional and interpersonal problems. These types of anxiety-provoking experiences, if prolonged, could impede exploration (e.g., seeking out interactions with others) and other positive coping strategies.

The developmental model describes a progression through successive stages (Breger 1974). These stages or phases serve to mark critical periods or "crises," initially involving interactions with parents and significant others but later involving interactions with society and peers (Erikson 1963). Ackerman (1983) and Beletis and Brown (1981) have outlined the developmental crises that purportedly occur for the COA according to Erikson's (1963) psychosocial stages. The psychological and emotional problems that occur in adulthood are tied to the specific psychosocial crises left unresolved during development (see Table 11.4). According to this model, failure at the initial stage (i.e., trust vs. mistrust) may result in the COA's inability to tolerate intimacy, confusion over locus of control, and unsuccessful differentiation of self (Beletis and Brown 1981). The inability to develop a basic sense of trust in oneself and others prevents successful management of the next stage, autonomy vs. shame and doubt. Lack of differentiation and insecure attachments can result in a dependent stance in which the COA is desperately eager to please and do things correctly. Due to ongoing insecure attachments, COAs are described as having difficulty negotiating separation from their families. Early isolation from peers may prevent the development of interpersonal skills, resulting in few support systems outside the family. These developmental failures may serve to further delay physical and emotional separation from the alcoholic family.

The development of autonomy is important during the adolescent years (Powers, Hauser, and Kilner 1989), as well as in early childhood. Strong relationships have been found between parental acceptance, empathy, and support, and adolescent ego development. Parents with greater awareness of self and appreciation of individual differences are likely to explain more to, and problem-solve with, their adolescent children. These types of interactions are presumed to be helpful in the development of autonomy and may well be absent in some alcoholic families.

Levels of development can be examined in many ways based on different psychological stages or phases (e.g., cognitive, moral). In this section the focus has been on attachment and psychosocial stages. Although there are many developmental influences that may contribute to emotional and psychological problems for ACOAs, there has been little empirical work in this area. Models are needed that specify subsets of both positive and negative developmental influences on COAs. Many parental influences can be disruptive in childhood experience (marital transitions [Hetheringon, Stanley-Hagan, and Anderson 1989], parental unemployment [McLoyd 1989], depression and other psychiatric conditions [Rutter and Quinton 1984]) and many of these factors can coexist with alcoholism. Even if the COA's emotional problems were found to be associated with parental alcoholism, this does not necessarily mean that alcoholism constitutes the key variable. The developmental concept of attachment is both global and descriptive, rather than explanatory (Alpher 1984). In all likelihood attachment is made up of more specific and dynamic constructs that can be empirically examined.

Developmental models would appear to have utility for clinicians working from a number of therapeutic approaches, although they would appear to have

Table 11.4 Psychosocial Crises Occurring at Differing Developmental Stages

Stage	Psychosocial Crises
Trust vs. Mistrust	Emotional unavailability of parent Inconsistent nurturing
Autonomy vs. Shame/Doubt	Inconsistent, excessive, or lax discipline/excessive dependency or lack thereof
Industry vs. Inferiority	Lack of recognition for achievement at school and in other pursuits
Identity vs. Identity Diffusion	Over-identification with ACOA roles
Intimacy vs. Isolation	Inability to manage closeness/dependency
Generativity vs. Self-absorption	Inability to give and care for others
Integrity vs. Despair	Blaming others/negative outlook on life

Source: Partially adapted from Ackerman (1983).

greatest relevance to those working from psychodynamic, interpersonal, and cognitive perspectives. Although there can be no discounting the general importance of a developmental perspective, the extent to which the construct of attachment is seriously confounded with temperament is a matter of continuing debate (e.g., Alpher 1984). Also, the relationship between attachment and drinking behavior, a key outcome domain for COAs, has yet to be demonstrated (Kwakman, Zuiker, Schippers, and de Wuffel 1988).

Therapeutic Approaches

Despite the lack of a consensually defined therapeutic target, many therapeutic approaches exist for treating COAs and ACOAs. Group therapy appears to be the treatment of choice, with family and individual therapy also prevalent. Self-help groups for ACOAs have flourished within the last ten years and educational/preventive programs have recently been organized for COAs. Controversy exists as to whether treatment should be long-term or short-term and whether the focus should be strictly educational or involve character restructuring. Also, clinicians are now questioning the assumption that all ACOAs are in need of treatment (Crandell 1989; Vannicelli 1989). This section examines some of the current approaches, including group therapy, object relations theory, family system therapy, cognitive orientations, self-help groups, and educational/prevention programs. Despite the fact that treatment for ACOAs is flourishing, there is little evidence concerning the effectiveness of any of these treatments, especially with respect to clearly defined outcomes.

Group Therapy Approaches

The interactional group therapy model has been described by Brown and Beletsis (1986) and Vannicelli (1989). This model was adapted from interactional group therapy for alcoholics (Brown and Yalom 1977). The goals of the therapy group include reducing the sense of isolation, instilling hope, learning from watching others, altering distorted self-concepts, creating a reparative family experience, and gaining understanding of the effects of parental alcoholism (Vannicelli 1989). As in other dynamic-oriented groups, the issue of family transference develops and is described as extremely powerful for ACOAs. Unresolved issues from the ACOA's family of origin are encouraged, and the validity of the ACOA's beliefs and perceptions about these core issues are challenged by group members (Brown and Beletsis 1986). Vannicelli (1989) describes a powerful countertransference reaction that often develops for ACOA group leaders. She indicates that this may arise because all therapists are "adult children" working on some dysfunctional aspect of their family of origin. The group serves to recreate powerful family dynamics for all participants. Initially the working alliance within the group is hindered by feelings of anger and hostile transferences toward group leaders (Brown 1988). Anger and hostility are presumed to protect the ACOA against intense feelings of dependence. The ability to form a working alliance early in the therapeutic process has been described as a necessary component for effective psychotherapy (Bordin 1975; Gelso and Carter 1985). This process (developing a working alliance) requires a capacity to form attachments and an ability to trust others. As described earlier, these may be difficult areas for some ACOAs and may contribute to therapeutic difficulties.

Object Relations Theory

A diagnosis of personality disorder (e.g., Borderline Personality) is often applied to ACOAs. Object relations theory has been utilized to explain the etiology of this disorder, and the appropriate treatment (Hibbard 1987, 1989; Richards 1980). Hibbard (1987) argues that posttraumatic stress disorder has been incorrectly applied to ACOAs in that this diagnosis fails to explain the underlying developmental pathology. Splitting and polarization are described as common developmental anomalies that occur with COAs (Hibbard 1987; Richards 1980). Hibbard (1987, p. 783) states that "parental alcoholism breeds an atmosphere which encourages the polarization of the instincts, rather than the blending and neutralization of these instincts." The child responds to significant others as part objects which are either "all good" or "all bad," rather than comprised of both qualities. This ambivalence toward parental figures is manifested in a basic sense of mistrust and results in ongoing pathological interactions. Richards (1980) indicates that progress in therapy requires: (a) a consistent, caring therapist who provides a "corrective emotional experience," (b) the development of repression (splitting at a higher level of ego development), and (c) an ongoing experience in which the client cannot destroy the new "object." Similar to the interactional group therapy approach, object relations therapy is usually a long-term undertaking. Crandell (1989) on the other hand, states that brief treatment is appropriate for ACOAs, even with characterologic disorders, as long as there is a specific identified conflict and good ego strength.

Family Systems Therapy

Systems theory is important for work with ACOAs due to several theoretical assumptions: (a) ACOA roles (Black 1982; Wegscheider 1981) are adopted within a family context in order to maintain equilibrium, (b) family members often become "enablers" or codependents (FitzGerald 1988), and (c) denial and other defenses are shared by all family members as unspoken rules (Wegscheider 1981). Some important aspects of systems include boundaries, rules, and communication (Constantine 1986), which are assumed to be distorted in the dysfunctional alcoholic family. At least three family therapy orientations have been used with alcoholic families: multiple couple group therapy, conjoint family therapy, and conjoint hospitalization (Steinglass et al. 1987).

Joan K. Jackson (1954) was instrumental in developing a family approach to working with the alcoholic family system. In her work she describes seven predictable stages that the family may go through in adjusting to alcoholism: (1) denying the problem, (2) trying to eliminate the problem, (3) family disorganization, (4) attempts to reorganize, (5) attempts to escape the problem, (6) actual escape of the problem, and (7) reorganization after the problem drinker seeks treatment. Family disorganization can last for indefinite periods of time and there is no assurance that a family will move through all stages.

Steinglass et al. (1987) have defined the alcoholic family as any family in which alcoholism has become a central organizing principle around which family life is structured. They suggest assessing the family to determine which stage of development they are in (i.e., early, middle or late) and basing the course of treatment accordingly. Krestan and Bepko (1988) have emphasized the need to consider "family developmental tasks" in the family life-cycle. The amount of disruption and stress that parental alcoholism creates for the COA is directly related to the amount of disruption of the normal family life-cycle. Krestan and Bepko (1988, p. 483) state "The life cycle model is clinically relevant to an understanding of alcohol problems because the family's developmental stage and the individual's developmental stage intersect to become a context in which an alcohol problem may become both a cause and effect of dysfunction." Early-onset problem drinking (i.e. occurring early in the family life-cycle) is considered more disruptive than late-onset problem drinking (occurring late in the family life-cycle). From this perspective, assessing the developmental level of the family may be as critical to treatment as is the assessment of the individual's developmental level. Specific family therapy interventions could be tailored for unique family life-cycle stages.

Although a great deal has been written about working with the alcoholic in a family context, little information exists for family therapy that focuses on COAs and ACOAs. Wegscheider (1981) describes the alcoholic family system as a closed system that does not admit communication from the outside and thus seals itself off from learning and change. Kantor and Lehr (1975) have described a "closed" family system in which there are strong external boundaries that maintain privacy and "family secrets." Rules, in this type of family system, are authoritarian and closed to input from other family members or outside influences. Roles and boundaries are fixed and strong, with strict adherence to established norms. On the other hand, the "random family" is characterized by chaos and fluctuation in rules and decision making. Alcoholic families may fluctuate between "closed" and "random," depending on the degree of activity or parental alcoholism.

Alcoholic families are often described as "dysfunctional families." The dysfunctional family has been characterized as extremely rigid, intensely hostile, and as having immense difficulty coping with change and separation (Beavers 1982). Applying the term "dysfunctional" to all alcoholic families is clearly an overgeneralization. Alcoholic families vary in their degree of dysfunction as do other types of families (Steinglass et al. 1987).

The disruption of the family ritual process has been identified as a contributing factor to ACOAs' later emotional and psychological problems (Bennett et al. 1987; Wolin et al. 1980). When family rituals such as holidays, birthdays, and other special occasions are disrupted by the alcoholic's drinking, increased family confrontation occurs, and neglect of ritual observances may increase the likelihood of family members developing psychological problems in adulthood (Bennett et al. 1987). Imber-Black (1989) has identified five ritual themes that are key factors in family rituals: (1) membership, (2) healing, (3) identity definition, (4) belief expression, and (5) negotiation. She incorporates the assignment of rituals into her family therapy approach but states that the family determines the form and meaning of any therapeutic ritual. Assigning family rituals may be especially important for alcoholic families undergoing therapy. Rituals may help the family to begin to bond together as a unit and to develop a unified therapeutic alliance.

Alcoholic families are heterogeneous, just as are individual COAs and ACOAs. From the clinical perspective, treatment approaches need to be adapted to the unique developmental stage of both the COA and the family unit. Family therapy issues (communication, boundaries, triangles, coalitions) are assumed to address the key underlying system-related problems. As with other therapy orientations, solid family-therapy outcome studies are needed to confirm or disconfirm divergent methods.

Cognitive Approaches

Although no formal cognitive therapy approach has been identified for working with ACOAs, cognitive-behavioral methods are used. Kern (1985) has outlined a cognitive information approach to treatment for ACOAs that focuses on providing accurate, reality-based data to help restructure beliefs. The focus is on gaining an understanding of the "disease" of alcoholism and the associated pathological behaviors. This treatment relies on relabeling of feelings, validating experiences, and providing hope for change. ACOAs often develop illogical/irrational beliefs, and the goal of cognitive approaches is to challenge and restructure these assumptions, thereby eradicating emotional problems.

The following general principles have been recommended for treatment of COAs (Kern 1985): (1) the COA should be treated as a primary client as well as a member of an alcoholic family system; (2) group therapy is the treatment of choice for COAs; (3) therapists must avoid focusing on one COA in the family (e.g., the "scapegoat") to the exclusion of others; (4) any COA who is a minor must have parental consent and participation; (5) all family members should be involved in the intake process in order for all to receive identical information, preventing family distortion; (6) clinical supervision is extremely important to avoid becoming entrapped in the "family dance"; (7) the length of treatment can vary from eight to ten weeks for educational approaches and can take up to three years for personality change; (8) COA treatment should be carried out in agencies specializing in alcohol and drug treatment; (9) COAs are often involuntary clients; (10) structuring "family rituals" into the treatment is important; and (11) clinicians should incorporate developmental information into the therapeutic process. These principles appear applicable to many of the currently employed treatment modalities.

Self-help Groups

Alcoholic-oriented self-help groups, such as Alcoholics Anonymous (AA), have a long, successful history. Self-help groups for COAs and ACOAs began more recently and are growing rapidly. Al-Anon family groups began in 1951 and now number some 25,000, including 3,000 Alateen groups (Pittman 1985). The group focus is on family members who have been affected by the negative aspects of alcoholism. These groups are similar to AA in that "group shared experience" is the primary therapeutic process. Members are encouraged to examine themselves and not dwell on the identified alcoholic. The goal is not to reform the alcoholic but to reform one's self through identifying a higher power and adopting the twelve steps and traditions of AA. Initially these groups were utilized primarily by spouses of alcoholics, but more recently ACOAs have been participating or forming groups of their own. Cutter and Cutter (1987) reported that the main problem areas discussed at "adult childrens" Al-Anon group sessions were: (a) depression and fear, (b) alcoholism-related problems, (c) feeling responsible for others, (d) difficulty expressing feelings and being assertive, (e) difficulty with intimacy and closeness, and (f) problems working the program. These authors report that the greatest improvement was noted in lowered depression and greater acceptance of one's self. The focus of most Al-Anon family groups is on pragmatic action rather than excessive introspection (Ablon 1974). Members are encouraged to take a "moral inventory," like that taken in AA groups. This inventory helps members to face the nature and implication of their actions on others. In a preliminary study of adolescent COAs, those who attended Alateen groups reported higher self-esteem and better school grades than those COAs who did not attend meetings (Hughes 1977).

Education and Prevention

There has been little research done on prevention for COAs. Many difficulties arise in establishing primary prevention programs for COAs, including the ethical implications of screening (Burk and Sher 1988; Heller et al. 1982), determining the best mode of intervention, and obtaining parental consent. The dangers of adversely labeling a child (see section below on labeling) may possibly outweigh any benefits of the intervention program. Although there is agreement that early intervention is needed to interrupt the development of emotional problems, few programs exist. The goals of most existing prevention programs are not tied into well-conceptualized theoretical models. School systems are the major institutions involved in alcohol abuse prevention and could provide the best opportunity for intervention with COAs. In this section we will briefly examine the educational and prevention programs that have been suggested and/or implemented.

Robinson (1989) has called for the early identification of COAs at the preschool level. The rationale being that the earlier the intervention, the greater the chance of interrupting the cycle before dysfunctional patterns become well established. He recommends assessing and implementing the programs in the school system, where ongoing contact is maintained. Since preschool children are unable to verbalize or give questionnaire responses, the following four areas are assessed: (1) daily routines such as sleeping, toilet habits, and developmental delays, (2) play, (3) emotional adjustment, and (4) parental relationships. Early assessment is unquestionably difficult, except in more severe cases.

The CASPAR (Cambridge-Somerville Program for Alcoholism Rehabilitation) program developed a standard curriculum that is used nationally by school systems (CASPAR 1978). CASPAR provides activities for all grade levels. Davis, Johnston, DiCicco, and Orenstein (1985) have described an elementary school program for sixth graders that is led by a guidance counselor and consists of puppet shows, storybooks, arts and crafts, and other activities adapted from CASPAR. Many of the children are recruited from special education services and from referrals by teachers and parents. Children are taught that they are not alone and that their parent's drinking is not their fault. They are also taught that it is important to take care of their own needs and that they deserve to have fun, as their friends do. Edwards and Zander (1985) recommend the following strategies for school counselors working with COAs: (a) establish a trusting relationship by demonstrating consistent care and interest, (b) help the child overcome his/her denial, (c) explain and discuss alcoholism as a disease, (d) help the child to identify and express diverse feelings, (e) help the child develop positive relationships, (f) incorporate success into all exercises and activities, (g) recognize the child's worth by providing praise, (h) provide the child with a sense of control for facing family situations, and (i) provide a realistic sense of hope.

The Student Assistance Program is a model developed to provide individual and group counseling to COA high school students, and appears to have been adopted in a number of localities. This program was developed by the Westchester County, New York, Department of Community Mental Health as a response to student alcohol problems and behavioral consequences of parental alcoholism and introduced into the Westchester County public schools in 1979 (Morehouse 1981). Goals of the program include promoting an understanding of alcoholism, improving coping skills, and reducing feelings of isolation and stigma.

Recently, evaluations of school-based prevention programs for COAs have begun to appear in the research literature (Emshoff and Moeti 1987; Roosa, Gensheimer, Short, Ayers, and Shell 1989). These programs are similar to those described above in providing information about alcoholism, attempting to foster the development of coping skills, and using self-esteem enhancement strategies. However, they are noteworthy for including a systematic evaluation component and appear to demonstrate some success in effecting desired behavior changes. At present, available data are insufficient for drawing strong conclusions concerning the effectiveness of school-based prevention programs for COAs. When well-designed, large-scale studies are completed and reported (e.g., Roosa, Gensheimer, Ayers, and Short 1990), we will begin to have a clearer idea of our current technology and of needed new directions.

Bibliotherapy is often recommended as an intervention approach for COAs and ACOAs (Manning and Manning 1984; Robinson 1989). This is a nonthreatening intervention that introduces the child to stories about parental alcoholism and provides appropriate models and ways of coping. Communication between adults and children can be stimulated by books, allowing for more open discussion about difficult topics. When using bibliotherapy one must be aware of the child's reading level and any reading problems they may have (Pardeck and Pardeck 1987). Robinson (1989) provides a comprehensive list of books and other resource materials for both adults and children.

Higher education has also implemented special group programs to address COA/ACOA concerns. These secondary prevention groups are aimed at high-risk college students who have not experienced the complete emotional and psychological impact of parental alcoholism (Downing and Walker 1987). The major goals of these group sessions are to (a) build universality and decrease denial, (b) gain information about alcoholism and codependency, and (c) recognize feelings. Initially the sessions are fairly structured but subsequent sessions are intended to deal with specific needs of participants. Donovan (1981) describes a structured support group developed at Brown University in which reading material, films, and open discussions were utilized to stimulate expression of feelings and identification with being an ACOA. The preceding review of treatment approaches is purely descriptive, and it is difficult to evaluate the state-of-the-art of intervention with COAs for a number of reasons. First, although it is known that COAs are at risk for a number of negative outcomes, the various pathways to each of these outcomes are still not well understood and it is not clear what variables are most important to target. Even if we could identify critical targets for intervention, the effectiveness of specific interventions for altering defined problem areas remains unknown.

A critical question for therapy research with COAs is whether COA-specific treatment is necessary. That is, if chief complaints center on "standard" clinical problems (low self-esteem, anxiety, depression, poor relationships, etc.), can treatment approaches developed for these specific problems be equally effective for COAs? If they are, treatment for COAs could then be targeted for specific symptoms, not necessarily global issues surrounding the alcoholic family-of-origin. Given the dramatic increase in problem-specific treatment approaches, effective treatment might best be provided by referral of COAs to therapists experienced in the specific disorder manifested by that client (affective disorders, anxiety disorders, substance abuse). Clearly, this is an empirical and clinical issue that needs further analysis. The possibility exists that some of the current strategies for COA treatment may provide elements for effective interventions that are lacking in standard clinical approaches. Perhaps, participation in a COA group holds unique therapeutic benefits for individuals suffering the effects of growing up in an alcoholic family. However, until such work is undertaken, the therapeutic benefits of participating in a COA treatment program are supported solely by clinical, anecdotal, and testimonial reports.

Social-Psychological Aspects of the COA Movement

The Widespread Acceptance of the COA Lore

As described above, there is little in the way of empirical evidence supporting the generalizations made about COAs by the media or by clinicians who write on this topic. Regardless, it is clear that many COAs appear to identify strongly with the generalizations made about them, suggesting that there is at least a kernel of truth surrounding the clinical lore. However, acceptance of personality descriptions, in and of itself, does not provide strong evidence for the validity of these descriptions. In order for personality descriptions to provide useful information, they must not only describe the individual or group, they must be able to differentiate the individual or group from appropriate comparison populations (Meehl 1956). Numerous studies conducted over the past two decades suggest there are a large number of personality descriptors that a majority of individuals find to be highly descriptive of themselves, and often uniquely so. This general phenomenon has been referred to in the psychological literature as the "Barnum effect," so-named because of P. T. Barnum's method of insuring the success of his circus—have a little something in it for everybody. Personality descriptions that tend to produce "Barnum effects" (i.e., are viewed as being accurate and uniquely descriptive) tend to be vague, doubleheaded, favorable, or have high-base rates in the general population (Dickson and Kelly 1985). Could the stereotypes of COAs promoted in the clinical and popular literature represent "Barnum effects"? Very possibly so. For example, some of the descriptions offered by Woititz (1983; see Table 11.2) appear vague (e.g., "guess at what normal is"), doubleheaded (e.g., "are super responsible or super irresponsible"), and probably have high-base rates in the general population (e.g., "have difficulty with intimate relationships"). In a recent article in the *New York Times Book Review* (February 11, 1990), Wendy Kaminer captures the essence of the high base-rate issue quite well when she states "Melody Beattie . . . defines codependency as being affected by someone else's behavior and obsessed with controlling it. *Who isn't?*" (italics added) (p. 26).

Logue and Sher (1990) recently conducted a study where a large sample of college-student COAs and nonCOAs completed a computer-administered battery of personality tests and were then provided a "computer-generated" paragraph describing their basic personality traits. Half of the subjects were provided a paragraph consisting of popular COA descriptions, the other half were provided a paragraph consisting of well-validated "Barnum" statements. (The COA and "Barnum" statements were first equated for social desirability.) All subjects were then asked to rate how accurately the paragraph described them personally. The results indicated that both COAs and nonCOAs found the "COA" paragraphs to be highly descriptive of them.

Also, the "Barnum" paragraphs were rated similarly to the "COA" paragraphs for both groups. Thus, this study demonstrated that the COA descriptors were highly descriptive of college students in general, and appeared to have properties similar to the well-validated "Barnum" descriptors. The implication of this study is that, *to some extent,* the widespread acceptance of the stereotypes from the clinical COA literature may be due to the Barnum effect.

It could be argued that observations of COAs by trained clinicians are not subject to the same self-rating biases that affect individuals when assessing their own personality. However, it is well known that all clinicians are subject to perceiving "illusory correlations" when none actually exist, especially when such correlations conform to their preconceived notions (Chapman and Chapman 1969). Confirmatory observations are very salient and remembered, disconfirmatory observations are less noticed and more quickly forgotten. For example, it is quite possible that clinicians specializing in COA issues notice a correlation between a client's family history and specific psychological traits, not because of a valid correlation, but because of their own belief systems and cognitive biases producing an "illusory correlation" effect. Although such an explanation is highly speculative, this is clearly an area in need of further investigation.

By raising the question of psychological processes that might lead clinicians and individuals to accept the stereotypes promoted in the COA literature, we do not mean cavalierly to discount a number of potentially important observations and insights. However, given the lack of empirically derived findings, reasons for the seemingly noncritical acceptance of many unsubstantiated generalizations must be considered.

Possible Labeling Effects on COAs

With the growth of the COA movement, many individuals have been assigned the label "COA" or "ACOA". Sometimes this labeling was designated by the individuals themselves, sometimes by others (teachers or therapists). Unfortunately, the popular generalizations that COAs are likely to have significant emotional problems and/or be in need of psychotherapy may be pernicious, providing the context for a negative labeling effect. Although social scientists have long recognized many possible negative affects of labeling (Goffman 1963), the question of labeling has received relatively little attention in the COA literature.

Burk and Sher (1988) recently reviewed the relevance of labeling theory and research for COAs, and noted that labeling can perpetuate inappropriate behavior in deviant individuals and initiate it in nondeviant individuals. This could come about by associating with deviant peer groups and by setting up self-fulfilling prophecies. Although focusing on the negative aspects of labeling, Burk and Sher (1988) noted the possibility that labeling might serve an important function by helping to direct individuals to appropriate interventions (self-help groups, bibliotherapy, professional treatment services), and by providing an external attribution for psychological distress. That is, the belief that the "source" of the difficulty stems from growing up in an alcoholic home might help the COA to organize a number of seemingly disparate complaints into one set of interrelated problems. This type of attribution would serve to minimize nonproductive self-blame. However, Burk and Sher (1988) also noted that "there is the potential that the attributional function of the COA label can be overgeneralized . . . and lead to an inappropriate denial of responsibility in important life areas" (p. 295).

Although we are not aware of studies looking at the consequences of labeling for COAs, two recent studies indicate that the "COA" label carries with it a number of negative stereotypes for both peers and mental health professionals. In the first study (Burk and Sher 1990; Study 1), high school students were asked to rate themselves as "mentally ill" teenagers, "typical" teenagers, and "teenagers with an alcoholic parent" on a series of bipolar adjective pairs. COAs were consistently rated as being significantly more deviant than typical teenagers, and were rated similar to mentally ill teenagers on several dimensions. Although the study did not determine if these stereotypes were based primarily on personal acquaintance or on more public sources of influence (e.g., the media), clear evidence for a strong stigma surrounding the label was obtained. Given, the negative social implications of being perceived as "different" during adolescence (Duck 1975), the COA label is regarded as having potentially serious negative effects on normal socialization.

A second study (Burk & Sher 1990; Study 2) used an experimental design to investigate the effects of the COA label on mental health workers (professionals and paraprofessionals). Subjects watched videotapes of an adolescent who was described as having either an alcoholic father or parents with no known problems and as possessing either a high degree of social success (school leader) or social problems (behavior problems). The behaviors of the two adolescents portrayed on the tape were the same across all four cells; only the description of the parents' alcoholism and the child's social functioning were manipulated. The major finding was that, independent of social functioning, the mental health workers rated the COA as more pathological than the nonCOA.

Taken together, these two studies indicate strong negative stereotypes associated with the COA label, both from the peer group and from mental health personnel, who are often responsible for treating COAs. These findings suggest that concerns about labeling COAs are well grounded, although the actual effects of such labeling have not been directly assessed. Nevertheless, these findings in conjunction with the literature on the negative psychosocial effects of labels argue for extreme caution when assessing or promoting services for COAs, especially those that are not experiencing current psychological difficulties. Especially for children and youth, innovative strategies that indirectly screen and recruit COAs (cf. Gensheimer, Roosa, and Ayers, in press) might circumvent some of the problems with labeling and stigmatization while still reaching the targeted population.

Summary

Intense interest in the problems of COAs exists in the public at-large and the treatment community. Although a number of theories concerning the nature and treatment of COA-related difficulties exist, these theories tend to rest on anecdotes, case-reports, and have a weak empirical base. While the number of treatment approaches for COAs and ACOAs have proliferated in recent years, virtually nothing is known about their efficacy. The general question of the value of COA-oriented treatment relative to other alternative treatment approaches is currently an open question. Additionally, interventions that have focused on prevention, not just on treatment for symptomatic individuals, have been a recent trend in providing services for COAs and raise a number of ethical questions, especially those surrounding potentially negative labeling effects in the context of interventions with unproven efficacy.

Although the tone of this chapter is somewhat skeptical, its intent is not to discount the clinical theories and associated intervention strategies that have emerged in recent years. There can be little doubt that countless individuals have been helped by their involvement with the COA movement and by their dedicated counselors, teachers, and therapists. However, whether the current modalities represent the most effective intervention strategies needs to be addressed. Furthermore, all interventions have the potential to result in negative treatment effects, and controlled outcome research is clearly needed to evaluate possible harmful effects of the interventions to which many COAs are currently being exposed (Burk and Sher 1988). As stated recently by Burk and Sher (1988, p. 298), "If services for COAs are to be maximally beneficial and minimally harmful, these services will have to take into account the possibilities that not all COAs need such services, that the services might prove harmful for some, and that the mere act of labeling someone a COA might have unintended negative personal and social consequences."

The relative lack of congruence between the clinical literature and the research literature is disturbing. Although there is little doubt that empirical research targeted at evaluating many of the clinical hypotheses is warranted, intervention strategies derived from the basic research are also needed. Some potential directions for such innovation are described in chapter 12.

12 Concluding Comments

Although we are still far from having a complete understanding of how genetic and environmental factors contribute to the etiology of alcoholism and a range of negative outcomes among COAs, definite progress has been made on a number of fronts. Estimates of the genetic contribution to risk are continually being refined. A host of *potential* biological and psychological markers of risk have been identified (neurophysiological and biochemical deficits, abnormal responses to ethanol, personality variables, and neuropsychological characteristics). We have an increasingly sophisticated understanding of the effects of parental alcoholism on family functioning and how this influences offspring psychological functioning.

Despite our increasing knowledge, it is still too early to draw firm conclusions concerning the etiology of alcoholism and psychological disorders among COAs, and the optimal strategies for preventing and treating these problems. First, relatively few findings have proven replicable across laboratories. Numerous reported findings are of uncertain reliability, and some of these are likely to be spurious. In large part, these inconsistent findings are probably attributable to methodological problems (especially sampling, ascertainment of family history, failure to consider the heterogeneity of alcoholism and comorbidity, and low statistical power). However, even among the more robust findings (those concerning attenuated P300, behavioral undercontrol, enhanced stress-response-dampening effects of alcohol, increased rates of psychopathology in childhood and adulthood), there remains considerable ambiguity concerning the extent to which these more consistent findings are specific to a family history of alcoholism.

Second, the scope of most research programs is usually limited to a relatively narrow set of variables, precluding our ability to statistically integrate findings across biological, psychological, and social domains. Undoubtedly, the lack of integrative theories that attempt to systematically organize and relate data at varying levels of biopsychosocial organization has hindered research efforts attempting to explain how diverse genetic and environmental influences are causally related to health-related outcomes among COAs. Without such an understanding, our attempts to predict who will suffer the adverse effects of parental alcoholism (and under what conditions) will be limited. Our ability to design effective interventions to prevent or treat these difficulties will also be hindered by theoretical views that fail to take the multivariate nature of parental alcohol effects into account.

Third, there is relatively little detailed prospective data which would permit analysis of developmental progressions and moderating influences operating at different developmental stages. Although a number of prospective studies of COAs have been reported (Drake and Vaillant 1988; McCord 1981; Miller and Jang 1977; Rydelius 1981; Werner 1986) and others are in progress (Schulsinger et al. 1986; Zucker, Baxter, Noll, Theado and Weil 1982), there is a relative paucity of detailed longitudinal data permitting quantitative analysis of the ontogenetic development of problems of COAs and factors that moderate the influences of presumed mediators at different developmental stages.

Not only are developmental data lacking, but developmental perspectives are lacking (although see Zucker 1987). Research on risk factors at various ages often assumes that deficits noted will have a direct linear effect on later outcome and developmental progressions are rarely considered. As research on COAs progresses, we can hope that the field will develop a greater appreciation of developmental processes and the multivariate nature of risk and moderating influences.

Clearly, broad-based prospective studies assessing the development of normal and abnormal behavior among COAs are ultimately needed. Furthermore, to the extent that these prospective studies can incorporate behavior-genetic strategies (e.g., twin and adoption studies, cf. Heath 1990), researchers can begin to partition genetic and environmental sources of variance on outcome, and gain a clearer understanding of the etiology of substance abuse and psychopathology.

To a large extent, the limitations of most existing COA research are beginning to be addressed by contemporary investigators. Continual improvement in the methodological soundness of COA-relevant research is clearly noticeable. Theoretical models addressing the etiological heterogeneity of alcoholism and encompassing a broad array of potentially relevant variables are being developed and refined (see chapter 9). Cross-sectional, prospective, and behavior-genetic investigations are moving away from merely predicting outcome, to modeling the effects of presumed mediators and moderators of risk and are increasingly theory-driven.

The need for careful assessment, consideration of heterogeneity, a developmental perspective, a multivariate framework, attention to issues of mediation and moderation, and multiple theoretical frameworks has been discussed throughout this book, and similar points have been cogently made in recent chapters on COAs (Windle and Searles 1990) and developmental psychopathology more generally (Garmezy 1990). To the extent that these general notions guide future work, the next era of research on COAs holds promise for greatly enhancing our understanding of the short- and long-term effects of parental alcoholism.

Underresearched Areas

Although basic research on etiology appears to be moving along at a rapid rate, investigators have tended to ignore a number of issues which clearly warrant greater attention. A few of these are briefly noted below.

The Relation between Race/Ethnicity and the Effects of Parental Alcoholism

Despite the multiracial and multicultural nature of our society, most of the published research fails to address the effects of parental alcoholism on individuals of different racial and ethnic backgrounds. To what extent do the findings concerning biological or psychosocial functioning generalize across racial and ethnic populations? At present this is unknown. One recent study (Russell, Cooper, and Frone 1990) demonstrated an important three-way interaction among family history, race, and gender. These authors found that, among whites, family history was a more significant risk factor for females than for males. For blacks, family history was a more significant risk factor for males than for females. As noted by Russell et al. (1990), these findings "illustrate the potential hazards involved in generalizing data on prevalence rates of alcoholism among COAs across subgroups differing with respect to race . . . and sex" (p. 226). The potential effect of parental alcoholism probably varies as a function of other important sociodemographic variables as well (e.g., one-parent and two-parent households), and a complete understanding of the intergenerational transmission will ultimately require a broader multiracial and multicultural perspective.

The Validity and Effects of the ACOA and Codependency Movements

As noted in chapter 11, despite the vagueness of the terms "ACOA" (as a clinical entity) and "codependent" and the absence of empirical validation of these and related concepts, the huge commercial success of self-help books and the proliferation of treatment programs (both self-help and professionally led) attest to the popularity and acceptance of these concepts in the general population. Unfortunately, there is relatively little opportunity for COAs to learn that these popular generalizations do not rest on sound empirical foundations, and that the routes to "recovery" advocated by many authorities are unproven treatments leading to uncertain outcomes. The point here is not that the common lay clinical perspectives on the ACOA or codependent is harmful or counterproductive. Indeed, as noted earlier, it is likely that the lives of many people have changed for the better as a result of their involvement in the ACOA movement and the dedicated work of their therapists. However, if this population is to be optimally served, the tenets of various clinical approaches need to be empirically tested and the effectiveness and potential negative side-effects of labeling and intervention need to be evaluated.

Development of Empirically Grounded Intervention

A number of potential mediators and moderators of the parental alcoholism/ offspring alcoholism relation have been identifed, although far from definitively (behavioral undercontrol, emotionality, alcohol expectancies, coping ability, parenting, ethanol sensitivity, school failure, neurophysiological dysfunction, attention deficits). Behavioral and psychological interventions have been developed for some of these problems (cognitive approaches to altering expectancies, parent training to reduce conduct problems and school problems, interventions that focus on problem-solving or other coping abilities), but most existing interventions (both preventive and treatment) are not based on established techniques for remediating these difficulties. This dissociation between established research findings and intervention may be due to the fact that most of the clinical practitioners conducting prevention and treatment with COAs are not well versed in either developmental psychopathology or cognitive/behavior interventions. In the next several years, outcome studies assessing the effectiveness of interventions targeted at the presumed mediators and moderators discussed in chapters 9 and 10 will, one hopes, be undertaken. Such studies will not only lay the foundation for a rational approach to intervention but could also serve to refine etiological models by experimentally manipulating presumed risk and protective factors and observing the effects on outcome.

A Final Note

The population of COAs has come under increased study in recent years by researchers from fields as diverse as molecular genetics, behavioral pharmacology, psychophysiology, developmental and personality psychology, child and adult psychopathology, family process, and epidemiology. As illustrated throughout this book, it appears that an adequate scientific explanation of the transmission of risk from alcoholics to their children will require an appreciation of diverse biological, psychological, and sociological factors, and no single vantage point holds a monopoly on "the truth." The challenge for future research is not only to clarify basic findings but, more important, to integrate these findings into coherent developmental, biopsychosocial models. In a nontrivial sense, understanding the mediational and moderational processes that determine the wide range of outcomes among COAs is akin to understanding the determinants of human psychological development more generally. This is no small undertaking.

References

Abel, E. L. (1981). Behavioral teratology of alcohol. *Psychological Bulletin, 90,* 564–581.

Abel, E. L. (1989). Paternal and maternal alcohol consumption: Effects on offspring in two strains of rats. *Alcoholism: Clinical and Experimental Research, 13,* 533–541.

Ablon, J. (1974). Al-Anon family groups: Impetus for learning and change through the presentation of alternatives. *American Journal of Psychotherapy, 28, 1,* 30–45.

Ackerman, R. J. (1983). *Children of alcoholics: A guidebook for educators, therapists, and parents.* Holmes Beach, Fla.: Learning Publications.

Ainsworth, M. D. S., Blehar, M. C., Waters, E., & Wall, S. (1978). *Patterns of attachment: A psychological study of the strange situation.* Hillsdale, N.J.: Lawrence Erlbaum Associates.

Aldenderfer, M. S., & Blashfield, R. K. (1984). *Cluster Analysis.* Beverly Hills, Calif.: Sage Publications.

Alexopoulos, G. S., Lieberman, K. W., & Frances, R. J. (1983). Platelet MAO activity in alcoholic patients and their first-degree relatives. *American Journal of Psychiatry, 140,* 1501–1503.

Alpher, V. S. (1984). Attachment: A reconsideration of its heterogeneity and construct validity. *Psychological Reports, 54,* 531–535.

Alterman, A. I., Bridges, K. R., & Tarter, R. E. (1986a). Drinking behavior of high-risk college men: Contradictory preliminary findings. *Alcoholism: Clinical and Experimental Research, 10,* 1–6.

Alterman, A. I., Bridges, K. R., & Tarter, R. E. (1986b). The influences of both drinking and familial risk statuses on cognitive functioning of social drinkers. *Alcoholism: Clinical and Experimental Research, 10,* 448–451.

Alterman, A. I., Searles, J. S., & Hall, J. G. (1989). Failure to find differences in drinking behavior as a function of familial risk for alcoholism: A replication. *Journal of Abnormal Psychology, 98,* 50–53.

American Psychiatric Association. (1980). *Diagnostic and statistical manual of mental disorders (third edition): DSM-III.* Washington, D.C.: American Psychiatric Association.

American Psychiatric Association. (1987). *Diagnostic and statistical manual of mental disorders (third edition—revised): DSM-III-R.* Washington, D.C.: American Psychiatric Association.

Andreasen, N. C., Endicott, J., Spitzer, R. L., & Winokur, G. (1977). The family history method using diagnostic criteria. *Archives of General Psychiatry, 34,* 1229–1235.

Andreasen, N. C., Rice, J., Endicott, J., Reich, T., Coryell, W. (1986). The family history approach to diagnosis: How useful is it? *Archives of General Psychiatry, 43,* 421–429.

Apfel, R. J., & Sifneos, P. E. (1979). Alexithymia: Concept and measurement. *Psychotherapy and Psychosomatics, 32,* 180–190.

Aronson, H., & Gilbert, A. (1963). Preadolescent sons of male alcoholics. *Archives of General Psychiatry, 20,* 47–53.

Babor, T. F., Berglas, S., Mendelson, J. H., Ellingboe, J., & Miller, K. (1983). Alcohol, affect, and disinhibition of verbal behavior. *Psychopharmacology, 80,* 53–60.

Ballenger, J. F., Goodwin, F. K., Major, L., & Brown, G. (1979). Alcohol and central serotonin metabolism in man. *Archives of General Psychiatry, 36,* 224–227.

Baribeau, J. M. C., Braun, C. M. J., & Dube, R. (1986). Effects of alcohol intoxication on visuospatial and verbal-contextual tests of emotion discrimination in familial risk for alcoholism. *Alcoholism: Clinical and Experimental Research, 10,* 496–499.

Barnes, G. E. (1983). Clinical and personality characteristics. In B. Kissin & H. Begleiter, eds., *The pathogenesis of alcoholism: Psychosocial factors* (Vol. 6, pp. 113–196). New York: Plenum Press.

Baron, R. M., and Kenny, D. A. (1986). The moderator-mediator variable distinction in social psychological research: Conceptual, strategic, and statistical considerations. *Journal of Personality and Social Psychology, 51,* 1173–1182.

Beattie, M. (1987). *Codependent no more.* San Francisco: Harper & Row.

Beattie, M. (1989). *Beyond Codependency.* San Francisco: Harper & Row.

Beavers, W. R. (1982). Healthy, midrange and severely dysfunctional families. In Walsh, F., ed., *Normal Family Processes.* New York: Guilford.

Begleiter, H., Porjesz, B., & Bihari, B. (1987). Auditory brainstem potentials in sons of alcoholic fathers. *Alcoholism: Clinical and Experimental Research, 11,* 1–4.

Begleiter, H., Porjesz, B., Bihari, B., & Kissin, B. (1984). Event-related brain potentials in boys at risk for alcoholism. *Science, 225,* 1493–1496.

Begleiter, H., Porjesz, B., Rawlings, R., & Eckardt, M. (1987). Auditory recovery function and P3 in boys at high risk for alcoholism. *Alcohol, 4,* 315–321.

Behar, D., Berg, C. J., Rapoport, J. L., Nelson, W., Linnoila, M., Cohen, M., Bozevich, C., & Marshall, T. C. (1983). Behavioral and physiological effects of ethanol in high-risk and control children: A pilot study. *Alcoholism: Clinical and Experimental Research, 7,* 404–410.

Beletsis, S., & Brown, S. (1981). A developmental framework for understanding the adult children of alcoholics. *Focus on Women: Journal of Addiction and Health, 2,* 187–203.

Bennett, L. A., Wolin, S. J., Reiss, D., & Teitelbaum, M. A. (1987). Couples at risk for transmission of alcoholism: Protective influences. *Family Process, 26,* 111–129.

Bennett, L. A., Wolin, S. J., & Reiss, D. (1988a). Deliberate family process: A strategy for protecting children of alcoholics. *British Journal of Addiction, 83,* 821–829.

Bennett, L. A., Wolin, S. J., & Reiss, D. (1988b). Cognitive, behavioral, and emotional problems among school-age children of alcoholic parents. *American Journal of Psychiatry, 145,* 185–190.

Benson, C. S., & Heller, K. (1987). Factors in the current adjustment of young adult daughters of alcoholic and problem drinking fathers. *Journal of Abnormal Psychology, 90,* 305–312.

Berkowitz, A., & Perkins, H. W. (1988). Personality characteristics of children of alcoholics. *Journal of Consulting and Clinical Psychology, 56,* 206–209.

Biek, J. D. (1981). Screening test for identifying adolescents adversely affected by a parental drinking problem. *Journal of Adolescent Health Care, 2,* 107–113.

Billings, A., Kessler, M., Gomberg, C., & Weiner, S. (1979). Marital conflict-resolution of alcoholic and nonalcoholic couples during sobriety and experimental drinking. *Journal of Studies on Alcohol, 40,* 193–195.

Black, C. (1982). *It will never happen to me.* Denver, Colo.: M.A.C. Printing and Publications.

Black, C., Bucky, S. F., & Wilder-Padilla, S. (1986). The interpersonal and emotional consequences of being an adult child of an alcoholic. *International Journal of the Addictions, 21,* 213–231.

Blau, M. (1990). Adult children: Tied to the past. *American Health, 9* (6), 56–65.

Blum, K., Noble, E. P., Sheridan, P. J., Montgomery, A., Ritchie, T., Jagadeeswaran, P., Nogami, H., Briggs, A. H., & Cohn, J. B. (1990). Allelic association of human dopamine D_2 receptor gene in alcoholism. *Journal of the American Medical Association, 263,* 2055–2060.

Bohman, M. (1978). Some genetics aspects of alcoholism and criminality: A population of adoptees. *Archives of General Psychiatry, 35,* 269–276.

Bohman, M., Cloninger, C. R., von Knorring, A. L., Sigvardsson, S. (1984). An adoption study of somatoform disorders: III. Cross-fostering analysis and genetic relationship to alcoholism and criminality. *Archives of General Psychiatry, 41,* 872–878.

Bohman, M., Sigvardsson, S., & Cloninger, C. R. (1981). Maternal inheritance of alcohol abuse: Cross-fostering analysis of adopted women. *Archives of General Psychiatry, 38,* 965–969.

Booz-Allen & Hamilton, Inc. (1974). *An assessment of the needs of and resources for children of alcoholic parents.* Rockville, Md.: National Institute on Alcohol Abuse and Alcoholics.

Bordin, E. S. (1975). The generalizability of the psychoanalytic concept of the working alliance. *Psychotherapy: Theory, Research, and Practice, 16,* 252–260.

Borgatta, E. G. (1965). A short test of personality: The S-ident Form. *Journal of Educational Research, 58,* 453–456.

Bowlby, J. (1969). *Attachment and loss.* Vol. 1: *Attachment.* New York: Basic Books.

Bowlby, J. (1980). *Attachment and loss.* Vol. 3: *Loss, sadness and depression.* London: Hogarth Press.

Breger, L. (1974). *From instinct to identity: The development of personality.* Englewood Cliffs, N.J.: Prentice-Hall.

Brown, J. B. (1977). Platelet MAO and alcoholism. *American Journal of Psychiatry, 134,* 206–207.

Brown, S. A. (1989). Life events of adolescents in relation to personal and parental substance abuse. *American Journal of Psychiatry, 146,* 484–489.

Brown, S. A., Creamer, V. A., & Stetson, B. A. (1987). Adolescent alcohol expectancies in relation to personal and parental drinking patterns. *Journal of Abnormal Psychology, 96,* 117–121.

Brown, S. A., Goldman, M. S., Inn, A., & Anderson, L. R. (1980). Expectations of reinforcement from alcohol: Their domain and relation to drinking patterns. *Journal of Consulting and Clinical Psychology, 48,* 419–426.

Brown, S. (1988). *Treating adult children of alcoholics: A developmental perspective.* New York: John Wiley & Sons.

Brown, S., & Beletsis, S. (1986). The development of family transference in groups for the adult children of alcoholics. *International Journal of Group Psychotherapy, 36,* 97–114.

Brown, S., & Yalom, I. D. (1977). Interactional group therapy with alcoholics. *Journal of Studies on Alcohol, 38,* 426–456.

Burk, J. P. (1985). Psychological correlates for children of alcoholics: Socialization as a moderator of adult alcoholism and symptoms of psychopathology. Master's thesis. University of Missouri, Columbia.

Burk, J. P., & Sher, K. J. (1988). The "forgotten children" revisited: Neglected areas of COA research. *Clinical Psychology Review, 8,* 285–302.

Burk, J. P., & Sher, K. J. (1990). Labeling the child of an alcoholic: Negative stereotyping by mental health professionals and peers. *Journal of Studies on Alcohol, 51,* 156–163.

Buss, A. H., & Plomin, R. (1984). *Temperament: Early developing personality traits.* Hillsdale, N.J.: Lawrence Erlbaum Associates.

Buydens-Branchey, L., Branchey, M., Noumair, D., & Lieber, C. S. (1989). Age of alcoholism onset: II. Relationship to susceptibility to serotonin precursor availability. *Archives of General Psychiatry, 46,* 231–236.

Cadoret, R. J., Cain, C. A., & Grove, W. M. (1980). Development of alcoholism in adoptees raised apart from alcoholic biologic relatives. *Archives of General Psychiatry, 78,* 561–563.

Cadoret, R. J., & Gath, A. (1978). Inheritance of alcoholism in adoptees. *British Journal of Psychiatry, 132,* 252–258.

Cadoret, R. J., O'Gorman, T. W., Troughton, E., & Heywood, E. (1985). Alcoholism and antisocial personality: Interrelationships, genetic, and environmental factors. *Archives of General Psychiatry, 42,* 161–167.

Cadoret, R. J., Troughton, E., & O'Gorman, T. W. (1987). Genetic and environmental factors in alcohol abuse and antisocial personality. *Journal of Studies on Alcohol, 48,* 1–8.

Cadoret, R. J., Troughton, E., O'Gorman, T. W., & Heywood, E. (1986). An adoption study of genetic and environmental factors in drug abuse. *Archives of General Psychiatry, 43*, 1131–1136.

Cadoret, R., Troughton, E., & Widmer, R. (1984). Clinical differences between antisocial and primary alcoholics. *Comprehensive Psychiatry, 25*, 1–8.

Callan, V. J., & Jackson, D. (1986). Children of alcoholic fathers and recovered alcoholic fathers: Personal and family functioning. *Journal of Studies on Alcohol, 47*, 180–182.

Caplan, G. (1981). Mastery of stress: Psychosocial aspects. *American Journal of Psychiatry, 138*, 413–420.

Cappell, H., & Greeley, J. (1987). Alcohol and tension reduction: An update on research and theory. In H. T. Blane and K. E. Leonard, eds., *Psychological theory of drinking and alcoholism*. New York: Guilford Press.

CASPAR, Inc. (1978). *Decisions about drinking*. Somerville, Mass.: CASPAR Alcohol Education Program.

Cattell, R. B., Eber, H. W., & Tatsuoka, M. M. (1970). *Handbook for the Sixteen Personality Factor Questionnaire (16PF)*. Champaign, Ill.: Institute for Personality Ability and Testing.

Cederlof, R., Friberg, L., & Lundman, T. (1977). The interactions of smoking, environment, and heredity and their implications for disease etiology. *Acta Medicae Scandinavia, 202*(Suppl. 612), 1–128.

Cermak, T. (1984). Children of alcoholics and the case for a new diagnostic category of co-dependency. *Alcohol, Health and Research World, 8*, 38–42.

Cermak, T. L. (1986). *Diagnosing and treating co-dependence*. Minneapolis: Johnson Institute Books.

Cermak, T. L. (1988). *A time to heal*. Los Angeles: Jeremey P. Tarcher.

Cermak, T. L., & Brown, S. (1982). Interactional group therapy with the adult children of alcoholics. *International Journal of Group Psychotherapy, 32*, 375–388.

Chapman, L. J., & Chapman, J. P. (1969). Illusory correlation as an obstacle to the use of valid psychodiagnostic signs. *Journal of Abnormal Psychology, 74*, 271–287.

Chapman, L. J., & Chapman, J. P. (1973). *Disordered thought in schizophrenia*. Englewood Cliffs, N.J.: Prentice-Hall.

Chapman, L. J., & Chapman, J. P. (1978). The measurement of differential deficit. *Journal of Psychiatric Research, 14*, 303–311.

Chassin, L., Mann, L. M., & Sher, K. J. (1988). Self-awareness theory, family history of alcoholism, and adolescent alcohol involvement. *Journal of Abnormal Psychology, 97*, 206–217.

Chassin, L., Rogosch, F., & Barrera, M. (1990). Substance use and symptomatology among adolescent children of alcoholics. Manuscript under review.

Chipperfield, B., & Vogel-Sprott, M. (1988). Family history of problem drinking among young male social drinkers: Modeling effects on alcohol consumption. *Journal of Abnormal Psychology, 97*, 423–438.

Christiansen, B. A., & Goldman, M. S. (1983). Alcohol-related expectancies vs. demographic/background variables in the prediction of adolescent drinking. *Journal of Consulting and Clinical Psychology, 51*, 249–257.

Christiansen, B. A., Goldman, M. S., & Brown, S. A. (1985). The differential development of adolescent alcohol expectancies may predict alcoholism. *Addictive Behaviors, 10,* 299–306.

Christiansen, B. A., Goldman, M. S., & Inn, A. (1982). Development of alcohol-related expectancies in adolescents: Separating pharmacological from social-learning influences. *Journal of Consulting and Clinical Psychology, 50,* 330–334.

Christiansen, B. A., Smith, G. T., Roehling, P. V., & Goldman, M. S. (1989). Using alcohol expectancies to predict adolescent drinking behavior after one year. *Journal of Consulting and Clinical Psychology, 57,* 93–99.

Chu, D. (1988). Breaking the bond of silence. *People,* April 18, 1988, p. 100.

Churchill, J. C., Broida, J. P., & Nicholson, N. (1990). Locus of control and self-esteem of adult children of alcoholics. *Journal of Studies on Alcohol, 51,* 373–376.

Ciraulo, D. A., Barnhill, J., Ciraulo, A. M., Greenblatt, D. J., & Shader, R. I. (1989). Parental alcoholism as a risk factor in benzodiazepine abuse: A pilot study. *American Journal of Psychiatry, 146,* 1333–1335.

Ciraulo, D. A., Sands, B. F., & Shader, R. I. (1988). Critical review of liability for benzodiazepine abuse among alcoholics. *American Journal of Psychiatry, 145,* 1501–1506.

Clair, D., & Genest, M. (1987). Variables associated with the adjustment of offspring of alcoholic fathers. *Journal of Studies on Alcohol, 48,* 345–355.

Claridge, G., Canter, S., & Hume, W. (1973). *Personality differences and biological variations: A study of twins.* New York: Pergamon Press.

Claydon, D. (1987). Self-reported alcohol, drug, and eating-disorder problems among male and female collegiate children of alcoholics. *Journal of American College Health, 36,* 111–116.

Clifford, C. A., Fulker, D. W., Gurling, H. M. D., & Murray, R. M. (1981). Preliminary findings from a twin study of alcohol use. *Twin research 3, part C: Epidemiological and clinical studies.* New York: A. R. Liss.

Cloninger, C. R. (1987a). Neurogenetic adaptive mechanisms in alcoholism. *Science, 236,* 410–416.

Cloninger, C. R. (1987b). A systematic method for clinical description and classification of personality variants. *Archives of General Psychiatry, 44,* 573–588.

Cloninger, C. R. (1987c). Tridimensional personality questionnaire (TPQ). Unpublished. St. Louis: Washington University.

Cloninger, C. R. (1988). Reply to "Sensation seeking and behavior disorders." *Archives of General Psychiatry, 45,* 503–504.

Cloninger, C. R., Bohman, M., & Sigvardsson, S. (1981a). Inheritance of alcohol abuse: Cross-fostering analysis of adopted men. *Archives of General Psychiatry, 38,* 861–868.

Cloninger, C. R., Martin, R. L., Clayton, P., et al. (1981b). Follow up and family study of anxiety neurosis. In D. F. Klein & J. Rabkin, eds., *Anxiety: New Research and changing comments.* New York: Raven Press.

Cloninger, C. R., Reich, T., and Wetzel, R. (1979). Alcoholism and adult depression: Familial associations and genetic models from alcoholism and adult depression. In D. W. Goodwin & C. K. Erickon, eds., *Alcoholism and affective disorders: Clinical, genetic, and biochemical studies* (pp. 57–86). New York: Spectrum Publications.

Cloninger, C. R., Sigvardsson, S., Reich, T., & Bohman, M. (1986). In *Genetic and biological markers for drug abuse and alcoholism*, NIDA/NIAAA Research Monograph. Washington, D.C.: U.S. Government Printing Office.

Cloninger, C. R., Sigvardsson, S., Reich, T., & Bohman, M. (1988). Childhood personality predicts alcohol abuse in young adults. *Alcoholism: Clinical and Experimental Research, 12,* 494–505.

Cohen, J. (1977). *Statistical power analysis for the behavioral sciences,* revised edition. New York: Academic Press.

Cohen, J., and Cohen, P. (1983). *Applied multiple regression/correlation analysis for the behavioral sciences.* Hillsdale, N.J.: Lawrence Erlbaum Associates.

Cohen, M. E., & White, P. D. (1951). Life situations, emotions and neurocirculatory asthenia. *Psychosomatic Medicine, 13,* 335–357.

Cohen, S., & Wills, T. A. (1985). Stress, social support, and the buffering hypothesis. *Psychological Bulletin, 98,* 310–357.

Compas, B. E. (1987). Coping with stress during childhood and adolescence. *Psychological Bulletin, 101,* 393–403.

Conger, J. J. (1956). Alcoholism: Theory, problem and challenge, II: Reinforcement theory and the dynamics of alcoholism. *Quarterly Journal of Studies on Alcohol, 13,* 296–305.

Conners, C. K. (1969). A teacher rating scale for use in drug studies with children. *American Journal of Psychiatry, 126,* 884–888.

Conners, C. K. (1970). Symptom patterns in hyperkinetic, neurotic, and normal children. *Child Development, 41,* 667–682.

Connors, G. J., & Maisto, S. A. (1983). Methodological issues in alcohol and stress research. In L. A. Pohorecky & J. Brick, eds., *Stress and alcohol use* (pp. 105–119). New York: Elsevier Biomedical.

Constantine, L. L. (1986). *Family paradigms: The practice of theory in family therapy.* New York: Guilford.

Cooper, J. R., Bloom, F. E., & Roth, R. H. (1982). *The biochemical basis of neuropharmacology, fourth edition.* New York: Oxford Press.

Cooper, L., Russell, M., & George, W. (1988). Coping, expectancies, and alcohol abuse: A test of social learning formulations. *Journal of Abnormal Psychology, 97,* 218–230.

Cork, M. (1969). *The forgotten children.* Toronto: Addiction Research Foundation.

Cotton, N. (1979). The familial incidence of alcoholism: A review. *Journal of Studies on Alcohol, 40,* 89–116.

Cox, N. J., & Suarez, B. K. (1985). Linkage analysis for psychiatric disorders. II. Methodological considerations. *Psychiatric Developments, 3,* 369–382.

Crabbe, J. C. (1989). Genetic animal models in the study of alcoholism. *Alcoholism: Clinical and Experimental Research, 13,* 120–127.

Crandell, J. S. (1989). Brief treatment for adult children of alcoholics: Accessing resources for self-care. *Psychotherapy, 26, 4,* 510–512.

Craven, D. (1988). Children of alcoholics: A neglected population. *Girl Scout Leader, 65,* 26–29.

Crowe, R. R., Pauls, D. L., Slymen, D. J., & Noyes, R. (1980). A family study of anxiety neurosis: Morbidity risk in families of patients with and without mitral valve prolapse. *Archives of General Psychiatry, 37,* 77–79.

Cutter, C. G., & Cutter H. S. G. (1987). Experience and change in Al-Anon family groups: Adult children of alcoholics. *Journal of Studies on Alcohol, 48,* 29–32.

Davis, R. B., Johnston, P. D., DiCicco, L., & Orenstein, A. (1985). Helping children of alcoholic parents: An elementary school program. *The School Counselor.* May, 357–363.

Dean, A., & Lin, N. (1977). The stress-buffering role of social support: Problems and prospects for systematic investigation. *Journal of Nervous and Mental Disease, 165,* 403–417.

Desmond, E. (1987). Out in the open. *Time,* 80–90.

Deutsch, C. (1982). *Broken bottles, broken dreams.* New York: Teachers College Press.

de Wit, H., & McCracken, S. G. (1990). Ethanol self-administration in males with and without an alcoholic first-degree relative. *Alcoholism: Clinical and Experimental Research, 14,* 63–70.

DiCicco, L., Davis, R., & Orenstein, A. (1984). Identifying the children of alcoholics from survey responses. *Journal of Drug and Alcohol Education, 30,* 1–17.

DiCicco, L., Davis, R., Travis, J., & Orenstein, A. (1983–1984). Recruiting children from alcoholic families into a peer education program. *Alcohol Health and Research World, 8,* 28–34.

Dickson, D. H., & Kelly, I. W. (1985). The "Barnum effect" in personality assessment: A review of the literature. *Psychological Reports, 57,* 367–382.

Digman, J. M., & Inouye, J. (1986). Further specification of the five robust factors of personality. *Journal of Personality and Social Psychology, 50,* 116–123.

Dishion, T. J., Patterson, G. R., & Reid, J. R. (1988). Parent and peer factors associated with drug sampling in early adolescence: Implications for treatment. In E. R. Rahdert & J. Grabowski, eds., *NIDA Research Monograph 77, Adolescent drug abuse: Analyses of treatment research* (pp. 69–93). Rockville, Md.: NIDA.

Donovan, B. E. (1981). A collegiate group for the sons and daughters of alcoholics. *Journal of the American College Health Association, 30,* 83–86.

Douglas, K. (1988). *The ragman's son.* New York: Simon and Schuster.

Downing, N. E., & Walker, M. E. (1987). A psychoeducational group for adult children of alcoholics. *Journal of Counseling and Development, 65,* 440–442.

Drake, R. E., & Vaillant, G. E. (1988). Predicting alcoholism and personality disorder in a 33-year longitudinal study of children of alcoholics. *British Journal of Addiction, 83,* 799–807.

Drejer, K., Theilgaard, A., Teasdale, T. W., Schulsinger, F., & Goodwin, D. W. (1985). A prospective study of young men at high risk for alcoholism: Neuropsychological assessment. *Alcoholism: Clinical and Experimental Research, 9,* 498–502.

Duck, S. W. (1975). Personality similarity and friendship choices by adolescents. *European Journal of Social Psychology, 5,* 351–365.

Dunn, N. J., Jacob, T., Hummon, N., & Seilhamer, R. A. (1987). Marital stability in alcoholic-spouse relationships as a function of drinking pattern and location. *Journal of Abnormal Psychology, 96,* 99–107.

Earls, F. J. (1987). On the familial transmission of child psychiatric disorder. *Journal of Child Psychology and Psychiatry and Allied Disciplines, 28,* 791–802.

Earls, F., Reich, W., Jung, K. G., & Cloninger, C. R. (1988). Psychopathology in children of alcoholic and antisocial parents. *Alcoholism: Clinical and Experimental Research, 12,* 481–487.

Edwards, D. M., & Zander, T. A. (1985). Children of alcoholics: Background and strategies for the counselor. *Elementary School Guidance and Counseling, 20,* 2.

Edwards, G. (1982). *The treatment of drinking problems: A guide for the helping professions.* New York: McGraw-Hill.

Edwards, G. (1986). The alcohol dependence syndrome: A concept as stimulus to enquiry. *British Journal of Addiction, 81,* 171–183.

Edwards, G., & Gross, M. (1976). Alcohol dependence: Provisional description of a clinical syndrome. *British Medical Journal, 1,* 1058–1061.

Edwards, P., Harvey, C., & Whitehead, P. C. (1973). Wives of alcoholics: A critical review and analysis. *Quarterly Journal of Studies on Alcohol, 34,* 112–132.

Ehlers, C. L., & Schuckit, M. A. (1988). EEG response to ethanol in sons of alcoholics. *Psychopharmacology Bulletin, 24,* 434–437.

Ehlers, C. L., & Schuckit, M. A. (in press). Evaluation of EEG alpha activity in sons of alcoholics. *Neuropsychopharmacology.*

Ehlers, C. L., & Schuckit, M. A. (1990). EEG fast frequency activity in the sons of alcoholics. *Biological Psychiatry, 27,* 631–641.

Ehlers, C. L., Wall, T., & Schuckit, M. A. (1989). EEG spectral characteristics following ethanol administration in young men. *Electroencephalography and Clinical Neurophysiology, 93,* 179–187.

Elderton, E. M., & Pearson, K. (1910). A first study of the influence of parental alcoholism on the physique and ability of the offspring. *Eugenics Laboratory Memoirs, Series X,* 1–46.

El-Guebaly, N., & Offord, D. R. (1977). The offspring of alcoholics: A critical review. *American Journal of Psychiatry, 134,* 357–365.

El-Guebaly, N., & Offord, D. R. (1979). On being the offspring of an alcoholic: An update. *Alcoholism: Clinical and Experimental Research, 3,* 148–157.

Elmasian, R., Neville, H., Woods, D., Schuckit, M. A., & Bloom, F. (1982). Event-related brain potentials are different in individuals at high and low risk for developing alcoholism. *Proceedings of the National Academy of Science USA, 79,* 7900–7903.

Elul, M. R. (1972). The genesis of the EEG. *International Review of Neurobiology, 15,* 227–272.

Emshoff, J. G., & Moeti, R. L. (1987, August). School-based prevention with children of alcoholics. Paper presented at the annual convention of the American Psychological Association, New York.

Endicott, J., Andreasen, N., & Spitzer, R. L. (1978). *Family History—Research Diagnostic Criteria (FH-RDC)*. New York: New York State Psychiatric Institute.

Epstein, S. (1979). The stability of behavior: I. On predicting most of the people much of the time. *Journal of Personality and Social Psychology, 37,* 1097–1126.

Epstein, S. (1980). The stability of behavior: II. Implications for psychological research. *American Psychologist, 35,* 790–806.

Erikson, E. H. (1963). *Childhood and society.* 2nd ed. New York: Norton.

Ervin, C. S., Little, R. E., Streissguth, A. P., & Beck, D. E. (1984). Alcoholic fathering and its relation to child's intellectual development: A pilot investigation. *Alcoholism: Clinical and Experimental Research, 8,* 362–365.

Eysenck, H. J. (1957). Drugs and personality, I: Theory and methodology. *Journal of Mental Science, 103,* 119–131.

Eysenck, H. J., & Eysenck, S. B. G. (1968). *Manual for the Eysenck Personality Inventory.* San Diego, Calif.: Educational and Industrial Testing Service.

Eysenck, H. J. & Eysenck, S. B. G. (1975). *Manual for the Eysenck Personality Questionnaire.* San Diego, Calif.: Educational and Industrial Testing Service.

Eysenck, H. J. (1978). Superfactors P, E, and N in a comprehensive factor space. *Multivariate Behavioral Research, 13,* 475–481.

Famularo, R., Stone, K., Barnum, R., & Wharton, R. (1986). Alcoholism and severe child maltreatment. *American Journal of Orthopsychiatry, 56,* 481–485.

Feighner, J. P., Robins, E., Guze, S. B., Woodruff, R. A., Winokur, G., & Munoz, R. (1972). Diagnostic criteria for use in psychiatric research. *Archives of General Psychiatry, 26,* 57–63.

Fenigstein, A., Scheier, M. F., & Buss, A. H. (1975). Public and private self-consciousness: Assessment and theory. *Journal of Consulting and Clinical Psychology, 43,* 522–527.

Filstead, W., McElfresh, O., & Anderson, C. (1981). Comparing the family environments of alcoholic and "normal" families. *Journal of Alcohol and Drug Education, 26,* 24–31.

Fine, E. W., Yudin, L. W., Holmes, J., & Heinemann, S. (1976). Behavioral disorders in children with parental alcoholism. *Annals of the New York Academy of Sciences, 23,* 507–517.

Finn, P. R., Martin, J. B., & Pihl, R. O. (1987). Alexithymia in males at high genetic risk for alcoholism. *Psychotherapy and Psychosomatics, 47,* 18–21.

Finn, P. R., & Phil, R. O. (1987). Men at high risk for alcoholism: The effect of alcohol on cardiovascular response to unavoidable shock. *Journal of Abnormal Psychology, 96,* 230–236.

Finn, P. R., & Pihl, R. O. (1988). Risk for alcoholism: A comparison between two different groups of sons of alcoholics on cardiovascular reactivity and sensitivity to alcohol. *Alcoholism: Clinical and Experimental Research, 12,* 742–747.

Finn, P. R., Zeitouni, N. C., & Pihl, R. O. (1990). Effects of alcohol on psychophysiological hyperreactivity to nonaversive and aversive stimuli in men at high risk for alcoholism. *Journal of Abnormal Psychology, 99,* 79–85.

Fischer, M. (1971). Psychoses in the offspring of schizophrenic monozygotic twins and their normal co-twins. *British Journal of Psychiatry, 118,* 43–52.

FitzGerald, K. W. (1988). *Alcoholism: The inside story.* Garden City, N.Y.: Doubleday.

Folkman, S., & Lazarus, R. S. (1980). An analysis of coping in a middle-aged community sample. *Journal of Health and Social Behavior, 21*, 219–239.

Fowler, C. J., von Knorring, L., & Oreland, L. (1980). Platelet monoamine oxidase activity in sensation seekers. *Psychiatry Research, 3*, 273–279.

Fowles, D. C. (1980). The three-arousal model: Implications of Gray's two-factor learning theory for heart rate, electrodermal activity, and psychopathy. *Psychophysiology, 17*, 87–104.

Frankenstein, W., Hay, W. M., & Nathan, P. E. (1985). Effects of intoxication on alcoholics' marital communications and problem solving. *Journal of Studies on Alcohol, 46*, 1–6.

Freed, E. X. (1978). Alcohol and mood: An updated review. *International Journal of the Addictions, 8*, 451–473.

Gabrielli, W. F., & Mednick, S. A. (1983). Intellectual performance in children of alcoholics. *The Journal of Nervous and Mental Disease, 171*, 444–447.

Gabrielli, W. F., Mednick, S. A., Volavka, J., Pollock, V. E., Schulsinger, F., & Itil, T. M. (1982). Electroencephalograms in children of alcoholic fathers. *Psychophysiology, 19*, 404–407.

Gabrielli, W. F., & Plomin, R. (1985). Drinking behavior in the Colorado adoptee and twin sample. *Journal of Studies on Alcohol, 46*, 24–31.

Garmezy, N. (1990). A closing note: Reflections on the future. In J. Rolf, A. Masten, D. Cicchetti, K. Nuechterlein, & S. Weintraub, eds., *Risk and protective factors in the development of psychopathology* (pp. 527–534). Cambridge: Cambridge University Press.

Gelso, C. J., & Carter, J. A. (1985). The relationship in counseling and psychotherapy: Components, consequences, and theoretical antecedents. *The Counseling Psychologist, 13, 2*, 155–243.

Gensheimer, L. K., Roosa, M. W., & Ayers, T. S. (in press). Children's self-selection into prevention programs: Evaluation of an innovative recruitment strategy for children of alcoholics. *American Journal of Community Psychology.*

Giller, E., Jr., & Hall, H. (1983). Platelet MAO activity in recovered alcoholics after long-term abstinence. *American Journal of Psychiatry, 140*, 114–115.

Gittelman, R., Mannuzza, S., Shenker, R., & Bonagura, N. (1985). Hyperactive boys almost grown up, I: Psychiatric status. *Archives of General Psychiatry, 45*, 937–947.

Glynn, T. J. (1981). From family to peer: Transitions of influence among drug-using youth. In D. J. Lettieri & J. P. Ludford, eds., *Drug abuse and the American adolescent. NIDA research monograph 38* (pp. 57–81). Rockville, Md.: National Institute on Drug Use.

Goff, W. R. (1974). Human average evoked potentials: Procedures for stimulating and recording. In R. F. Thompson and M. M. Patterson, eds., *Bioelectric recording techniques,* part B. New York: Academic Press.

Goffman, E. (1963). *Stigma: Notes on the management of spoiled identity.* Englewood Cliffs, N.J.: Prentice-Hall.

Goglia, L. R. (1986). Personality characteristics of adult children of alcoholics. Doctoral dissertation, Georgia State University.

Goldman, M. S. (1989, November). Expectancies and alcoholism risk in adolescence. Paper presented at the annual convention of the *Association for Advancement of Behavior Therapy*. Washington, D.C.

Goodwin, D. W. (1988). *Is alcoholism hereditary?* 2d ed. New York: Balantine Books.

Goodwin, D. W., Schulsinger, F., Hermansen, L., Guze, S. B., & Winokur, G. (1973). Alcohol problems in adoptees raised apart from alcoholic biological parents. *Archives of General Psychiatry, 28,* 238–243.

Goodwin, D. W., Schulsinger, F., Knop, J., Mednick, S., & Guze, S. B. (1977). Alcoholism and depression in adopted-out daughters of alcoholics. *Archives of General Psychiatry, 34,* 751–755.

Goodwin, D. W., Schulsinger, F., Moller, N., Hermansen, L., Winokur, G., Guze, S. B. (1974). Drinking problems in adopted and nonadopted sons of alcoholics. *Archives of General Psychiatry, 31,* 164–169.

Gorenstein, E. E. (1987). Cognitive-perceptual deficit in an alcoholism spectrum disorder. *Journal of Studies on Alcohol, 48,* 310–318.

Gorenstein, E. E., & Newman, J. P. (1980). Disinhibitory psychopathology: A new perspective and a model for research. *Psychological Review, 87,* 301–315.

Gottfries, C. G., Oreland, L., Wiberg, A., & Winblad, B. (1975). Lowered monoamine oxidase activity in brains from alcoholic suicides. *Journal of Neurochemistry, 25,* 667–673.

Gottesman, I. I., & Bertelsen, A. (1989). Confirming unexpressed genotypes for schizophrenia. *Archives of General Psychiatry, 46,* 867–872.

Greenberg, G. S., Zucker, R. A., Noll, R. B. (1985, August). The development of cognitive structures about alcoholic beverages among preschoolers. Paper presented at the annual meeting of the American Psychological Association, Los Angeles, California.

Greist, D., Forehand, R., Wells, K., & McMahon, R. (1980). Examination of differences between nonclinic and behavior-problem clinic-referred children and their mothers. *Journal of Abnormal Psychology, 89,* 497–500.

Grove, W. M., & Cadoret, R. J. (1983). Genetic factors in alcoholism. In B. Kissin, & H. Begleiter, eds., *The pathogenesis of alcoholism: Biological factors* (Vol. 7, pp. 31–56). New York: Plenum Press.

Gurling, H. M. D., & Murray, R. M. (1984). Alcoholism and genetics: old and new evidence. In N. Krasner, J. S. Madden, & R. J. Walker, eds., *Alcohol-related problems* (pp. 127–136). New York: John Wiley & Sons.

Gurling, H. M. D., Murray, R. M., & Clifford, C. (1981). Genetic contributions to alcohol dependence and its effect on brain function. In G. L. Parisi & W. A. Nance, eds., *Twin Research* (Vol. 3, pp. 77–87). New York: A. R. Liss.

Halikas, J. A., Herzog, M. A., Mirassou, M., & Lyttle, M. D. (1981). Psychiatric diagnosis among female alcoholics. *Currents in Alcoholism, 8,* 283–291.

Hall, R., Hesselbrock, V. M., & Stabenau, J. R. (1983a). Familial distribution of alcohol use: I. Assortative mating in the parents of alcoholics. *Behavior Genetics, 13,* 361–372.

Hall, R., Hesselbrock, V. M., & Stabenau, J. R. (1983b). Familial distribution of alcohol use: II. Assortative mating of alcoholics probands. *Behavior Genetics, 13,* 373–382.

Hamilton, C. J., & Collins, J. J., Jr. (1985). The role of alcohol in wife beating and child abuse: A review of the literature. In J. J. Collins, ed., *Drinking and crime: Perspectives on the relationship between alcohol consumption and criminal behavior* (pp. 253–287). New York: Guilford.

Harada, S., Agarwal, D. P., & Goedde, H. W. (1985). Aldehyde dehydrogenase polymorphism and alcohol metabolism in alcoholics. *Alcohol, 2,* 391–392.

Harada, S., Agarwal, D. P., Goedde, H. W., & Ishikawa, B. (1983). Aldehyde dehydrogenase isoenzyme variation and alcoholism in Japan. *Pharmacology, Biochemistry, and Behavior* (Suppl. 1), *18,* 151–153.

Harada, S., Agarwal, D. P., Goedde, H. W., Tagaki, S., & Ishikawa, B. (1982). Possible protective role against alcoholism for aldehyde dehydrogenase isoenzyme deficiency in Japan. *Lancet, ii,* 827.

Harburg, E., Davis, D. R., & Caplan, R. (1982). Parent and offspring alcohol use: Imitative and aversive transmission. *Journal of Studies on Alcohol, 43,* 497–516.

Hare, R. (1970). *Psychopathy: Theory and research.* New York: Wiley.

Hare, R. (1985). *The psychopathy checklist.* Manuscript. University of British Columbia, Vancouver, Canada.

Hassett, J. (1978). *A primer of psychophysiology.* San Francisco: W. H. Freeman.

Hayduk, L. A. (1987). *Structural equation modeling with LISREL.* Baltimore, Md.: Johns Hopkins University Press.

Heath, A. (1990, May). Alternative research designs. Working group: Longitudinal studies of children at high risk. Prevention Research Branch, National Institute on Alcohol Abuse and Alcoholism, Rockville, Md.

Hegedus, A. M., Alterman, A. I., & Tarter, R. E. (1984). Learning achievement in sons of alcoholics. *Alcoholism: Clinical and Experimental Research, 8,* 330–333.

Hegedus, A. M., Tarter, R. E., Hill, S. Y., Jacob, T., & Winsten, N. E. (1984). Static Ataxia: A possible marker for alcoholism. *Alcoholism: Clinical and Experimental Research, 8,* 580–581.

Heller, K., Sher, K. J., & Benson, C. S. (1982). Problems associated with risk overprediction in studies of offspring of alcoholics: Implications for prevention. *Clinical Psychology Review, 2,* 183–200.

Helzer, J. E. (1987). Epidemiology of alcoholism. *Journal of Consulting and Clinical Psychology, 55,* 284–292.

Helzer, J. E., & Pryzbeck, T. R. (1988). The co-occurrence of alcoholism with other psychiatric disorders in the general population and its impact on treatment. *Journal of Studies on Alcohol, 49,* 219–224.

Hennecke, L. (1984). Stimulus augmenting and field dependence in children of alcoholic fathers. *Journal of Studies on Alcohol, 45,* 486–492.

Hesselbrock, M. N., Hesselbrock, V. M., & Stabenau, J. R. (1985a). Minimal brain dysfunction and neuropsychological test performance in children of alcoholics. *Recent Developments on Alcohol, 3,* 65–82.

Hesselbrock, M. N., Meyer, R. E., Keener, J. J. (1985b). Psychopathology in hospitalized alcoholics. *Archives of General Psychiatry, 42,* 1050–1055.

Hesselbrock, V., & Hesselbrock, M. (1986, August). Substance abuse among the adult offspring of alcoholic parents. Paper presented at the annual meeting of the American Psychological Association, New York.

Hesselbrock, V. M., O'Brien, J., Weinstein, M., & Carter-Menendez, N. (1987). Reasons for drinking and alcohol use in young adults at high risk and at low risk for alcoholism. *British Journal of Addictions, 82*, 1335–1339.

Hetherington, E. M., Stanley-Hagan, M., & Anderson, E. R. (1989). Marital transitions. *American Psychologist, 44, 2*, 303–312.

Hibbard, S. (1987). The diagnosis and treatment of adult children of alcoholics as a specialized therapeutic population. *Psychotherapy, 24*, 779–785.

Hibbard, S. (1989). Personality and object relational pathology in young adult children of alcoholics. *Psychotherapy, 26*, 504–509.

Hill, S. Y., Armstrong, J., Steinhauer, S. R., Baughman, T., & Zubin, J. (1987). Static ataxia as a psychobiological marker for alcoholism. *Alcoholism: Clinical and Experimental Research, 11*, 345–348.

Hill, S. Y., Aston, C., & Rabin, B. (1988). Suggestive evidence of genetic linkage between alcoholism and the MNS blood group. *Alcoholism: Clinical and Experimental Research, 12*, 811–814.

Hill, S. Y., Cloninger, C. R., & Ayre, F. R. (1977). Independent familial transmission of alcoholism and opiate abuse. *Alcoholism: Clinical and Experimental Research, 1*, 335–342.

Hill, S. Y., Goodwin, D. W., Cadoret, R., Osterland, K., & Doner, S. M. (1975). Association and linkage between alcoholism and eleven serological markers. *Journal of Studies on Alcoholism, 36*, 981–992.

Hill, S. Y., Steinhauer, S. R., Zubin, J., & Baughman, T. (1988). Event-related potentials as markers for alcoholism risk in high density families. *Alcoholism: Clinical and Experimental Research, 12*, 545–554.

Hill, S. Y., Steinhauer, S., Park, J., & Zubin, J. (1990). Event-related potential characteristics in children of alcoholics from high density families. *Alcoholism: Clinical and Experimental Research, 14*, 6–16.

Hinshaw, S. (1987). On the distinction between attentional deficits/hyperactivity and conduct problems/aggression in child psychopathology. *Psychological Bulletin, 101*, 443–463.

Hirsch, B. J., & Reischl, T. M. (1985). Social networks and developmental psychopathology: A comparison of adolescent children of a depressed, arthritic, or normal parent. *Journal of Abnormal Psychology, 94*, 272–281.

Holden, M. G., Brown, S. A., & Mott, M. A. (1988). Social support network of adolescents: Relation to family alcohol abuse. *American Journal of Drug and Alcohol Abuse, 14*, 487–498.

Hops, H., Sherman, L., Tildesley, E., Andrews, J., Ary, D., & Lichtenstein, E. (1987, November). Family influence on adolescent substance use. Paper presented at the annual meeting of the *Association for Advancement of Behavior Therapy*. Boston.

House, J. S., & Kahn, R. L. (1985). Measures and concepts of social support. In S. Cohen & S. L. Syme, eds., *Social support and health* (pp. 83–108). New York: Academic Press.

Hrubec, Z., & Omenn, G. S. (1981). Evidence of genetic predisposition to alcoholic cirrhosis and psychosis. *Alcoholism: Clinical and Experimental Research, 5,* 207–215.

Hughes, J. M. (1977). Adolescent children of alcoholic parents and the relationship of Alateen to these children. *Journal of Consulting and Clinical Psychology, 45,* 946–947.

Imber-Black, E. (1989). Creating rituals in therapy. *The Family Therapy Networker, 13, 4,* 39–46.

Irwin, M., Schuckit, M., & Smith, T. (1990). Clinical importance of age at onset in type 1 and type 2 primary alcoholics. *Archives of General Psychiatry, 47,* 320–324.

Jackson, J. K. (1954). The adjustment of the family to the crisis of alcoholism. *Quarterly Journal of Studies on Alcohol, 15,* 562–586.

Jacob, T., Favorini, A., Meisel, S. S., & Anderson, C. M. (1978). The alcoholic's spouse, children and family interactions. *Journal of Studies on Alcohol, 39,* 1231–1251.

Jacob, T., & Krahn, G. (1988). Marital interactions of alcoholic couples: Comparison with depressed and nondistressed couples. *Journal of Consulting and Clinical Psychology, 56,* 73–79.

Jacob, T., & Leonard, K. (1986). Psychological functioning in children of alcoholic fathers, depressed fathers, and control fathers. *Journal of Studies on Alcohol, 47,* 373–380.

Jacob, T., & Leonard, K. (1988). Alcoholic-spouse interaction as a function of alcoholism subtype and alcohol consumption interaction. *Journal of Abnormal Psychology, 97,* 231–237.

Jacob, T., Ritchey, D., Cvitkovic, J., & Blane, H. (1981). Communication styles of alcoholic and nonalcoholic families when drinking and not drinking. *Journal of Studies on Alcohol, 42,* 466–482.

Jacob, T., & Seilhamer, R. A. (1987). Alcoholism and family interaction. In T. Jacob, ed., *Family interaction and psychopathology: Theories, methods, and findings* (pp. 535–580). New York: Plenum.

Jardine, R. E., & Martin, N. G. (1984). Causes of variation in drinking habits in a large twin sample. *Acta Geneticae Medicae et Gemellologiae, 33,* 435–450.

Jellinek, E. M. (1960). *The disease concept of alcoholism.* New Haven: Hillhouse.

Johnson, J. L., & Rolf, J. (1988). Cognitive functioning in children from alcoholic and non-alcoholic families. *British Journal of Addiction, 83,* 849–857.

Johnson, R. (1989a). Auditory and visual P300s in temporal lobectomy patients: Evidence for modality specific generators. *Psychophysiology, 26,* 633–650.

Johnson, R. (1989b). Developmental evidence for modality-dependent P300 generators: A normative study. *Psychophysiology, 26,* 651–667.

Johnson, R. C., Nagoshi, C. T., Danko, G. P., Honbo, K. A., & Chau, L. L. (1990). Familial transmission of alcohol use norms and expectancies and reported alcohol use. *Alcoholism: Clinical and Experimental Research, 14,* 216–220.

Johnson, S., Leonard, K. E., & Jacob, T. (1989). Drinking, drinking styles, and drug use in children of alcoholics, depressives, and controls. *Journal of Studies on Alcohol, 50,* 427–531.

Jones, B. M. (1974). Circadian variation in the effects of alcohol on cognitive performance. *Quarterly Journal of Studies on Alcohol, 35,* 1212–1219.

Jones, J. W. (1983). *The Children of Alcoholics Screening Test (CAST).* Chicago: Camelot Unlimited.

Jones, M. C. (1968). Personality correlates and antecedents of drinking patterns in adult males. *Journal of Consulting and Clinical Psychology, 32,* 2–12.

Jones, M. C. (1971). Personality antecedents and correlates of drinking patterns in women. *Journal of Consulting and Clinical Psychology, 36,* 61–69.

Jonsson, E., & Nilsson, T. (1968). Alkoholkonsumtion hos monozygota och dizygota tvilling par. *Nordisk Hygienisk Tidskrift, 49,* 21–25.

Kaij, L. (1960). *Alcoholism in twins.* Stockholm: Almqvist & Wiksell.

Kalin, R., McClelland, D. C., & Kahn, M. (1965). The effect of male social drinking on fantasy. *Journal of Personality and Social Psychology, 1,* 441–452.

Kaminer, W. (1990). Chances are you're codependent too. *New York Times Book Review,* February, 1.

Kandel, D. B. (1985). On processes of peer influences in adolescent drug use: A developmental perspective. *Advances in Alcohol and Substance Abuse, 4,* 139–163.

Kantor, K., & Lehr, W. (1975). *Inside the family.* New York: Harper.

Kaplan, H. B. (1975). Increase in self-rejection as an antecedent of deviant responses. *Journal of Youth and Adolescence, 4,* 281–292.

Kaplan, R. F., Hesselbrock, V. M., O'Connor, S., & DePalma, N. (1988). Behavioral and EEG responses to alcohol in nonalcoholic men with a family history of alcoholism. *Progress in Neuro-Psychopharmacology and Biological Psychiatry, 12,* 873–885.

Kaprio, J., Koskenvuo, M., Langinvainio, H., Romanov, K., Sarna, S., & Rose, R. J. (1987). Genetic influences on use and abuse of alcohol: A Study of 5638 adult Finnish twin brothers. *Alcoholism: Clinical and Experimental Research, 11,* 349–356.

Kern, J. C. (1985). Management of children of alcoholics. In S. Zinberg, J. Wallace, and S. Blume, eds., *Practical approaches to alcoholism psychotherapy.* New York: Plenum.

Kern, J. C., Hassett, C. A., Collipp, P. J., Bridges, C., Solomon, M., & Condren, R. J. (1981). Children of alcoholics: Locus of control, mental age, and zinc level. *Journal of Psychiatric Treatment and Evaluation, 3,* 169–173.

Keynes, J. M. (1910–1911). Influence of parental alcoholism (correspondence). *Journal of the Royal Statistical Society, 74,* 339–345.

Knight, R. P. (1937). The dynamics and treatment of chronic alcohol addiction. *Bulletin of the Menninger Clinic, 1,* 233–250.

Knop, J., Teasdale, T. W., Schulsinger, F., & Goodwin, D. W. (1985). A prospective study of young men at high risk for alcoholism: School behavior and achievement. *Journal of Studies on Alcohol, 46,* 273–278.

Knowles, E., & Schroeder, D. A. (1989). Familial and personality correlates of alcohol-related problems. *Addictive Behaviors, 14,* 537–543.

Kojic, T., Dojcinova, A., Dojcinova, D., Stojanovic, O., Jakulic, S., Susakovic, N., & Gligorovic, V. (1977). Possible genetic predisposition for alcohol addiction. In M. M. Gross, ed., *Biological aspects of ethanol III A: Alcohol intoxication and withdrawal.* New York: Plenum.

Krestan, J., & Bepko, C. (1988). Alcohol problems and the family life cycle. In B. Carter & M. McGoldrick, eds. (2nd ed.), *The changing family life cycle: A framework for family therapy* (pp. 483–511). New York: Gardner Press.

Kubicka, L., Kozeny, J., & Roth, Z. (1990). Alcohol abuse and its psychosocial correlates in sons of alcoholics as young men and in the general population of young men in Prague. *Journal of Studies on Alcohol, 51,* 49–58.

Kushner, M. (1990). Moderators of the alcohol anxiety relation. Doctoral dissertation. University of Missouri.

Kushner, M., Sher, K. J., & Beitman, B. (1990). The relation between alcohol problems and the anxiety disorders. *American Journal of Psychiatry, 147,* 685–695.

Kwakman, A. M., Zuiker, F. A. J. M., Schippers, G. M., & de Wuffel, F. J. (1988). Drinking behavior, drinking attitudes, and attachment relationship of adolescents. *Journal of Youth and Adolescence, 17,* 247–253.

Lahey, B., Hartdagen, S., Frick, P., McBurnett, K., Connor, R., & Hynd, G. W. (1988). Conduct disorder: Parsing the confounded relation to parental divorce and antisocial personality. *Journal of Abnormal Psychology, 97,* 334–337.

Lander, E. S., & Botstein, D. (1989). Mapping Mendelian factors underlying quantitative traits using RFLP linkage maps. *Genetics, 121,* 185–199.

Lang, A. R., Pelham, W. E., Johnston, C., & Gelertner, S. (1989). Levels of adult alcohol consumption induced by interactions with child confederates exhibiting normal versus externalizing behaviors. *Journal of Abnormal Psychology, 98,* 294–299.

Lawson, D. M., Nathan, P. E., & Lipscomb, T. R. (1980). Guidelines for the administration of alcohol to human subjects in behavioral research. *Journal of Studies on Alcohol, 41,* 871–881.

Lazarus, R. S., & Folkman, S. (1984). *Stress, appraisal and coping.* New York: Springer.

Leerhsen, C., & Namuth, T. (1988). Alcohol and the family. *Newsweek, 111,* January 18, 62–68.

Lester, D., & Carpenter, J. A. (1985). Physiological measures in adolescents and their parentage. *Alcoholism: Clinical and Experimental Research, 9,* 212. Abstract.

Levenson, R. W., Oyama, O. N., & Meek, P. S. (1987). Greater reinforcement from alcohol for those at risk: Parental risk, personality risk, and gender. *Journal of Abnormal Psychology, 96,* 242–253.

Lex, B. W. (1985). Alcohol problems in special populations. In J. Mendelson & N. K. Mello, eds., *The diagnosis and treatment of alcoholism,* 2nd ed. (pp. 89–187). New York: McGraw-Hill.

Lex, B. W., Lukas, S. E., Greenwald, N. E., & Mendelson, H. H. (1988). Alcohol-induced changes in body sway in women at risk for alcoholism: A pilot study. *Journal of Studies on Alcohol, 49,* 346–356.

Li, T.-K., Lumeng, L., McBride, W. J., Waller, M. B. (1981). Indiana selection studies on alcohol-related behaviors. In G. E. McClearn, R. A. Deitrich, & V. G. Erwin, eds., *Development of animal models as pharmacologic tools, NIAAA Research Monograph No. 60.* (pp. 171–191). Rockville, Md.: NIAAA.

Lipscomb, R. R., Carpenter, J. A., & Nathan, P. E. (1979). Static ataxia: A predictor of alcoholism. *British Journal of Addictions, 74,* 289–294.

Loeber, R. (1990). Development and risk factors of juvenile antisocial behavior and delinquency. *Clinical Psychology Review, 10,* 1–41.

Loehlin, J. C. (1972). An analysis of alcohol-related questionnaire items from the national twin merit study. *Annals of the New York Academy of Science, 197,* 117–120.

Logue, M. B., & Sher, K. J. (1990, November). Children of alcoholics and the "Barnum" effect. Presented at the annual convention of the Association for Advancement of Behavior Therapy, San Francisco.

Loney, J. (1980). The Iowa theory of substance abuse among hyperactive adolescents. In D. J. Lettieri, M. Sayers, & H. W. Pearson, eds., *Theories of drug abuse: Selected contemporary perspectives, NIDA Research Monograph 30.* Rockville, Md.: National Institute on Drug Abuse.

Loper, R. G., Kammeier, M. I., & Hoffmann, H. (1973). MMPI characteristics of college freshman males who later became alcoholics. *Journal of Abnormal Psychology, 82,* 159–162.

Lund, C. A., & Landesman-Dwyer, S. (1979). Pre-delinquent and disturbed adolescents. The role of paternal alcoholism. In M. Galanter, ed., *Currents in alcoholism* (vol. 5), *Biomedical issues and clinical effects of alcoholism* (pp. 339–348). New York: Grune & Stratton.

MacAndrew, C. A. (1965). The differentiation of male alcoholic outpatients from nonalcoholic psychiatric outpatients by means of the MMPI. *Quarterly Journal of Studies on Alcohol, 26,* 238–246.

MacDonald, D. I., & Blume, S. B. (1986). Children of alcoholics. *American Journal of Diseases of Children, 140,* 750–754.

MacNicholl, T. A. (1905). A study of the effects of alcohol on school children. *The Quarterly Journal of Inebriety, 27,* 113–117.

Magnusson, D., & Endler, N. (1977). *Personality at the crossroads: Current issues in interactional psychology.* Hillsdale, N.J.: Lawrence Erlbaum and Associates.

Main, M., & Solomon, J. (1986). Discovery of an insecure disorganized/disoriented attachment pattern: Procedures, findings, and implications for the classification of behavior. In M. Yogman & T. B. Brazelton, eds., *Affective development in infancy* (pp. 95–124). Norwood, N.J.: Ablex.

Maisto, S. A., Connors, G. J., & Vuchinich, R. E. (1978). Methodological considerations in alcohol research with human subjects. *Addictive Behaviors, 3,* 243–251.

Major, L. F., Goyer, P. F., & Murphy, D. L. (1981). Changes in platelet monoamine oxidase activity during abstinence. *Journal of Studies on Alcohol, 42,* 1052–1057.

Major, L. F., Hawley, R. J., Saini, N., Garrick, N. A., & Murphy, D. L. (1985). Brain and liver monoamine oxidase type A and type B activity in alcoholics and controls. *Alcoholism: Clinical and Experimental Research, 9,* 6–9.

Major, L. F., & Murphy, D. L. (1978). Platelet and plasma amine oxidase activity in alcoholic individuals. *British Journal of Psychiatry, 132,* 548–554.

Mann, L. M., Chassin, L., & Sher, K. J. (1987). Alcohol expectancies and the risk for alcoholism. *Journal of Consulting and Clinical Psychology, 55,* 411–417.

Mann, R. E., Sobell, L. C., Sobell, M. B., & Pavan, D. (1985). Reliability of a family tree questionnaire for assessing family history of alcohol problems. *Drug and Alcohol Dependence, 15,* 61–67.

Manning, D. T., Balson, P. M., Xenakis, S. (1986). The prevalence of Type A personality in the children of alcoholics. *Alcoholism: Clinical and Experimental Research, 10,* 184–189.

Manning, O., & Manning, B. (1984). Bibliotherapy for children of alcoholics. *Journal of Reading, 27,* 720–725.

Mannuzza, S., Fryer, A. J., Endicott, J., & Klein, D. F. (1985). *Family Informant Schedule and Criteria* (FISC). New York: New York State Psychiatric Institute.

Marcus, A. M. (1986). Academic achievement in elementary school children of alcoholic mothers. *Journal of Clinical Psychology, 42,* 372–376.

Marlatt, G. A. (1987, May). Prevention with high risk drinkers. Paper presented at the third annual Indiana University Conference for Research on Clinical Problems: Psychological Models of Addictions. Nashville, Ind.

Marlatt, G. A., Collins, R. L., Hillman, R. S., Roffman, R., Steele, C., & Summers, D. (1981). Proposed guidelines for experiments involving the administration of alcohol to human subjects. *Alcoholism and Drug Abuse Institute Technical Report.* Seattle, Wash.: Alcohol and Drug Abuse Institute, University of Washington.

Marlatt, G. A., & Gordon, J., eds. (1985). *Relapse prevention: Maintenance strategies in the treatment of addictive behaviors.* New York: Guilford.

Marlatt, G. A., & Rohsenow, D. J. (1980). Cognitive process in alcohol use: Expectancy and the balanced placebo design. In N. K. Mello, ed., *Advances in substance abuse: Behavioral and biological research* (Vol. 1, pp. 159–199). Greenwich, Conn.: JAI Press.

Martin, N. G., & Boomsma, D. (1989). Willingness to drive when drunk and personality: A twin study. *Behavior Genetics, 19,* 97–111.

McClearn, G. E., & Kakihana, R. (1981). Selective breeding for ethanol sensitivity: Short-sleep vs. long-sleep mice. In G. E. McClearn, R. A. Deitrich, & V. G. Erwin, eds., *Development of animal models as pharmacologic tools, NIAAA Research Monograph No. 60.* (pp. 147–159). Rockville, Md.: NIAAA.

McCord, J. (1981). Alcoholism and criminality: Confounding and differentiating factors. *Journal of Studies on Alcohol, 42,* 739–748.

McCord, J. (1988). Identifying developmental paradigms leading to alcoholism. *Journal of Studies on Alcoholism, 49,* 357–362.

McCord, W., & McCord, J. (1962). A longitudinal study of the personality of alcoholics. In D. J. Pittman, & C. R. Snyder, eds., *Society, culture, and drinking patterns* (pp. 413–430). New York: Wiley.

McCrae, R. R., & Costa, P. T., Jr. (1985). Updating Norman's ''adequate taxonomy'': Intelligence and personality dimensions in natural language and in questionnaires. *Journal of Personality and Social Psychology, 49,* 710–721.

McDougall, W. (1929). The chemical theory of temperament applied to introversion and extraversion. *Journal of Abnormal and Social Psychology, 24,* 293–309.

McGue, M., & Gottesman, I. I. (1989). Genetic linkage in schizophrenia: Perspectives from genetic epidemiology. *Schizophrenia Bulletin, 15,* 453–464.

McKearn, J. (1988). Post-traumatic stress disorder: Implications for the treatment of family members of alcoholics. *Alcoholism Treatment Quarterly, 5*, 141–144.

McLoyd, V. C. (1989). Socialization and development in a changing economy. *American Psychologist, 44, 2*, 293–302.

McNeil, T. F., & Kaij, L. (1979). Etiological relevance of comparisons of high-risk and low-risk groups. *Acta Psychiatrica Scandinavica, 59*, 545–560.

Mednick, S. A., & McNeill, T. F. (1968). Current methodology in research on the etiology of schizophrenia: Serious difficulties which suggest the use of the high-risk group method. *Psychological Bulletin, 70*, 681–693.

Meehl, P. E. (1956). Wanted—a good cookbook. *American Psychologist, 11*, 263–272.

Meller, W. H., Rinehart, R., Cadoret, R. J., & Troughton, E. (1988). Specific familial transmission in substance abuse. *International Journal of the Addictions, 23*, 1029–1039.

Mendelson, J. H., Babor, T. F., Mello, N. K., & Pratt, H. (1986). Alcoholism and prevalence of medical and psychiatric disorders. *Journal of Studies on Alcohol, 47*, 361–366.

Merikangas, K. R., Leckman, J. F., Prusoff, B. A., Pauls, D. L., & Weisman, M. M. (1985). Familial transmission of depression and alcoholism. *Archives of General Psychiatry, 42*, 367–372.

Mershon, B., & Gorsuch, R. L. (1988). Number of factors in the personality sphere: Does increase in factors increase predictability of real-life criteria? *Journal of Personality and Social Psychology, 55*, 675–680.

Miller, D., & Jang, M. (1977). Children of alcoholics: A 20-year longitudinal study. *Social Work Research and Abstracts, 13*, 23–29.

Miller, W. R. (1987). Adult cousins of alcoholics. *Psychology of Addictive Behaviors, 1*, 74–76.

Mischel, W. (1968). *Personality and assessment.* New York: Wiley.

Molina, B., Chassin, L., Sher, K., Crews, T., & Hepworth, J. (1990). A comparison of three measurement models of personality risk for adolescent substance use. Manuscript. Arizona State University.

Monroe, S. M., & Steiner, S. C. (1986). Social support and psychopathology: Interrelations with preexisting disorder, stress, and personality. *Journal of Abnormal Psychology, 95*, 29–39.

Monteiro, M. G., Schuckit, M. A., Hauger, R., Irwin, M., & Duthie, L. A. (1990). Growth hormone response to intravenous diazepam and placebo in 82 healthy men. *Biological Psychiatry, 27*, 702–710.

Monteiro, M. G., Schuckit, M. A., & Irwin, M. (1990). Subjective feelings of anxiety in young men after ethanol and diazepam infusions. *Journal of Clinical Psychology, 51*, 12–16.

Moos, R. H., & Billings, A. G. (1982). Children of alcoholics during the recovery process: Alcoholic and matched control families. *Addictive Behaviors, 7*, 155–164.

Moos, R. H., & Moos, B. S. (1984). The process of recovery from alcoholism: III. Comparing functioning in families of alcoholics and matched control families. *Journal of Studies on Alcohol, 45*, 111–118.

Morehouse, E. R. (1981). Working with children of alcoholic parents in an outpatient alcoholism treatment facility and in the schools. In *National Institute on Alcohol Abuse and Alcoholism Research Monograph 4: Services for children of alcoholics* (pp. 138–151). Rockville, Md.: National Institute on Alcohol Abuse and Alcoholism.

Morey, L. C., & Blashfield, R. K. (1981). Empirical classifications of alcoholism: A review. *Journal of Studies on Alcohol, 42,* 925–937.

Morey, L. C., Skinner, H. A., & Blashfield, R. K. (1984). A typology of alcohol abusers: Correlates and implications. *Journal of Abnormal Psychology, 93,* 408–417.

Morrison, C., & Schuckit, M. A. (1983). Locus of control in young men with alcoholic relatives and controls. *Journal of Clinical Psychiatry, 44,* 306–307.

Moss, H. B., Guthrie, S., & Linnoila, M. (1986). Enhanced thyrotropin response to thyrotropin releasing hormone in boys at risk for development of alcoholism. *Archives of General Psychiatry, 43,* 1137–1142.

Moss, H. B., Yao, J. K., & Maddock, J. M. (1989). Responses by sons of alcoholic fathers to alcoholic and placebo drinks: Perceived mood, intoxication, and plasma prolactin. *Alcoholism: Clinical and Experimental Research, 13,* 252–257.

Mukherjee, A. B., Svoronos, S., Ghazanfari, A., Martin, P. R., Fisher, A., Roecklein, B., Rodbard, D., Staton, R., Behar, D., Berg, C. J., & Manjunath, M. (1987). Transketolase abnormality in cultured fibroblasts from familial chronic alcoholic men and their male offspring. *The Journal of Clinical Investigation, 79,* 1039–1043.

Munjack, K. J., & Moss, H. B. (1981). Affective disorder and alcoholism in families of agoraphobics. *Archives of General Psychiatry, 38,* 869–871.

Murphy, D. L., Belamker, R. H., Buchsbaum, M., Marin, N. F., Ciarnello, R., & Wyatt, R. J. (1977). Biogenic amine related enzymes and personality variations in normals. *Psychological Medicine, 7,* 149–157.

Murphy, J. M., McBride, W. J., Lumeng, L., & Li, T.-K. (1982). Regional brain levels of monoamines in alcohol-preferring and -nonpreferring lines of rats. *Pharmacology, Biochemistry, and Behavior, 16,* 145–149.

Murphy, J. M., McBride, W. J., Lumeng, L., & Li, T.-K. (1987). Contents of monoamines in forebrain regions of alcohol-preferring (P) and -nonpreferring (NP) lines of rats. *Pharmacology, Biochemistry, and Behavior, 26,* 389–392.

Murphy, J. M., McBride, W. J., Lumeng, L., & Li, T.-K. (1988). Effects of serotonin and dopamine agents on ethanol intake of alcohol-preferring P rats. *Alcoholism: Clinical and Experimental Research, 12,* 306. (Abstract.)

Murphy, J. M., Waller, M. B., Gatto, G. J., McBride, W. J., Lumeng, L., & Li, T.-K. (1985). Monoamine uptake inhibitors attenuate ethanol intake in alcohol-preferring (P) rats. *Alcohol, 2,* 340–352.

Murray, R. M., Clifford, C. A., & Gurling, H. M. (1983). Twin and adoption studies: How good is the evidence for a genetic role? In M. Galanter, ed., *Recent developments in alcoholism* (Vol. 1, pp. 25–48). New York: Plenum Press.

Murray, R. M., & Gurling, H. M. (1980). Genetic contributions to normal and abnormal drinking. In M. Sandler, ed., *Psychopharmacology of Alcohol* (pp. 89–105). New York: Raven Press.

Nagoshi, C. T., & Wilson, J. R. (1987). Influence of family alcoholism history on alcohol metabolism, sensitivity, and tolerance. *Alcoholism: Clinical and Experimental Research, 11,* 392–398.

Nagoshi, C. T., & Wilson, J. R. (1988). One-month repeatability of emotional responses to alcohol. *Alcoholism: Clinical and Experimental Research, 12,* 691–697.

Nagoshi, C. T., & Wilson, J. R. (1989). Long-term repeatability of human alcohol metabolism, sensitivity and acute tolerance. *Journal of Studies on Alcohol, 50,* 162–169.

Nardi, P. M. (1981). Children of alcoholics: A role-theoretical perspective. *Journal of Social Psychology, 115,* 237–245.

Nathan, P. (1988). The addictive personality is the behavior of the addict. *Journal of Consulting and Clinical Psychology, 56,* 183–188.

National Advisory Council on Alcohol Abuse and Alcoholism (1989). *Recommended council guidelines on ethyl alcohol administration in human experimentation.* Rockville, Md.: National Institute on Alcohol Abuse and Alcoholism.

National Council on Alcoholism (1972). Criteria for the diagnosis of alcoholism. *American Journal of Psychiatry, 129,* 127–135.

National Institute on Alcohol Abuse and Alcoholism (1985). *Alcoholism: An inherited disease.* Rockville, Md.: NIAAA.

Neale, M. C., & Martin, N. G. (1989). The effects of age, sex, and genotype on self-report drunkenness following a challenge dose of alcohol. *Behavior Genetics, 19,* 63–78.

Neville, H. J., & Schmidt, A. L. (1985). Event-related brain potentials in subjects at risk for alcoholism. In N. C. Chang, & H. M. Chao, eds., *Early identification of alcohol abuse: NIAAA research monograph no. 17* (pp. 228–239). Rockville, Md.: NIAAA.

Newlin, D. B. (1985). Offspring of alcoholics have enhanced antagonistic placebo response. *Journal of Studies on Alcohol, 46,* 490–494.

Newlin, D. B., & Aldrich, K. (1986). Reverse tolerance to alcohol in sons of alcoholics. *Alcoholism: Clinical and Experimental Research, 10,* 98. Abstract.

Newlin, D. B., & Thomson, J. B. (1990). Alcohol challenge with sons of alcoholics: A critical review and analysis. *Psychological Bulletin, 108,* 383–402.

Nixon, P. F. (1984). Is there a genetic component to the pathogenesis of the Wernicke-Korsakoff syndrome? *Alcohol and Alcoholism, 19,* 219–221.

Noller, P., Law, H., & Comrey, A. L. (1987). Cattell, Comrey, and Eysenck Personality factors compared: More evidence for the five robust factors? *Journal of Personality and Social Psychology, 53,* 775–782.

Noyes, R., Jr., Clancy, J., Crowe, R., Hoenk, P. R., & Slymen, D. J. (1978). The familial prevalence of anxiety neurosis. *Archives of General Psychiatry, 37,* 173–178.

Noyes, R., Jr., Crowe, R. R., Harris, E. L., Hamra, B. J., McChesney, C. M., & Chaudhry, D. R. (1986). Relationship between panic disorder and agoraphobia: A family study. *Archives of General Psychiatry, 43,* 227–232.

Nylander, I., & Rydelius, P.-A. (1982). A comparison between children of alcoholic fathers from excellent versus poor social conditions. *Acta Paediatrica Scandinavica, 71,* 809–813.

O'Connor, M. J., Sigman, M., & Brill, N. (1987). Disorganization of attachment in relation to maternal alcohol consumption. *Journal of Consulting and Clinical Psychology, 55,* 831–836.

O'Connor, S., Hesselbrock, V., & Tasman, A. (1986). Correlates of increased risk for alcoholism in young men. *Progress in Neuro-Psychopharmacology & Biological Psychiatry, 10,* 211–218.

O'Connor, S., Hesselbrock, V., Tasman, A., & DePalma, N. (1987). P3 amplitudes in two distinct tasks are decreased in young men with a history of paternal alcoholism. *Alcohol, 4,* 323–330.

O'Farrell, T. J., & Birchler, G. R. (1985, August). Marital relationships of alcoholic, conflicted, and nonconflicted couples. Paper presented at the American Psychological Association, Los Angeles.

O'Malley, S. S., Carey, K., & Maisto, S. A. (1986). Validity of young adults' reports of parental drinking practices. *Journal of Studies on Alcohol, 47,* 433–435.

O'Malley, S. S., & Maisto, S. A. (1985). Effects of family drinking history and expectancies on responses to alcohol in men. *Journal of Studies on Alcohol, 46,* 289–297.

Offord, D., Allen, N., & Abrams, N. (1978). Parental psychiatric illness. *Journal of the American Academy of Child Psychiatry, 17,* 224–238.

Orme, T., & Rimmer, J. (1981). Alcoholism and child abuse: A review. *Journal of Studies on Alcohol, 42,* 273–287.

Pandina, R. J., & Johnson, V. (1989). Familial drinking history as a predictor of alcohol and drug consumption among adolescent children. *Journal of Studies on Alcohol, 50,* 245–253.

Paolino, T., McCrady, B., Diamond, S., & Longabaugh, R. (1976). Psychological disturbances in spouses of alcoholics: An empirical study. *Journal of Studies on Alcohol, 37,* 1600–1608.

Pardeck, J. T., & Pardeck, J. A. (1987). Using bibliotherapy to help children cope with the changing family. *Social Work in Education, 9,* 107–116.

Parker, D. A., & Harford, T. C. (1987). Alcohol-related problems of children of heavy-drinking parents. *Journal of Studies on Alcohol, 48,* 265–268.

Partanen, J., Bruun, K., & Markkanen, T. (1966). *Inheritance of drinking behavior.* Helsinki: Finnish Foundation for Alcohol Studies.

Partington, J. T., & Johnson, F. G. (1969). Personality types among alcoholics. *Quarterly Journal of Studies on Alcohol, 30,* 21–34.

Patterson, B. W., Williams, H. L., McLean, G. A., Smith, L. T., & Schaeffer, K. W. (1987). Alcoholism and family history of alcoholism: Effects on visual and auditory event-related potentials. *Alcohol, 4,* 265–274.

Patterson, G. (1982). *Coercive family process.* Eugene, Ore.: Castalia Publishing.

Patterson, G., DeBaryshe, B. D., & Ramsey, E. (1989). A developmental perspective on antisocial behavior. *American Psychologist, 44,* 329–335.

Pearlin, L. I., & Schooler, C. (1978). The structure of coping. *Journal of Health and Social Behavior, 22,* 337–356.

Pederson, N. L. (1980). Genetic and environmental factors for usage of common drugs. Doctoral dissertation, University of Colorado, Denver.

Pedhazur, E. J. (1982). *Multiple regression in behavioral research.* New York: CBS College Publishing.

Peele, S. (1986). The implications and limitations of genetic models of alcoholism and other addictions. *Journal of Studies on Alcohol, 47,* 63–73.

Penick, E., Powell, B. J., Liskow, B. I., Jackson, J., & Nickel, E. J. (1988). The stability of coexisting psychiatric syndromes in alcoholic men after one year. *Journal of Studies on Alcohol, 49,* 395–405.

Penick, E., Read, M. R., Crowley, P. A., & Powell, B. J. (1978). Differentiation of alcoholics by family history. *Journal of Studies on Alcohol, 39,* 1944–1948.

Perris, C., Jacobson, L., von Knorring, L., Oreland, L., Perris, H., & Ross, S. B. (1980). Enzymes related to biogenic amine metabolism and personality characteristics in depressed patients. *Acta Psychiatrica Scandinavica, 61,* 477–484.

Perry, A. (1973). The effect of heredity on attitudes toward alcohol, cigarettes and coffee. *Journal of Applied Psychology, 58,* 275–277.

Petrie, A. (1967). *Individuality in pain and suffering,* Chicago: University of Chicago Press.

Pickens, R. W., & Svikis, D. S. (1988). The twin method in the study of vulnerability to drug abuse. In R. W. Pickens & D. S. Svikis, eds., *Biological vulnerability to drug abuse, NIDA Research Monograph 89.* Rockville, Md.: National Institute on Drug Abuse.

Pihl, R. O. (1990, May). A biobehavioral model for the inherited predisposition to alcoholism. Paper presented at the Eleventh Annual Meeting of the Society of Behavioral Medicine. Chicago.

Pihl, R. O., Peterson, J., & Finn, P. (1990a). An heuristic model for the inherited predisposition to alcoholism. *Psychology of Addictive Behavior, 4,* 12–25.

Pihl, R. O., Peterson, J., & Finn, P. (1990b). The inherited predisposition to alcoholism: Characteristics of sons of male alcoholics. *Journal of Abnormal Psychology.*

Pittman, W. (1985). The Al-Anon family group story: A legacy of love. *Alcoholism and Addiction, 6,* 49–52.

Pliner, P., & Cappell, H. (1974). Modification of affective consequences of alcohol: A comparison of solitary and social drinking. *Journal of Abnormal Psychology, 83,* 418–425.

Plomin, R., Defries, J. C., Loehlin J. C. (1977). Genotype-environment interaction and correlation in the analysis of human behavior. *Psychology Bulletin, 84,* 309–322.

Polich, J., & Bloom, F. E. (1988). Event-related brain potentials in individuals at high and low risk for developing alcoholism: Failure to replicate. *Alcoholism: Clinical and Experimental Research, 12,* 368–373.

Polich, J., Burns, T., & Bloom, F. E. (1988). P300 and the risk for alcoholism: Family history, task difficulty, and gender. *Alcoholism: Clinical and Experimental Research, 12,* 248–254.

Polich, J., Haier, R. J., Buchsbaum, M., & Bloom, F. E. (1988). Assessment of young men at risk for alcoholism with P300 from a visual discrimination task. *Journal of Studies on Alcohol, 49,* 186–190.

Pollock, V. E., Gabrielli, W., Mednick, S., & Goodwin, D. (1988b). EEG identification of subgroups of men at risk for alcoholism? *Psychiatry Research, 26,* 101–114.

Pollock, V. E., Schneider, L. S., Gabrielli, W. F., & Goodwin, D. W. (1987). Sex of parent and offspring in the transmission of alcoholism: A meta-analysis. *Journal of Nervous and Mental Disease, 173*, 668–673.

Pollock, V. E., Teasdale, T. W., Gabrielli, W. F., & Knop, J. (1986). Subjective and objective measures of response to alcohol among young men at risk for alcoholism. *Journal of Studies on Alcohol, 47*, 297–304.

Pollock, V. E., Volavka, J., Gabrielli, W. F., Mednick, S. A., Knop, J., & Goodwin, D. W. (1988a). Pattern reversal visual evoked potentials among men at risk for alcoholism. *Acta Psychiatrica Scandinavica, 78*, 276–282.

Pollock, V. E., Volavka, J., Goodwin, D. W., Gabrielli, W. F., Mednick, S. A., Knop, J., & Schulsinger, F. (1988c). Pattern reversal visual evoked potentials after alcohol administration among men at risk for alcoholism. *Psychiatry Research, 26*, 191–202.

Pollock, V. E., Volavka, J., Goodwin, D. W., Mednick, S. A., Gabrielli, W. F., Knop, J., & Schulsinger, F. (1983). The EEG after alcohol administration in men at risk for alcoholism. *Archives of General Psychiatry, 40*, 857–861.

Pollock, V. E., Volavka, J., Mednick, S. A. Goodwin, D. W., Knop, J., & Schulsinger. (1984). A prospective study of alcoholism: Electroencephalographic findings. In D. W. Goodwin, K. T. Van Dusen, & S. A. Mednick, eds., *Longitudinal research in alcoholism* (pp. 125–145). Hingham, Mass.: Kluwer-Nijhoff Publishing.

Powell, B. J., Penick, E., & Othmer, E. (1982). Prevalence of additional psychiatric syndromes among male alcoholics. *Journal of Clinical Psychiatry, 43*, 404–407.

Powers, S. I., Hauser, S. T., & Kilner, L. A. (1989). Adolescent mental health. *American Psychologist, 44, 2*, 200–208.

Prewett, M., Spence, R., & Chaknis, M. (1981). Attribution of causality by children with alcoholic parents. *International Journal of the Addictions, 16*, 367–370.

Pritchard, W. S. (1986). Cognitive event-related potential correlates of schizophrenia. *Psychological Bulletin, 100*, 43–66.

Puchall, L. B., Coursey, R. D., Buchsbaum, M. S., & Murphy, D. L. (1980). Parents of high-risk subjects defined by levels of monoamine oxidase activity. *Schizophrenia Bulletin, 6*, 338–346.

Raine, A., & Venables, P. H. (1987). Contingent negative variation, P3, evoked potentials, and antisocial behavior. *Psychophysiology, 24*, 191–199.

Raine, A., & Venables, P. H. (1988). Enhanced P3 evoked potentials and longer P3 recovery times in psychopaths. *Psychophysiology, 25*, 30–38.

Rearden, J. J., & Markwell, B. S. (1989). Self concept and drinking problems of college students raised in alcohol abused homes. *Addictive Behaviors, 14*, 225–227.

Regier, D. A., Myers, J. K., Kramer, M., Robins, L. N., Blazer, D. G., Hough, R. L., Eaton, W. W., & Locke, B. Z. (1984). The NIMH Epidemiological Catchment Area program. *Archives of General Psychiatry, 41*, 934–941.

Reich, T., Cloninger, C. R., Van Eerdewegh, P., Rice, J. P., & Mullaney, J. (1988). Secular trends in the familial transmission of alcoholism. *Alcoholism: Clinical and Experimental Research, 12*, 458–464.

Revelle, W., Humphreys, M. S., Simon, L., & Gilliland, K. (1980). The interactive effect of personality, time of day, and caffeine: A test of the arousal model. *Journal of Experimental Psychology: General, 109*, 1–31.

Rhodes, J. (1984). Differences in character roles between adolescents from alcoholic and nonalcoholic families. Doctoral dissertation. Arizona State University.

Richards, T. M. (1980). Splitting as a defense mechanism in children of alcoholic parents. In M. Galanter, ed., *Currents in Alcoholism: Recent Advances in Research and Treatment, 1,* 239–245.

Rieder, R. O., & Kaufmann, C. A. (1988). Genetics. In J. A. Talbott, R. E. Hales, & S. C. Yudofsky, eds., *Textbook of psychiatry* (pp. 33–65). Washington, D.C.: American Psychiatric Association Press.

Rimmer, J., Reich, T., & Winokur, G. (1972). Alcoholism V: Diagnosis and clinical variation among alcoholics. *Quarterly Journal of Studies on Alcohol, 33,* 658–666.

Roberts, S. (1990). A marker gene for alcoholism? *The Journal of NIH Research, 2* (5), 24–25.

Robins, L., Bates, W., & O'Neal, P. (1962). Adult drinking patterns of former problem children. In D. Pittman, & C. R. Snyder, eds., *Society, culture, and drinking patterns,* (pp. 395–412). New York: Wiley.

Robins, L. N., West, P. A., Ratcliff, K. S., & Herjanic, B. M. (1979). Father's alcoholism and children's outcomes. In F. A. Seixas, ed., *Currents in alcoholism.* Vol. 4: *Psychiatric, psychological, social, and epidemiological studies* (pp. 313–327). New York: Grune & Stratton.

Robins, L. N., Helzer, J. E., Weissman, M. M., Orvaschel, H., Gruenberg, E., Burke, J. D., Jr., & Regier, D. A. (1984). Lifetime prevalence of specific psychiatric disorders in three sites. *Archives of General Psychiatry, 41,* 949–958.

Robins, L. N., Murphy, G. E., & Breckenridge, M. B. (1968). Drinking behavior of young urban negro men. *Quarterly Journal of Studies on Alcohol, 29,* 657–684.

Robinson, B. E. (1989). *Working with children of alcoholics: The practitioner's handbook.* Lexington, Mass.: Lexington Books.

Roe, A. (1945). The adult adjustment of children of alcoholic parents raised in foster homes. *Quarterly Journal of Studies on Alcohol, 5,* 378–393.

Rogosch, F., Chassin, L., & Sher, K. J. (1990). Personality variables as mediators and moderators of family history risk for alcoholism: Conceptual and methodological issues. *Journal of Studies on Alcohol, 51,* 310–318.

Rohsenow, D. J., & Marlatt, G. A. (1981). The balanced placebo design: Methodological considerations. *Addictive Behaviors, 6,* 107–122.

Roosa, M. W., Gensheimer, L. K., Short, J., Ayers, T. S., & Shell, R. (1989). A preventive intervention for children in alcoholic families: Results of a pilot study. *Family Relations, 38,* 295–300.

Roosa, M. W., Gensheimer, L. K., Short, J., Ayers, T. S., & Short, J. L. (1990). Development of a school-based prevention program for children in alcoholic families. *Journal of Primary Prevention, 11,* 119–141.

Roosa, M. W., Sandler, I. N., Beals, J., & Short, J. L. (1988). Risk status of adolescent children of problem drinking parents. *American Journal of Community Psychology, 16,* 225–239.

Roosa, M. W., Sandler, I. N., Gehring, M., Beals, J., & Cappo, L. (1988). The Children of Alcoholics Life Events Schedule: A stress scale for children of alcohol-abusing parents. *Journal of Studies on Alcohol, 49,* 422–429.

Ross, H. E., Glaser, F. B., & Germanson, T. (1988). The prevalence of psychiatric disorders in patients with alcohol and other drug problems. *Archives of General Psychiatry, 45,* 1023–1031.

Rowe, D., & Plomin, R. (1977). Temperament in early childhood. *Journal of Personality Assessment, 41,* 150–156.

Russell, M., Cooper, M. L., & Frone, M. R. (1990). The influence of sociodemographic characteristics on familial alcohol problems: Data from a community sample. *Alcoholism: Clinical and Experimental Research, 14,* 221–226.

Russell, M., Henderson, C., & Blume, S. (1985). *Children of alcoholics: A review of the literature.* New York: Children of Alcoholics Foundation.

Rutter, M. (1987). Psychosocial resilience and protective mechanisms. *American Journal of Orthopsychiatry, 57,* 316–331.

Rutter, M., & Quinton, D. (1984). Parental psychiatric disorder: Effects on children. *Psychological Medicine, 14,* 853–880.

Rydelius, P.-A. (1981). Children of alcoholic fathers: Their social adjustment and their health status over 20 years. *Acta Paediatrica Scandinavica, 286,* 1–89.

Sameroff, A., & Chandler, M. (1974). Reproductive risk and the continuum of caretaking casualty. F. D. Horowitz, M. Hetherington, S. Scarr-Salapatek, & G. Siegel, eds., *Review of child development research* (vol. 4) (pp. 187–244). Chicago: University of Chicago Press.

Saunders, G. R., & Schuckit, M. A. (1981). MMPI scores in young men with alcoholic relatives and controls. *Journal of Nervous and Mental Disease, 169,* 456–458.

Saunders, L. B., & Williams, R. (1983). The genetics of alcoholism: Is there an inherited susceptibility to alcohol-related problems? *Alcohol and Alcoholism, 18,* 189–217.

Savoie, T. M., Emory, E. K., & Moody-Thomas, S. (1988). Acute alcohol intoxication in socially drinking female and male offspring of alcoholic fathers. *Journal of Studies on Alcohol, 49,* 430–435.

Schaeffer, K., Parsons, O., & Yohman, J. (1984). Neuropsychological differences between male familial and nonfamilial alcoholics and nonalcoholics. *Alcoholism: Clinical and Experimental Research, 8,* 347–351.

Schandler, S. L., Brannock, J. C., Cohen, M. J., Antick, J., & Caine, K. (1988). Visuospatial learning in elementary school children with and without a family history of alcoholism. *Journal of Studies on Alcohol, 49,* 538–545.

Schmidt, A. L., & Neville, H. J. (1985). Language processing in men at risk for alcoholism: An event-related potential study. *Alcohol, 2,* 529–533.

Schooler, C., Zahn, T. P., Murphy, D. L., & Buchsbaum, M. S. (1978). Psychological correlates of monoamine oxidase in normals. *Journal of Nervous and Mental Disease, 166,* 177–186.

Schuckit, M. A. (1973). Alcoholism and sociopathy: Diagnostic confusion. *Quarterly Journal of Studies on Alcoholism, 34,* 157–164.

Schuckit, M. A. (1980a). Self-ratings of alcohol intoxication by young men with and without family histories of alcoholism. *Journal of Studies on Alcohol, 41,* 242–249.

Schuckit, M. A. (1980b). Alcoholism and genetics: Possible biological mediators. *Biological Psychiatry, 15,* 437–447.

Schuckit, M. A. (1981). Peak blood-alcohol levels in men at high-risk for the future development of alcoholism. *Alcoholism: Clinical and Experimental Research, 5,* 64–66.

Schuckit, M. A. (1982a). A study of young men with alcoholic close relatives. *American Journal of Psychiatry, 139,* 791–794.

Schuckit, M. A. (1982b). Anxiety and assertiveness in sons of alcoholics and controls. *Journal of Clinical Psychiatry, 43,* 238–239.

Schuckit, M. A. (1983). Extroversion and neuroticism in young men at higher or lower risk for alcoholism. *American Journal of Psychiatry, 140,* 1223–1224.

Schuckit, M. A. (1984a). Subjective responses to alcohol in sons of alcoholics and control subjects. *Archives of General Psychiatry, 41,* 879–884.

Schuckit, M. A. (1984b). Differences in plasma cortisol after ingestion of ethanol in relatives of alcoholics and controls: Preliminary results. *Journal of Clinical Psychiatry, 45,* 324–376.

Schuckit, M. A. (1985a). Genetics and the risk for alcoholism. *Journal of the American Medical Association, 253,* 2614–2617.

Schuckit, M. A. (1985b). Ethanol-induced changes in body sway in men of high alcoholism risk. *Archives of General Psychology, 42,* 375–379.

Schuckit, M. A. (1987). Biological vulnerability to alcoholism. *Journal of Consulting and Clinical Psychology, 55,* 301–309.

Schuckit, M. A., Butters, N., Lyn, L., & Irwin, M. (1987a). Neuropsychologic deficits and the risk for alcoholism. *Neuropsychopharmacology, 1,* 50–53.

Schuckit, M. A., & Chiles, J. (1978). Family history as a diagnostic aid in two samples of adolescents. *Journal of Nervous and Mental Disease, 166,* 165–176.

Schuckit, M. A., & Duby, J. (1982). Alcohol-related flushing and the risk for alcoholism in sons of alcoholics. *Journal of Clinical Psychiatry, 43,* 415–418.

Schuckit, M. A., Engstrom, D., Alpert, R., & Duby, J. (1981). Differences in muscle-tension response to ethanol in young men with and without family histories of alcoholism. *Journal of Studies on Alcohol, 42,* 918–924.

Schuckit, M. A., & Gold, E. O. (1988). A simultaneous evaluation of multiple markers of ethanol/placebo challenges in sons of alcoholics and controls. *Archives of General Psychiatry, 45,* 211–216.

Schuckit, M. A., & Gold, E. O., Croot, F., Finn, P., & Polich, J. (1988a). P300 latency after ethanol ingestion in sons of alcoholics and in controls. *Biological Psychiatry, 24,* 310–315.

Schuckit, M. A., Gold, E., & Risch, C. (1987a). Serum prolactin levels in sons of alcoholics and control subjects. *American Journal of Psychiatry, 144,* 854–859.

Schuckit, M. A., Gold, E., & Risch, C. (1987b). Plasma cortisol levels following ethanol in sons of alcoholics and controls. *Archives of General Psychiatry, 44,* 942–945.

Schuckit, M. A., Goodwin, D. A., & Winokur, G. (1972). A study of alcoholism in half siblings. *American Journal of Psychiatry, 128,* 1132–1136.

Schuckit, M. A., Irwin, M., & Mahler, H. I. M. (1990). Tridimensional Personality Questionnaire scores of sons of alcoholic and nonalcoholic fathers. *American Journal of Psychiatry, 147,* 481–487.

Schuckit, M. A., Li, T. K., Cloninger, C. R., & Deitrich, R. A. (1985). University of California, Davis, conference: Genetics of alcoholism. *Alcoholism: Clinical and Experimental Research, 9*, 475–492.

Schuckit, M. A., O'Connor, D. T., Duby, J., Vega, R., & Moss, M. (1981). Dopamine-beta-hydroxylase activity levels in men at high risk for alcoholism and controls. *Biological Psychiatry, 16*, 1067–1075.

Schuckit, M. A., Parker, D. C., Rossman, L. R. (1983). Ethanol-related prolactin responses and risk for alcoholism. *Biological Psychiatry, 18*, 1153–1159.

Schuckit, M. A., & Penn, N. E. (1985). Performance on the Rod and Frame for men at elevated risk for alcoholism and controls. *American Journal of Drug and Alcohol Abuse, 3*, 113–118.

Schuckit, M. A., & Rayses, V. (1979). Ethanol ingestion: Differences in blood acetaldehyde concentrations in relatives of alcoholics and controls. *Science, 203*, 54–55.

Schuckit, M. A., Rimmer, J., Reich, T., & Winokur, G. (1970). Alcoholism: Antisocial traits in male alcoholics. *British Journal of Psychiatry, 117*, 575–576.

Schuckit, M. A., Risch, S. C., & Gold, E. O. (1988b). Alcohol consumption, ACTH level, and family history of alcoholism. *American Journal of Psychiatry, 145*, 1391–1395.

Schuckit, M. A., Shaskan, E., Duby, J., Vega, R., & Moss, M. (1982). Platelet monoamine activity in relatives of alcoholics. *Archives of General Psychiatry, 39*, 137–140.

Schuckit, M. A., & Sweeney, S. (1987). Substance use and mental health problems among sons of alcoholics and controls. *Journal of Studies on Alcohol, 48*, 528–534.

Schulsinger, F., Knop, J., Goodwin, D. W., Teasdale, T. W., & Mikkelson, U. (1986). A prospective study of young men at high risk for alcoholism. *Archives of General Psychiatry, 43*, 755–760.

Scott, E. M. (1970). *Struggles in an alcoholic family.* Springfield, Ill.: Charles C. Thomas.

Searles, J. S. (1988). The role of genetics in the pathogenesis of alcoholism. *Journal of Abnormal Psychology, 97*, 153–167.

Seilhamer, R. A., & Jacob, T. (1990). Family factors and adjustment of children of alcoholics. In M. Windle & J. S. Searles, eds., *Children of alcoholics: Critical perspectives* (pp. 168–186). New York: Guilford.

Seixas, J. S., & Youcha, G. (1985). *Children of alcoholism; A survivor's manual.* New York: Harper & Row.

Selzer, M. (1971). The Michigan Alcoholism Screening Test: the quest for a new diagnostic instrument. *American Journal of Psychology, 172*, 1653–1658.

Selzer, M., Vinokur, A., and van Rooijen, L. (1975). A self-administered Short Michigan Alcoholism Screening Test (SMAST). *Journal of Studies on Alcohol, 36*, 117–126.

Sher, K. J. (1983). Platelet monoamine oxidase activity in relatives of alcoholics. *Archives of General Psychiatry, 40*, 466.

Sher, K. J. (1985a). Excluding problem drinkers in high-risk studies of alcoholism: Effect of screening criteria on high-risk vs. low-risk comparisons. *Journal of Abnormal Psychology, 94*, 106–109.

Sher, K. J. (1985b). Subjective effects of alcohol: The influence of setting and individual differences in alcohol expectancies. *Journal of Studies on Alcohol, 46,* 137–146.

Sher, K. J. (1986). [Personality test for alcoholism and MAO activity in a college student sample.] Unpublished raw data.

Sher, K. J. (1987). Stress response dampening. In H. T. Blane & K. E. Leonard, eds., *Psychological theories of drinking and alcoholism* (pp. 227–271). New York: Guilford Press.

Sher, K. J., Bylund, D. B., Hartmann, J., Walitzer, K. S., & Ray-Prenger, C. (1987). *MAO activity, personality, substance use, and family history of alcoholism.* Unpublished manuscript.

Sher, K. J., & Descutner, C. (1986) Reports of paternal alcoholism: Reliability across siblings. *Addictive Behaviors, 11,* 25–30.

Sher, K. J., & Levenson, R. W. (1982). Risk for alcoholism and individual differences in the stress-response-dampening effect of alcohol. *Journal of Abnormal Psychology, 91,* 350–368.

Sher, K. J., & Walitzer, K. S. (1986). Individual differences in the stress-response-dampening effect of alcohol. *Journal of Abnormal Psychology, 95,* 159–167.

Sher, K. J., & Walitzer, K. S. (1989, November). Children of alcoholics and the search for mediators of risk. Paper presented at the annual convention of the Association for Advancement of Behavior Therapy. Washington, D.C.

Sher, K. J., Walitzer, K. S., Wood, P., & Brent, E. E. (in press). Characteristics of children of alcoholics: Putative risk factors, substance use and abuse, and psychopathology. *Journal of Abnormal Psychology.*

Sher, K. J., Walitzer, K. S., Bylund, D. B., & Hartmann, J. (1989). Alcohol, stress, and family history of alcoholism. *Alcoholism: Clinical and Experimental Research, 13,* 337.

Shiffman, S., & Wills, T. A., eds. (1985). *Coping and substance abuse.* New York: Academic Press.

Smith, S. S., & Newman, J. P. (1990). Alcohol and drug abuse/dependence disorders in psychopathic and nonpsychopathic criminal offenders. *Journal of Abnormal Psychology, 99,* 430–439.

Sommers, S. (1988). *Keeping secrets.* New York: Warner Books.

Spielberger, C. D., Gorsuch, R. L., & Lushene, R. E. (1970). *Manual for the State-Trait Anxiety Inventory.* Palo Alto: Consulting Psychologists Press.

Spivack, G., Spotts, J., Haimes, P. E. (1967). *The Devereux Adolescent Behavior Rating Scale Manual.* Devon, Pa.: The Devereux Foundation Press.

Spohr, H.-L., & Steinhausen, H.-C. (1987). Follow-up studies of children with fetal alcohol syndrome. *Hippokrates Verlag GmbH, 18,* 13–17.

Sram, R. J., Kocisova, J., Marecek, P., & Nerad, J. (1986). Geneticke riziko pri zavislosti na alcoholu. *Ceskoslovenska Psychiatrie, 82,* 113–117. (Abstract in English.)

Stark, E. (1987, January). Forgotten victims: Children of alcoholics. *Psychology Today,* pp. 58–62.

Steinglass, P. (1979). The alcoholic family in the interaction laboratory. *Journal of Nervous and Mental Disease, 167,* 428–436.

Steinglass, P. (1981a). The impact of alcoholism on the family. *Journal of Studies on Alcohol, 42,* 288–303.

Steinglass, P. (1981b). The alcoholic family at home: Patterns of interaction in dry, wet, and transitional stages of alcoholism. *Archives of General Psychiatry, 38,* 578–584.

Steinglass, P., Bennett, L. A., Wolin, S. J., & Reiss, D. (1987). *The alcoholic family.* New York; Basic Books.

Steinglass, P., Davis, D., & Berenson, D. (1977). Observations of conjointly hospitalized "alcoholic couples" during sobriety and intoxication: Implications for theory and therapy. *Family Process, 16,* 1–16.

Steinglass, P., & Robertson, A. (1983). The alcoholic family. In B. Kissin, & H. Begleiter, eds., *The pathogenesis of alcoholism: Psychosocial factors* (pp. 243–307). New York: Plenum Press.

Steinglass, P., Weiner, S., & Mendelson, J. H. (1971). A systems approach to alcoholism: A model and its clinical application. *Archives of General Psychiatry, 24,* 401–408.

Steinhauer, S. R., Hill, S. Y., & Zubin, J. (1987). Event-related potentials in alcoholics and their first-degree relatives. *Alcohol, 4,* 307–314.

Steinhausen, H.-C., & Spohr, H.-L. (1986). Fetal alcohol syndrome. In B. B. Lahey & A. E. Kazdin, eds., *Advances in Clinical Child Psychology,* Vol 9 (pp. 217–243). New York: Plenum Press.

Stern, R. M., Ray, W. J., & Davis, C. M. (1980). *Psychophysiological recording.* New York: Oxford University Press.

Streissguth, A. P., Landesman-Dwyer, S., Martin, J. C., & Smith, D. W. (1980). Teratogenic effects of alcohol in humans and laboratory animals. *Science, 209,* 353–354.

Suarez, B. K., & Cox, B. K. (1985). Linkage analysis for psychiatric disorders. I. Basic concepts. *Psychiatric Developments, 3,* 219–243.

Sullivan, J. L., Cavenar, J. O., Maltbie, A. A., Lister, P., & Zung, W. W. K. (1979). Familial, biochemical, and clinical correlates of alcoholics with low platelet monoamine oxidase activity. *Biological Psychiatry, 14,* 385–394.

Sullivan, J. L., Stanfield, C. N., Maltbie, A. A., Hammett, E., & Cavenar, J. O. (1978). Stability of low blood platelet monoamine oxidase activity in human alcoholics. *Biological Psychiatry, 13,* 391–397.

Sullivan, W. C. (1899). A note on the influence of maternal inebriety on the offspring. *Journal of Mental Science, 45,* 489–503.

Swartz, C. M., Drews, V., & Cadoret, R. (1987). Decreased epinephrine in familial alcoholism. *Archives of General Psychiatry, 44,* 938–941.

Swinson, R. P., & Madden, J. S. (1973). ABO blood groups and ABH substance secretion in alcoholics. *Quarterly Journal of Studies in Alcohol, 34,* 64–70.

Tabakoff, B., Hoffman, P., Lee, J. M., Saito, T., Willard, B., & De Leon-Jones, F. (1988). Differences in platelet enzyme activity between alcoholics and nonalcoholics. *New England Journal of Medicine, 318* (3), 134–139.

Takahashi, S., Tani, N., & Yamane, H. (1976). Monoamine oxidase activity in blood platelets in alcoholism. *Folia Psychiatria Neurologia Japon, 30,* 455–462.

Tanna, V. L., Wilson, A. F., Winokur, G., & Elston, R. C. (1988). Possible linkage between alcoholism and esterase-D. *Journal of Studies on Alcohol, 49,* 472–476.

Tarter, R. E. (1978). Etiology of alcoholism: Interdisciplinary perspectives. In P. E. Nathan, G. A. Marlatt, and T. Loberg, eds., *Alcoholism: New directions in behavioral research and treatment* (pp. 41–70). New York: Plenum.

Tarter, R. E. (1988). Are there inherited behavioral traits that predispose to substance abuse? *Journal of Consulting and Clinical Psychology, 56,* 189–196.

Tarter, R. E., Alterman, A. I., & Edwards, K. L. (1985). Vulnerability to alcoholism in men: A behavior-genetic perspective. *Journal of Studies on Alcohol, 46,* 329–356.

Tarter, R. E., Hegedus, A. M., Goldstein, G., Shelly, D., & Alterman, A. I. (1984). Adolescent sons of alcoholics: Neuropsychological and personality characteristics. *Alcoholism: Clinical and Experimental Research, 8,* 216–221.

Tarter, R. E., Jacob, T., Bremer, D. A. (1989). Cognitive status of sons of alcoholic men. *Alcoholism: Clinical and Experimental Research, 13,* 232–235.

Tarter, R. E., Jacob, T., Hill, S., Hegedus, A. M., & Carra, J. (1986). Perceptual field dependency: Predisposing trait or consequence of alcoholism. *Journal of Studies on Alcohol, 47,* 498–499.

Tarter, R. E., Kabene, M., Escallier, E. A., Laird, S. B., & Jacob, T. (1990). Temperament deviation and risk for alcoholism. *Alcoholism: Clinical and Experimental Research, 14,* 380–382.

Thomas, A., & Chess, S. (1977). *Temperament and development.* New York: Brunner/Mazel.

Thompson, W. D., Orvaschel, H., Prusoff, B. A., & Kidd, K. (1982). An evaluation of the family history method for ascertaining psychiatric disorders. *Archives of General Psychiatry, 39,* 53–58.

Ticku, M. K., & Kulkarni, S. K. (1988). Molecular interactions of ethanol with the GABAergic system and potential of R)!%-4513 as an ethanol antagonist. *Pharmacology, Biochemistry, & Behavior, 30,* 501–510.

Tsuang, M. T., Fleming, J. A., Kendler, K. S., & Gruenberg, A. S. (1988). Selection of controls for family studies: Biases and implications. *Archives of General Psychiatry, 45,* 1006–1008.

Tyndel, M. (1974). Psychiatric study of one thousand alcoholic patients. *Canadian Psychiatric Association Journal, 19,* 21–24.

Utne, H. E., Hansen, F. V., Winkler, K., & Schulsinger, F. (1977). Alcohol elimination rates in adoptees with and without alcoholic parents. *Journal of Studies on Alcohol, 38,* 1219–1223.

Vaillant, G. E. (1983). Natural history of male alcoholism V: Is alcoholism the cart or the horse to sociopathy? *British Journal of Addiction, 78,* 317–326.

Vaillant, G. E. (1989). The pendulum swings the other way: The role of environment obscured by genes. *Archives of General Psychiatry, 46,* 1151.

Vannicelli, M. (1989). *Group psychotherapy with adult children of alcoholics: Treatment techniques and countertransference considerations.* New York: Guilford.

Vogel-Sprott, M., & Chipperfield, B. (1987). Family history of problem drinking among male social drinkers: Behavioral effects of alcohol. *Journal of Studies on Alcohol, 48,* 430–436.

Vogel-Sprott, M., Chipperfield, B., & Hart, D. M. (1985). Family history of problem drinking among young male social drinkers: Reliability of the Family Tree Questionnaire. *Drug and Alcohol Dependence, 16,* 251–256.

von Knorring, A-L., Bohman, M., von Knorring, L., & Oreland, L. (1985). Platelet MAO activity as a biological marker in subgroups of alcoholism. *Acta Psychiatrica Scandanavica, 72,* 51–58.

von Knorring, L., Oreland, L., Haggendal, J., Magnusson, T., Almay, B., & Johansson, F. (1986). *Journal of Neural Transmission, 66,* 37–46.

von Knorring, L., Oreland, L., & von Knorring, A-L. (1987). Personality traits and platelet MAO activity in alcohol and drug abusing teenage boys. *Acta Psychiatrica Scandanavica, 75,* 307–314.

Walitzer, K. (1990). Personality and the transmission of familial risk for alcoholism. Doctoral dissertation. University of Missouri—Columbia.

Walitzer, K. S., & Sher, K. J. (1990). Alcohol cue reactivity and ad lib drinking in young men at risk for alcoholism. *Addictive Behaviors, 15,* 29–46.

Warheit, G. J., & Auth, J. B. (1985). Epidemiology of alcohol abuse in adulthood. In J. O. Cavenar, ed., *Psychiatry* (Vol. 3, pp. 1–18). Philadelphia: Lippincott.

Warren, G., & Raynes, A. (1972). Mood changes following three conditions of alcohol intake. *Quarterly Journal of Studies on Alcohol, 33,* 979–988.

Wegscheider, S. (1977). *Families in stress.* Crystal, Minn.: Nurturing Networks.

Wegscheider, S. (1981). *Another chance: Hope and health for the alcoholic family.* Palo Alto: Science and Behavior Books.

Wegscheider-Cruse, S. (1985). *Choices.* Pompano Beach, Fla.: Health Communications.

Weinberg, J. R., & Schnapps, B. (1987). Adult pets of alcoholics: Another underserved population. *Psychology of Addictive Behaviors, 1,* 131.

Weingartner, H., Rudorfer, M. V., Buchsbaum, M. S., & Linnoila, M. (1983). Effects of serotonin on memory impairment produced by ethanol. *Science, 221,* 472–474.

Weissman, M. M., Merikangas, K. R., John, K., Wickramaratne, P., Prusoff, B. A., & Kidd, K. K. (1986). Family-genetic studies of psychiatric disorders: Developing technologies. *Archives of General Psychiatry, 43,* 1104–1116.

Werner, E. E. (1986). Resilient offspring of alcoholics: A longitudinal study from birth to age 18. *Journal of Studies on Alcohol, 47,* 34–40.

West, M. O., & Prinz, R. J. (1987). Parental alcoholism and childhood psychopathology. *Psychological Bulletin, 102,* 204–218.

Whipple, S. C., Parker, E. S., Noble, E. P. (1988). An atypical neurocognitive profile in alcoholic fathers and their sons. *Journal of Studies on Alcohol, 49,* 240–244.

Wiberg, A., Gottfries, C. G., & Oreland, L. (1977). Low platelet monoamine oxidase activity in human alcoholics. *Medical Biology, 55,* 181.

Wilson, C., & Orford, J. (1978). Children of alcoholics: reports of a preliminary study and comments on the literature. *Journal of Studies on Alcohol, 39,* 121–142.

Wilson, G. T. (1988). Alcohol and anxiety. *Behaviour Research and Therapy, 26,* 369–381.

Wilson, J. R., & Nagoshi, C. T. (1988). Adult children of alcoholics: cognitive and psychomotor characteristics. *British Journal of Addiction, 83,* 809–820.

Windle, M. (1990). Temperament and personality attributes among children of alcoholics. In M. Windle & J. S. Searles, eds., *Children of alcoholics: Critical perspectives* (pp. 129–167). New York: Guilford.

Windle, M., & Searles, J. S. (1990). Summary, integration, and future directions: Toward a life-span perspective. In M. Windle & J. S. Searles, eds., *Children of alcoholics: Critical perspectives* (pp. 217–238). New York: Guilford.

Winokur, G., Reich, T., Rimmer, J., & Pitts, F. N. (1970). Alcoholism: III. Diagnosis and familial psychiatric illness in 259 alcoholic probands. *Archives of General Psychiatry, 23*, 104–111.

Winokur, G., Rimmer, J., and Reich, T. (1971) Alcoholism: IV. Is there more that one type of alcoholism? *British Journal of Psychiatry. 118*, 525–531.

Winokur, G., Tanna, V., Elston, R., & Go, R. (1976). Lack of association of genetic traits with alcoholism: C3, Ss, and ABO systems. *Journal of Studies on Alcohol, 36*, 981–992.

Witkin, H. A., Dyk, R. B., Faterson, H. F., Goodenough, D. R., & Karp, S. A. (1962). *Psychological differentiation.* New York: Wiley.

Woititz, J. G. (1983). *Adult children of alcoholics.* Pompano Beach, Fla.: Health Communications.

Woititz, J. G. (1984). Adult children of alcoholics. *Alcoholism Treatment Quarterly, 1*, 71–99.

Wolf, A. W., Schubert, D., Patterson, M. B., Grande, T. P., Brocco, K. J., & Pendleton, L. (1988). Associations among major psychiatric diagnoses. *Journal of Consulting and Clinical Psychology, 56*, 292–294.

Wolin, S. J., Bennett, L. A., & Noonan, D. L. (1979). Family rituals and the reoccurrence of alcoholism over generations. *American Journal of Psychiatry, 136*, 589–593.

Wolin, S. J., Bennett, L. A., Noonan, D. L., & Teitelbaum, M. A. (1980). Disrupted family rituals: A factor in the intergenerational transmission of alcoholism. *Journal of Studies on Alcohol, 41*, 199–214.

Wood, B. L. (1987). *Children of alcoholism: The struggle for self and intimacy in adult life.* New York: New York University Press.

Woodruff, R. A., Guze, S. B., and Clayton, P. J. (1973). Alcoholics who see a psychiatrist compared to those who do not. *Quarterly Journal of Studies on Alcoholism, 34*, 1162–1171.

Woodside, M. (1983). Children of alcoholic parents: Inherited and psychosocial influences. *Journal of Psychiatric Treatment & Evaluation, 5*, 531–537.

Woodside, M. (1984). *Children of alcoholics.* New York: Children of Alcoholics Foundation.

Workman-Daniels, K. L., & Hesselbrock, V. M. (1987). Childhood problem behavior and neuropsychological functioning in persons at risk for alcoholism. *Journal of Studies on Alcohol, 48*, 187–193.

Young, W. F., Laws, E. R., Sharbrough, F. W., & Winshilboum, R. (1986). Human monoamine oxidase: Lack of brain and platelet correlation. *Archives of General Psychiatry, 43*, 604–612.

Zahn, T. P. (1986). Psychophysiological approaches to psychopathology. In M. G. H. Coles, E. Donchin, & S. W. Porges, eds., *Psychophysiology: Systems, processes, and applications* (pp. 508–610). New York: Guilford.

Zimmerman, M., Coryell, W., Pfohl, B., & Stangl, D. (1988). The reliability of the family history method for psychiatric diagnoses. *Archives of General Psychiatry, 45*, 320–322.

Zucker, R. A. (1976). Parental influences upon drinking patterns of their children. In M. Greenblatt & M. A. Schuckit, eds., *Alcoholism and problems in women and children* (pp. 211–238). New York: Grune & Stratton.

Zucker, R. A. (1987). The four alcoholisms: A developmental account of the etiologic process. In P. C. Rivers, ed., *Nebraska symposium on motivation, 1986: Alcohol & addictive behavior* (pp. 27–83). Lincoln: University of Nebraska Press.

Zucker, R. A., Baxter, J. A., Noll, R. B., Theado, D. P., & Weil, C. M. (1982, August). An alcoholic risk study: Design and early health-related findings. Paper presented at the annual meeting of the *American Psychological Association*. Washington, D.C.

Zucker, R. A., & Gomberg, E. S. L. (1986). Etiology of alcoholism reconsidered: The case for a biopsychosocial process. *American Psychologist, 41,* 783.

Zuckerman, M. (1988). Sensation seeking and behavior disorders. *Archives of General Psychiatry, 45,* 502–503.

Zuckerman, M., Buchsbaum, M., & Murphy, D. (1980). Sensation seeking and its biological correlates. *Psychological Bulletin, 88,* 187–214.

Zuckerman, M., Kuhlman, D. M., & Camac, C. (1988). What lies beyond E and N? Factor analyses of scales believed to measure basic dimensions of personality. *Journal of Personality and Social Psychology, 54,* 96–107.

Zuckerman, M., Neary, R. S., & Brustman, B. A. (1970). Sensation-seeking scale correlates in experience (smoking, drugs, alcohol, "hallucinations," and sex) and preference for complexity (designs). *Proceedings of the 78th Annual Convention of the American Psychological Association, 5,* 317–318 (Summary).

Index of Names

Abel, E. L., 24, 35
Ablon, J., 164
Abrams, N., 36
Ackerman, R. J., 157, 158, 159
Agarwal, D. P., 124
Ainsworth, M. D. S., 156, 157
Aldenderfer, M. S., 8
Aldrich, K., 125
Alexopolous, G. S., 102
Allen, N., 36
Alpert, R., 99, 111
Alpher, V. S., 158, 159
Alterman, A. I., 45, 74, 75, 80, 86, 89, 121, 126
American Psychiatric Association, 152
Anderson, C., 27
Anderson, E. R., 158
Andreasen, N., 56
Andreasen, N. C., 55
Apfel, R. J., 81
Armstrong, J., 87
Aronson, H., 74
Aston, C., 22
Auth, J. B., 5
Ayers, T. S., 165, 170
Ayre, F. R., 35

Babor, T. F., 11, 124
Ballenger, J. F., 102
Balson, P. M., 82
Baribeau, J. M. C., 91, 110
Barnes, G. E., 72, 80
Barnhill, J., 35, 117

Baron, R. M., 43, 47, 48
Barrera, M., 29
Bates, W., 72
Beals, J., 81
Beattie, M., 148, 151
Beavers, W. R., 162
Begleiter, H., 96, 97
Behar, D., 87, 107, 109, 116
Beitman, B., 37
Beletis, S., 148, 157, 158, 159, 160
Bennett, L. A., 29, 30, 77, 81, 86, 142, 162
Benson, C. S., 27, 34, 77, 78, 144
Bepko, C., 161
Berenson, D., 27
Berglas, S., 124
Berkowitz, A., 58, 75, 78, 81
Bertelsen, A., 18
Biek, J. D., 58
Bihari, B., 96
Billings, A., 28
Billings, A. G., 27, 29, 40, 78
Birchler, G. R., 28
Black, C., 30, 31, 39, 40, 148, 149, 152, 153, 155
Blashfield, R. K., 8, 9
Blau, M., 150
Blehar, M. C., 156, 157
Bloom, F. E., 97, 101
Blum, K., 22
Blume, S. B., 2

Bohman, M., 19, 37, 102
Boomsma, D., 18
Booz-Allen and Hamilton Inc., 154
Bordin, E. S., 160
Borgotta, E. G., 78
Botstein, D., 22
Bowlby, J., 156, 157
Branchey, M., 102
Brannock, J. C., 89
Braun, C. M. J., 91
Breckenridge, M. B., 36
Breger, L., 157
Bremer, D. A., 86
Brent, E. E., 74
Bridges, K. R., 74, 89
Brill, N., 157
Broida, J. P., 81
Brown, J. B., 101
Brown, S., 148, 151, 153, 154, 157, 158, 159, 160
Brown, S. A., 83, 84, 92, 124, 137, 144
Brustman, B. A., 126
Bruun, K., 18
Buchsbaum, M., 97, 126
Buchsbaum, M. S., 102, 118
Bucky, S. F., 40, 153
Burk, J. P., 31, 39, 156, 164, 168, 169, 170
Burns, T., 97
Buss, A. H., 73, 77, 78, 79, 130
Butters, N., 89
Buydens-Branchey, L., 102

Bylund, D. B., 70, 102, 108

Cadoret, R., 103
Cadoret, R. J., 16, 19, 20, 22, 35, 37, 117, 126
Cain, C. A., 19
Callan, V. J., 27, 81
Camac, C., 73, 76
Canter, S., 83
Caplan, G., 143
Caplan, R., 31
Cappell, H., 67, 111
Carey, K., 56
Carpenter, J. A., 87
Carter, J. A., 160
Cattell, R. B., 73
Cavenar, J. O., 102
Cederlof, R., 17
Cermak, T. L., 148, 151, 152, 153, 154
Chaknis, M., 80
Chandler, M., 136
Chapman, J. P., 63, 65, 168
Chapman, L. J., 63, 65, 168
Chassin, L., 29, 35, 43, 74, 75, 82, 92, 145
Chess, S., 136
Chiles, J., 36
Chipperfield, B., 32, 56, 108, 110, 123
Christiansen, B. A., 83
Chu, D., 148
Churchill, J. C., 81
Ciraulo, A. M., 35, 117
Ciraulo, D. A., 35, 117
Clair, D., 27, 30, 78, 126, 144, 146
Clancy, J., 37
Claridge, G., 83
Claydon, D., 58
Clayton, P. J., 11
Clifford, C., 17
Clifford, C. A., 18, 23
Cloniger, C. R., 8, 9, 10, 13, 15, 16, 19, 20, 35, 36, 37, 45, 48, 72, 73, 74, 82, 83, 98, 116, 121, 126, 130, 131, 132, 133, 141, 144
Cohen, J., 51, 75

Cohen, M. E., 37
Cohen, M. J., 89
Cohen, P., 51
Cohen, S., 143, 144
Coles, Robert, 150
Collins, J. J., Jr., 26
Compas, B. E., 157
Comrey, A. L., 76
Conger, J. J., 110
Connors, C. K., 77
Connors, G. J., 66, 68, 71
Constantine, L. L., 161
Cooper, J. R., 101
Cooper, L., 127, 138
Cooper, M. L., 173
Cork, Margaret, 149
Coryell, W., 55
Costa, P. T., Jr., 76
Cotton, N., 16, 54, 55
Coursey, R. D., 102
Cox, N. J., 21
Crabb, J. C., 23, 24
Crandell, J. S., 159
Craven, D., 148
Creamer, V. A., 84
Croot, F., 97
Crowe, R. R., 37
Crowley, P. A., 8
Cvitkovic, J., 28

Danko, G. P., 83
Davis, C. M., 96
Davis, D., 27
Davis, D. R., 31
Davis, R., 58
Davis, R. B., 165
Dean, A., 143
DeBaryshe, B. D., 128
DeFries, J. C., 25
Descutner, C., 56, 58
Desmond, E., 148
Deutsch, C., 30, 32, 39, 155, 156
De Wit, H., 108, 123
Diamond, S., 60
DiCicco, L., 58, 165
Dickson, D. H., 167
Dietrich, R. A., 16
Digman, J. M., 76
Dishion, T. J., 136
Donovan, B. E., 166

Douglas, Kirk, 148
Downing, N. E., 166
Drake, R. E., 30, 34, 36, 62, 172
Drejer, K., 80, 88, 89, 90
Drews, V., 103
Dube, R., 91
Duby, J., 67, 101, 103, 107, 111
Duck, S. W., 169
Dunn, N. J., 28
Dyk, R. B., 80

Earls, F., 39
Earls, F. J., 34
Eber, H. W., 73
Edwards, D. M., 165
Edwards, G., 2, 3
Edwards, K. L., 46, 121
Edwards, P., 60
Ehlers, C. L., 95, 107, 114
Elderton, E. M., 86
El-Guebaly, N., 2, 34, 149
Elmasian, R., 96, 97, 114, 115
Elul, M. R., 94
Emory, E. K., 107
Emshoff, J. G., 165
Endicott, J., 55, 56
Endler, N., 68
Engstrom, D., 99, 111
Epstein, S., 71
Erikson, E. H., 157, 158
Ervin, C. S., 86, 88, 90
Escallier, E. A., 79
Eysenck, H. J., 73, 74, 76, 77, 83
Eysenck, S. B. G., 74, 77

Famularo, R., 26
Faterson, F. H., 80
Favorini, A., 27
Feighner, J. P., 3
Fenigstein, A., 78
Filstead, W., 27
Finn, P. R., 8, 59, 67, 77, 78, 79, 82, 99, 100, 104, 111, 112, 113, 120, 123, 125, 133
Fischer, M., 18
FitzGerald, K. W., 161

Folkman, S., 146
Forehand, R., 25
Fowler, C. J., 102
Fowles, D. C., 111
Frances, R. J., 102
Frankenstein, W., 28
Freed, E. X., 107
Friberg, L., 17
Frone, M. R., 173
Fryer, A. J., 56
Fulker, D. W., 18

Gabrielli, W., 114
Gabrielli, W. F., 16, 18, 88, 90, 91, 95, 108
Garmezy, N., 173
Gath, A., 19
Gatto, G. J., 102
Gehring, M., 58
Gelso, C. J., 160
Genest, M., 27, 30, 78, 126, 144, 146
Gensheimer, L. K., 165, 170
George, W., 127
Germanson, T., 11
Gilbert, A., 74
Giller, E., Jr., 101
Gittelman, R., 36
Glaser, F. B., 11
Glynn, T. J., 31, 32
Goedde, H. W., 124
Goffman, E., 61, 168
Goglia, L. R., 74
Gold, E. O., 46, 97, 103, 109
Goldman, M. S., 83, 85, 92
Goldstein, G., 58
Gomberg, C., 28
Gomberg, E. S. L., 72, 75, 76
Goodwin, D. W., 16, 19, 20, 22, 25, 38, 74, 114, 124
Goodwin, F. K., 102
Gordon, J., 127
Gorenstein, E. E., 38, 98
Gorsuch, R. L., 76, 78
Gottesman, I. I., 18, 22
Gottfries, C. G., 101
Goyer, P. F., 101

Greeley, J., 111
Greenberg, G. S., 85
Greenwald, N. E., 70
Greist, D., 25
Gross, M., 3
Grove, W. M., 16, 19, 20, 22
Gurling, H. M. D., 16, 17, 18, 23, 24
Guthrie, S., 103
Guze, S. B., 11

Haggendal, J., 101
Haier, R. J., 97
Haimes, P. E., 77
Halikas, J. A., 11
Hall, H., 101
Hall, J. G., 74
Hall, R., 61
Hamilton, C. J., 26
Hansen, F. V., 107
Harada, S., 124
Harburg, E., 31, 69, 128
Hare, R., 39, 75
Hart, D. M., 56
Hartmann, J., 102
Harvey, C., 60
Hassett, J., 95
Hauger, R., 117
Hauser, S. T., 158
Hawley, R. J., 101
Hay, W. M., 28
Hayduk, L. A., 45, 52
Heath, A., 172
Hegedus, A. M., 58, 86, 87
Heller, K., 27, 34, 77, 78, 144, 156, 164
Helzer, J. E., 5, 12, 13
Henderson, C., 2
Hennecke, L., 79, 80
Hermansen, L., 19
Herzog, M. A., 11
Hesselbrock, M. N., 8, 11, 35, 88, 89, 90
Hesselbrock, V. M., 8, 35, 61, 64, 84, 88, 89, 90, 96
Hetherington, E. M., 158
Hibbard, S., 148, 160
Hill, S., 80
Hill, S. Y., 22, 35, 87, 90, 97

Hinshaw, S., 36
Hirsch, B. J., 144
Hoffmann, H., 72
Holden, M. G., 144
Hops, H., 33
House, J. S., 143
Hrubec, Z., 17
Hughes, J. M., 164
Hume, W., 83
Humphreys, M. S., 70

Imber-Black, E., 162
Inn, A., 83
Inouye, J., 76
Irwin, M., 117, 131

Jackson, D., 27, 81
Jackson, J. K., 149, 161
Jacob, T., 27, 28, 29, 35, 40, 77, 80, 86
Jang, M., 30, 86, 172
Jardine, R. E., 18
Jellinek, E. M., 3, 8, 9
Johnson, F. G., 8, 9
Johnson, J. L., 86, 88
Johnson, R., 98
Johnson, R. C., 83
Johnson, S., 35
Johnson, V., 35, 69
Johnston, C., 25
Johnston, P. D., 165
Jones, B. M., 69
Jones, J. W., 57
Jones, M. C., 72, 77, 78, 79, 126
Jonsson, E., 18
Jung, K. G., 39

Kabene, M., 79
Kahn, M., 67
Kahn, R. L., 143
Kaij, L., 17, 54
Kakihana, R., 23
Kalin, R., 67
Kaminer, W., 150, 151, 167
Kammeier, M. I., 72
Kandel, D. B., 128
Kantor, K., 162
Kaplan, H. B., 136
Kaplan, R. F., 84, 95, 108, 114

Kaprio, J., 17, 18
Kaufmann, C. A., 21
Keener, J. J., 11
Kelly, I. W., 167
Kenny, D. A., 43, 47, 48
Kern, J. C., 80, 148, 163
Kessler, M., 28
Keynes, J. M., 86
Kilner, L. A., 158
Knight, R. P., 8, 9
Knop, J., 74, 86, 89
Knowles, E., 73
Kojic, T., 22
Krahn, G., 29
Krestan, J., 161
Kuhlman, D. M., 73, 76
Kulkarni, S. K., 117
Kushner, M., 37, 127, 138
Kwakman, A. M., 159

Lahey, B., 32
Lander, E. S., 22
Landesman-Dwyer, S., 35, 77
Lang, A. R., 25, 50
Law, H., 76
Laws, E. R., 101
Lawson, D. M., 66
Lazarus, R. S., 146
Leckman, J. F., 13
Leerhsen, C., 148
Lehr, W., 162
Leonard, K., 35, 40, 77
Lester, D., 87
Levenson, R. W., 56, 83, 99, 100, 111, 112, 113, 120, 123, 136
Lex, B. W., 70, 109, 110
Li, T. K., 16, 23, 102
Lieberman, K. W., 102
Lin, N., 143
Linnoila, M., 103
Lipscomb, R. R., 87, 109
Lipscomb, T. R., 66
Little, R. E., 86
Loeber, R., 128
Loehlin, J. C., 18, 32
Logue, M. B., 167
Loney, J., 36
Loper, R. G., 72
Lukas, S. E., 70

Lumeng, L., 23, 102
Lund, C. A., 77
Lundman, T., 18
Lushene, R. E., 78
Lyn, L., 89
Lyttle, M. D., 11

MacAndrew, C. A., 73
McBride, W. J., 23, 102
McClean, G. A., 97
McClearn, G. E., 23
McClelland, D. C., 67
McCord, J., 32, 38, 72, 128, 142, 143, 172
McCord, W., 72
McCracken, S. G., 108, 109, 123
McCrady, B., 60
McCrae, R. R., 76
MacDonald, D. I., 2
McDougall, W., 83
McElfresh, O., 27
McGue, M., 22
McKearn, J., 154
McLoyd, V. C., 158
McNeill, T. F., 53, 54
MacNicholl, T. A., 149
Madden, J. S., 22
Maddock, J. M., 103
Magnusson, D., 68
Mahler, H. I. M., 131
Main, M., 157
Maisto, S. A., 56, 66, 68, 71, 84, 87, 107, 109, 110, 123
Major, L., 102
Major, L. F., 101
Maltbie, A. A., 101, 102
Mann, L. M., 74, 82, 84, 120, 124, 127
Mann, R. E., 56
Manning, B., 165
Manning, D. T., 82
Manning, O., 165
Mannuzza, S., 36, 56
Marcus, A. M., 86
Markkanen, T., 18
Marlatt, G. A., 67, 85, 127
Martin, J. B., 81
Martin, J. C., 35
Martin, N. G., 18

Mednick, S., 114
Mednick, S. A., 53, 54, 88, 90, 91
Meehl, P. E., 167
Meek, P. S., 56, 83, 99
Meller, W. H., 35
Mello, N. K., 11
Mendelson, J. H., 11, 27, 124
Merikangas, K. R., 13, 37, 38
Mershon, B., 76
Meyer, R. E., 11
Miller, D., 30, 86, 172
Miller, W. R., 150
Mirassou, M., 11
Mischel, W., 82
Moeti, R. L., 165
Molina, B., 75
Monroe, S. M., 144
Monteiro, M. G., 117
Moody-Thomas, S., 107
Moos, B. S., 27
Moos, R. H., 27, 29, 40, 78
Morehouse, E. R., 165
Morey, L. C., 8, 9
Morrison, C., 81
Moss, H. B., 37, 103, 104, 107, 108, 115, 123
Mott, M. A., 144
Mukherjee, A. B., 103
Munjack, K. J., 37
Murphy, D., 126
Murphy, D. L., 101, 102
Murphy, G. E., 36
Murphy, J. M., 102
Murray, R. M., 16, 17, 18, 23, 24

Nagoshi, C. T., 64, 71, 83, 84, 87, 89, 90, 107, 108, 109, 110, 111, 123
Namuth, T., 148
Nardi, P. M., 154
Nathan, P., 76
Nathan, P. E., 28, 66, 87
National Advisory Council on Alcohol Abuse and Alcoholism, 67, 69, 70
National Council on Alcoholism, 3

National Institute on Alcohol Abuse and Alcoholism, 16
Neale, M. C., 18
Neary, R. S., 126
Neville, H., 96
Neville, H. J., 96, 97
Newlin, D. B., 67, 68, 70, 71, 99, 108, 111, 118, 119, 120, 124, 125, 129, 133, 135
Newman, J. P., 38, 75, 98
Nicholson, N., 81
Nilsson, T., 18
Nixon, P. F., 125
Noble, E. P., 80
Noll, R. B., 85
Noller, P., 76
Noonan, D. L., 30
Noumair, D., 102
Noyes, R. J., 37
Nylander, I., 141

O'Brien, J., 84
O'Connor, D. T., 103
O'Connor, M. J., 157
O'Connor, S., 84, 96
O'Farrell, T. J., 28
Offord, D., 36
Offord, D. R., 2, 34, 149
O'Gorman, T. W., 19, 35, 38
O'Malley, S. S., 56, 84, 87, 107, 109, 110, 123
Omenn, G. S., 17
O'Neal, P., 72
Oreland, L., 101, 102
Orenstein, A., 58
Orford, J., 27, 154
Orme, T., 26
Orvaschel, H., 55
Othmer, E., 11
Oyama, O. N., 56, 83, 99

Pandina, R. J., 35, 69
Paolino, T., 60
Pardeck, J. A., 166
Pardeck, J. T., 166
Park, J., 90
Parker, D. C., 103
Parker, E. S., 80
Parsons, O., 66, 88

Partanen, J., 18
Partington, J. T., 8, 9
Patterson, B. W., 97
Patterson, G., 25, 128
Patterson, G. R., 136
Pauls, D. L., 37
Pearson, K., 86
Pederson, N. L., 18
Pedhazur, E. J., 52
Peele, S., 16, 18
Pelham, W. E., 25
Penick, E., 8, 9, 11
Penn, N. E., 80, 110
Perkins, H. W., 58, 75, 78, 81
Perris, C., 102
Perry, A., 18, 83, 124
Peterson, J., 100, 104, 133
Petrie, A., 79, 80
Pfohl, B., 55
Pickens, R. W., 17
Pihl, R. O., 8, 59, 67, 77, 78, 79, 81, 82, 99, 100, 104, 111, 112, 113, 120, 123, 125, 133, 136
Pittman, W., 163
Pliner, P., 67
Plomin, R., 18, 32, 51, 73, 77, 79, 130
Polich, J., 97
Pollock, V. E., 16, 95, 96, 107, 108, 110, 113, 114, 123
Porjesz, B., 96
Powell, B. J., 8, 11
Powers, S. I., 158
Pratt, H., 11
Prewett, M., 80
Prinz, R. J., 26, 27, 34, 36, 37, 39, 50
Pritchard, W. S., 98
Prusoff, B. A., 13, 55
Pryzbeck, T. R., 12, 13
Puchall, L. B., 102

Quinton, D., 158

Rabin, B., 22
Raine, A., 98
Ramsey, E., 128
Ratcliff, K. S., 139

Rawlings, R., 96
Ray, W. J., 96
Raynes, A., 67
Rayses, V., 107
Read, M. R., 8
Regier, D. A., 5
Reich, T., 6, 13, 16, 38, 72
Reich, W., 39
Reid, J. R., 136
Reischl, T. M., 144
Reiss, D., 30, 77, 142
Revelle, W., 70
Rhodes, J., 155
Rice, J., 55
Richards, T. M., 160
Reider, R. O., 21
Rimmer, J., 13, 26, 38
Rinehart, R., 35
Risch, S. C., 103
Ritchey, D., 28
Roberts, S., 22
Robertson, A., 26, 27
Robins, L., 72
Robins, L. N., 5, 6, 7, 36, 139
Robinson, B. E., 164, 165, 166
Roe, A., 19
Roehling, P. V., 83
Rogosch, F., 29, 43, 49, 141, 145
Rohsenow, D. J., 67
Rolf, J., 86, 88
Roosa, M. W., 58, 81, 137, 165, 170
Ross, H. E., 11
Rossman, L. R., 103
Roth, R. H., 101
Rowe, D., 130
Rudorfer, M. V., 118
Russell, M., 2, 5, 23, 26, 27, 31, 32, 34, 36, 38, 127, 173
Rutter, M., 47, 158
Rydelius, P. -A., 141, 172

Saini, N., 101
Sameroff, A., 136
Sandler, I. N., 58, 81
Sands, B. F., 117
Saunders, G. R., 73

Saunders, L. B., 125
Savoie, T. M., 107, 123
Schaeffer, K., 66, 88, 89, 90
Schandler, S. L., 89
Scheier, M. F., 78
Schippers, G. M., 159
Schmidt, A. L., 96, 97
Schnapps, B., 150
Schneider, L. S., 16
Schooler, C., 102
Schroeder, D. A., 73
Schuckit, M., 131
Schuckit, M. A., 13, 16, 19, 35, 36, 38, 46, 67, 68, 73, 77, 78, 79, 80, 81, 82, 84, 87, 90, 95, 97, 99, 101, 102, 103, 107, 108, 109, 110, 111, 114, 115, 116, 117, 122, 123, 124, 125
Schulsinger, F., 19, 74, 78, 172
Scott, E. M., 30
Searles, J. S., 2, 16, 18, 23, 74, 173
Seilhamer, R. A., 27
Seixas, J. S., 39
Selzer, M., 56
Shader, R. I., 117
Sharbrough, F. E., 101
Shaskan, E., 101
Shenker, R., 36
Sher, K. J., 34, 35, 37, 39, 43, 56, 58, 62, 63, 67, 68, 69, 70, 74, 75, 77, 78, 79, 81, 82, 83, 84, 88, 89, 90, 91, 92, 99, 102, 107, 108, 111, 112, 120, 123, 124, 125, 126, 127, 136, 156, 164, 167, 168, 169, 170
Shiffman, S., 137
Short, J., 165
Sifneos, P. E., 81
Sigman, M., 157
Sigvardsson, S., 16, 19, 72
Simon, L., 70
Skinner, H. A., 8, 9
Slymen, D. J., 37
Smith, G. T., 83

Smith, S. S., 75
Smith, T., 131
Sobell, L. C., 56
Sobell, M. B., 56
Solomon, J., 157
Sommers, Suzanne, 148
Spence, R., 80
Spielberger, C. D., 78
Spitzer, R. L., 55, 56
Spivack, G., 77
Spohr, H. -L., 35
Spotts, J., 77
Stabenau, J. R., 8, 61, 88
Stanfield, C. N., 101
Stanley-Hagan, M., 158
Stark, E., 150
Steiner, S. C., 144
Steinglass, P., 26, 27, 161, 162
Steinhauer, S., 90
Steinhauer, S. R., 87, 97
Steinhausen, H. -C., 35
Stern, R. M., 96
Stetson, B. A., 84
Streissguth, A. P., 35, 86
Suarez, B. K., 21
Sullivan, J. L., 101, 102
Sullivan, W. C., 149
Svikis, D. S., 17
Swartz, C. M., 103, 116
Sweeney, S., 35
Swinson, R. P., 22

Takahashi, S., 101
Tani, N., 101
Tanna, V. L., 22
Tarter, R. E., 36, 45, 58, 73, 74, 75, 76, 79, 80, 82, 87, 88, 89, 90, 91, 92, 98, 121, 130, 133
Tasman, A., 96
Tatsuoka, M. M., 73
Teasdale, T. W., 74, 80, 107
Teitelbaum, M. A., 30
Theilgaard, A., 80
Thomas, A., 136
Thompson, W. D., 55
Thomson, J. B., 67, 68, 70, 71, 108, 118, 119, 120, 124, 125, 129, 133, 135
Ticku, M. K., 117

Travis, J., 58
Troughton, E., 19, 35, 38
Tyndel, M., 11

Utne, H. E., 107

Vaillant, G. E., 30, 34, 36, 38, 62, 132, 172
Vannicelli, M., 148, 159, 160
Van Rooijen, L., 56
Venables, P. H., 98
Vinokur, A., 56
Vogel-Sprott, M., 32, 56, 108, 110, 123
Volavka, J., 114
Von Knorring, A. L., 19, 102
Von Knorring, L., 101, 102
Vuchinich, R. E., 66

Walitzer, K., 69, 145
Walitzer, K. S., 35, 36, 70, 74, 83, 84, 99, 108, 123, 124
Walker, M. E., 166
Wall, T., 114
Waller, M. B., 102
Warheit, G. J., 5
Warren, G., 67
Waters, E., 156, 157
Wegscheider, S., 1, 30, 31, 149, 155, 156, 161
Wegschneider-Cruse, S., 151
Weinberg, J. R., 150
Weiner, S., 27
Weingartner, H., 118
Weinstein, M., 84
Wells, K., 25
Werner, E. E., 30, 49, 75, 91, 141, 143, 144, 145, 146, 172
West, M. O., 26, 27, 34, 36, 37, 39, 50
West, P. A., 139
Wetzel, R., 13, 38
Whipple, S. C., 80, 89, 90, 96
White, P. D., 37
Whitehead, P. C., 60
Wiberg, A., 101

Wilder-Padilla, S., 40, 153
Williams, H. L., 97
Williams, R., 125
Wills, T. A., 137, 143, 144
Wilson, A. F., 22
Wilson, C., 27, 154
Wilson, G. T., 111
Wilson, J. R., 64, 71, 84, 87, 89, 90, 107, 108, 109, 110, 111, 123
Windle, M., 2, 75, 76, 173
Winkler, K., 107
Winokur, G., 13, 19, 22, 38
Witkin, H. A., 80
Woititz, J. G., 1, 39, 148, 149, 153, 154, 167

Wolf, A. W., 11
Wolin, S. J., 29, 30, 32, 49, 78, 141, 142, 162
Wood, B. L., 153
Wood, P., 35, 74
Woodruff, R. A., 11
Woods, D., 96
Woodside, M., 2
Workman-Daniels, K. L., 64, 88, 89, 90

Xenakis, S., 82

Yalom, I. D., 160
Yamane, H., 101

Yao, J. K., 103
Yohman, J., 66, 88
Youcha, G., 39
Young, W. F., 101

Zahn, T. P., 98, 102
Zander, T. A., 165
Zeitouni, N. C., 99
Zimmerman, M., 55
Zubin, J., 97
Zucker, R. A., 9, 31, 32, 72, 75, 76, 85, 121, 132
Zuckerman, M., 73, 76, 126, 131
Zuiker, F. A. J. M., 159

Index of Subjects

Abstraction, 90–91
Academic achievement, 86, 128, 133
Acetaldehyde, 107, 124
ACOA. *See* Adult child of an alcoholic
ACOA movement, 150–51, 173–74
ACTH. *See* Adrenocorticotropic trophic hormone
Activity level, 79
ADHD. *See* Attention deficit hyperactivity disorder
Adjustment, 156
Adoption
 and alcoholism, 19–20
 and gene X environment interactions, 25
Adrenocorticotropic trophic hormone (ACTH), 103, 104, 116
Adult child of an alcoholic (ACOA), 148
 bibliotherapy for, 165–66
 and Borderline Personality, 160
 characteristics and roles of, 153–56
 and codependency, 152
 cognitive therapy for, 163
 developmental theories applied to, 157
 family systems therapy for, 161–63
 and family transference, 160
 labeling effects on, 168
 movement, 150–51, 173–74
 self-help groups for, 163–64
 therapeutic approaches to, 159–66
Adult Children of Alcoholics (Woititz), 149
Al-Anon, 163, 164
Alateen, 163, 164
Alcohol. *See* Ethanol
Alcohol abuse
 DSM-III-R diagnostic criteria for, 3–5
 genetic determination of, 16

 prevalence of, 14
 prevention of, 164
 and psychopathology, 12, 13
Alcohol consumption. *See* Alcohol use
Alcohol dependence
 defined, 2–3
 DSM-III-R diagnostic criteria for, 3–5
 genetic determination of, 16
 prevalence of, 14
 and psychopathology, 12, 13
Alcohol effects, model of, 129
Alcohol expectancies, 83–85, 124–25, 127, 138
Alcoholics Anonymous, 163–64
Alcoholism. *See also* Alcoholism comorbidity; Parental alcoholism
 and allele A1, 22
 animal studies, 22–25
 antisocial, 9, 132
 and antisocial personality disorder, 38–39
 and anxiety, 37
 and behavioral undercontrol, 73–74
 biological variables for, 93
 in children of alcoholics, 16
 cluster analysis of, 8
 and cognitive style, 79
 defined, 2–5
 and depression, 37–38
 developmentally cumulative, 9, 132
 developmentally limited, 9, 132
 and drug use, 13, 14
 and emotionality, 76–78
 epidemiology of, 5–7
 family environment and psychosocial influence on, 25–33
 and family violence, 26
 in first-degree relatives of alcoholics, 16

gene for, 21–22
genetic influences on, 16–25, 41, 51, 73, 125
heterogeneity of, 48–49, 59–60
high-risk research in, 54
and hyperactivity, 79
intergenerational transmission of, 29–30
and MAO activity, 101
mediators of risk of children of alcoholics to, 43–47
negative affect, 9, 132
personality traits and prototypic types of, 10, 72–83
prevalence of, 5–7
primary and secondary, 12–14
psychopathology in, 11–12, 34–40
scope of term, 5, 14
and sociability, 78–79
and spontaneous EEG activity, 94
subtypes, 7, 8–10, 14, 15
transmissibility of, 6
in twins, 17–19
vulnerability of children of alcoholics to, 41–43, 48, 49, 121–39
Alcoholism comorbidity, 11–12, 15
in alcoholic population, 29
and alcoholism subtypes, 7
depression and alcoholism, 37
and psychopathology in children of alcoholics, 34
P3 attenuation and alcoholism, 98
Alcoholism subtypes, 14, 15
approaches to, 8–10
heterogeneity of alcoholism, 7
Alcohol-related consequences
defined, 2–3
parental modeling of, 31–33
and types of alcoholism, 10
Alcohol use. *See also* Alcohol use disorders
affective consequences of, 110
and cognitive performance, 92
family interaction affected by, 28–29
maternal, 61
pathological, 2–15
and platelet MAO activity, 101
studies of, 106–20
voluntary in children of alcoholics, 123
Alcohol use disorders. *See also* Alcohol abuse; Alcohol dependence
DSM-III-R diagnostic criteria for, 3–5

heterogeneity of, 7–10
selected typologies of, 9
Alexithymia, 81, 82
Alpha alcoholism (Jellinek), 9
Alpha energy, 113–14
Alprazolam, 35, 117
Altered states of consciousness, 126
Animal studies, 22–25
Antisocial alcoholism (Zucker), 9, 132
Antisocial personality disorder
in alcoholics, 13, 14, 38–39, 98
and Type 2 alcoholism, 20
Anxiety
and alcoholism, 37
in children of alcoholics, 37
ASP. *See* Antisocial personality disorder
Attachment, 156, 157–58
Attention deficit hyperactivity disorder (ADHD)
activity level, 79
in children of alcoholics, 36
in integrative model, 133
and personality of children of alcoholics, 73
and P3 attenuation, 98
and stress-response dampening effects of alcohol, 113
Autonomic activity, 99–100, 110–13
Autonomy, 158
Aversive stimulation, 100

Barnum effect, 167–68
Basal autonomic and electromyographic levels, 99
Behavioral undercontrol, 72–76, 82, 84–85, 102, 145
Benzodiazepine, 117
Beta alcoholism (Jellinek), 9
Beverage cues, 99
Bibliotherapy, 165–66
Biochemical substances, 100–104, 115–17
Biological markers, 21, 93
Body sway, 87–88, 92, 109–10
Borderline Personality, 160

California Psychological Inventory, 73
Cambridge-Somerville Program for Alcoholism Rehabilitation (CASPAR), 164–65

CAST. *See* Children of Alcoholics Screening
    Test
Causality, 50
Child abuse, 26
Children of alcoholics (COAs). *See also*
    Adult child of an alcoholic; Sons of
    male alcoholics
    abstraction and conceptual reasoning in,
        90–91
    academic achievement of, 86, 128
    and active alcoholism, 29
    activity level in, 79
    adjustment of, 156
    alcohol expectancies in, 84–85, 124–25,
        127
    alcoholism in, 16
    alexithymia in, 81, 82
    antisocial personality disorder in, 38–39
    anxiety and depression in, 37
    attention deficit hyperactivity disorder in,
        36, 73
    autonomic characteristics of, 99
    basal autonomic and EMG levels of, 99
    behavioral undercontrol in, 72–76, 82
    bibliotherapy for, 165–66
    biochemical characteristics of, 100–104
    biological characteristics of, 93–105
    body sway in, 87–88, 92, 110
    child abuse among, 26
    children of depressed parents compared to,
        40, 61–62
    clinical literature on, 148–70
    codependency in, 151–53
    cognitive functioning in, 86–92
    cognitive style of, 80
    cognitive therapy for, 163
    conduct problems in, 36–37
    and control groups, 61–62
    correlational research on, 50
    depression in, 37
    differential deficit in, 65–66
    differential effects of alcohol on, 117–20
    drinking motivation in, 125–29
    drug abuse in, 35, 117
    electromyographic characteristics of, 99
    emotionality in, 77–78, 82
    emotional processing in, 91–92
    endocrine hormones in, 103–4, 115–16
    ethanol absorption, elimination, and
        metabolism in, 106–7
    ethanol sensitivity of, 113–14

event-related potentials in, 96–99, 104,
    114–15
and exposure to alcohol, 128
and family alcoholism, 59–60
family history method for identifying, 56
family systems therapy for, 161–63
heart rate in, 111
heterogeneity among, 20
high-risk research on, 55–56
impaired coping in, 127
impulsivity in, 74, 126–27
inclusion/exclusion for, 62–63
interest in, 1–2, 170
interpersonal difficulties in, 39–40
labeling effects on, 168–79
learning and memory in, 89–90
limb of the blood alcohol curve in, 68–
    69, 118, 119, 120
locus of control in, 80–81
and maternal alcoholism, 60, 61
mediators of risk of alcoholism in, 43–47,
    50, 121–39
moderators of risk of alcoholism in, 47,
    49, 50, 140–47
movement, 149–51, 167–70
negative mood states in, 125–26
neurophysiological characteristics of, 94–99
neuropsychological functioning in, 86–92
orienting response in, 112
and parental modeling of alcohol use,
    31–33
perceptual-motor functioning in, 88
personality traits and later alcoholism in,
    72–83
personality traits ascribed to, 167–68
and placebo controls, 67
platelet MAO activity in, 105, 116–17
prevalence of, 5, 14
prevention for, 164
psychological characteristics of, 72–92
psychopathology in, 34–35
reactivity to aversive stimulation in, 100
reactivity to nonaversive stimulation in,
    99–100
reinforcing effects of alcohol in, 122–24,
    129
research on, 53–71
responses to alcohol of, 106–20
responses to drugs of, 117
role reversal and role conflict in, 154–55
roles adopted by, 30–31

sampling of, 58–59, 63–64
school counselors working with, 165
scope of term, 5
self-esteem of, 81, 128
self-help groups for, 163–64
sensation seeking in, 126
sociability in, 78–79, 130
spontaneous EEG in, 95–96
and spousal psychopathology, 60–61
stress response in, 112–13, 118
subjective experience of alcohol in, 68
subjective intoxication in, 108
therapeutic approaches to, 159
tolerance development in, 125
and types of alcoholism, 10
verbal ability in, 88–89
visuospatial ability in, 89
voluntary alcohol consumption in, 123
vulnerability to alcoholism, 41–43, 66
Children of Alcoholics Screening Test (CAST), 57–58
Children of depressed parents (COD), 40, 61–62
Class, social. *See* Social class
Clinical literature, 148–70
Closed family system, 162
Cluster analysis, 8
CNS activity, 113–14
Coalcoholism, 151
COA movement, 149–51
and labeling of children of alcoholics, 168
social-psychological aspects of, 167–70
COAs. *See* Children of alcoholics
COD. *See* Children of depressed parents
Codependency, 151–53, 173–74
Codependent Personality Disorder, 151, 152
Cognitive functioning, 86, 98, 109–10
Cognitive-motor functioning, 109–10
Cognitive style, 79–80
Cognitive therapy, 163
Cohort effects, 6
Comorbidity, alcoholism. *See* Alcoholism comorbidity
Conceptual reasoning, 90–91
Conduct problems
in children of alcoholics, 36–37
in integrated model, 133
Conjoint family therapy, 161

Conjoint hospitalization, 161
Control groups, 61–62, 67
Coping
attachment as, 157
impaired, 127
as moderator of risk, 146–47
Correlational research, 50–52
Cortisol, 103, 116
Courtesy stigma, 61

DBH. *See* Dopamine-beta-hydroxylase
Defensive mechanisms, 153
Delinquency. *See* Conduct problems
Delta alcoholism (Jellinek), 9
Depression
and alcoholism, 37–38
in children of alcoholics, 37
children of depressed parents, 40
Development. *See* Social development theory
Developmentally cumulative alcoholism (Zucker), 9, 132
Developmentally limited alcoholism (Zucker), 9, 132
Developmental model, 132–33
Deviance-prone submodel, 136–37
Diagnostic and Statistical Manual of Mental Disorders (DSM-III-R)
diagnostic criteria for alcohol abuse disorders, 3–5
and psychopathology in alcoholics, 11
Diagnostic criteria for pathological alcohol use, 3–5
Diagnostic Interview Schedule (DIS), 5, 11
Differential deficit, 65–66
DIS. *See* Diagnostic Interview Schedule
Diversiform somatization, 20
Dizygotic twins (DZ twins; fraternal twins), 17–18
Dopamine-beta-hydroxylase (DBH), 103, 117
Dose of alcohol, 66–67
Drinking motivation, 125
Drug use
in alcoholics, 13, 14
in children of alcoholics, 35, 117DSM-III-R. See *Diagnostic and Statistical Manual of Mental Disorders*
Dysfunctional families, 162
DZ twins, 17–18

EAS. *See* Emotionality-Activity-Sociability scale
ECA. *See* Epidemiology Catchment Area survey
EEG. *See* Electroencephalographic activity
Electroencephalographic activity (EEG), 94–96, 113–14
Electromyographic activity (EMG), 99–100, 110–13
EMG. *See* Electromyographic activity
Emotionality, 76–78, 82, 130
Emotionality-Activity-Sociability scale (EAS), 77
Emotional processing, 91–92
Endocrine hormones, 103–4, 115–16
Enhanced reinforcement submodel, 135
Environment influences on alcoholism, 25–33
  in developmental model, 133
  and personality variables, 83
Enzymes, 101–3, 116–17
EPI. *See* Eysenck Personality Inventory
Epidemiology Catchment Area survey (ECA), 5, 6
Epidemiology of alcoholism, 5–7
Epinephrine, 103
Epsilon alcoholism (Jellinek), 9
ERPs. *See* Event-related potentials
Error, types 1 and 2, 64–65
Essential alcoholism (Knight), 8, 9
Ethanol
  absorption, elimination, and metabolism of, 106–7
  autonomic and electromyographic effects of, 110–13
  biochemical effects of, 115–17
  challenge studies, 66–71
  and CNS activity, 113–14
  dose of, 66–67
  exposure to, 128
  pharmacological effects of, 122–25
  reinforcing effects of, 122–24, 129
  responses of children of alcoholics to, 106–20
Ethanol challenge studies, 66–71
Ethnicity, 173
Event-related potentials, 94, 96–99, 104, 114–15
Evoked potentials, 94
Evoked responses, 94

Exacerbating factors, 47–49, 140
Exposure to alcohol, 128
Eysenck Personality Inventory (EPI), 77

Factorial design, 66
Familial alcoholism (Penick), 8, 9
Families
  alcohol expectancies in, 84–85
  alcoholism and psychopathology, 34–40
  environment and alcoholism, 25–33
  environment and interaction, 27–31
  factorial design research on, 66
  family life-cycle, 161–62
  family systems therapy, 161–63
  genetic linkage studies, 21–22
  overarching model of transmission of alcoholism in, 134–38
  and platelet MAO activity, 102
  rituals and alcoholism, 30, 162
  studies of genetic influence on alcoholism, 16–20
  variables of risk moderation, 142
  violence and alcoholism, 26
Family Environment Scale (FES), 27
Family history method, 55–58
Family History—Research Diagnostic Criteria (FH-RDC), 56, 57
Family Informant Schedule and Criteria (FISC), 56
Family life-cycle, 161–62
Family systems therapy, 161–63
Family transference, 160
FAS. *See* Fetal alcohol syndrome
Females. *See* Women
FES. *See* Family Environment Scale
Fetal alcohol syndrome (FAS)
  and maternal alcoholism, 35
  and paternal alcoholism, 61
FH-RDC. *See* Family History—Research Diagnostic Criteria
Field dependence-independence, 80, 89
FISC. *See* Family Informant Schedule and Criteria
Forgotten Children, The (Cork), 149
Fraternal twins, 17–18
Frontalis muscle tension, 111–12

Gamma alcoholism (Jellinek), 9
Gender. *See also* Men; Women
  and ethanol challenges, 70–71

in high-risk alcohol consumption studies,
112
Gene for alcoholism, 21–22
Genetic influence on alcoholism, 16–25
adoption studies on, 19–20
animal studies, 22–25
genotype-environment correlation, 51
linkage studies, 21–22
and medical consequences of alcoholism,
125
and personality traits, 73
twin studies on, 17–19
vulnerability of children of alcoholics, 41
Genetic markers, 21, 22
Genotype-environment correlation, 51
Group therapy, 159–60
Growth hormone, 103

Halstead-Reitan Neuropsychological Battery,
89
Harm avoidance, 130–31
Heart rate, 111
High-frequency somatization, 20
High-risk design, 53–55
Hyperactivity. *See* Attention deficit
hyperactivity disorder

Identical twins. *See* Monozygotic twins
Illusory correlations, 168
Impaired coping, 127
Impulsivity, 74, 76, 126–27
Incest, 26
Inclusion/exclusion criteria, 62–63, 69
Integrative model, 133
Intellectual deficits, 145–46
Interpersonal difficulties, 39–40
Intoxication
judgments of, 109
observer impressions of, 108–9
subjective, 107–8

Labeling, 168–70
Learning, 89–90
Limb of the blood alcohol curve, 68–69,
108, 118–20, 124, 129, 135
Linkage analysis, 21–22
Locus of control, 80–81

MAC. *See* MacAndrew alcoholism scale
MacAndrew alcoholism scale (MAC), 73–74

Major depression, 13
Male-limited alcoholism. *See* Type 2
alcoholism
Males. *See* Men
Mania, 13
MAO. *See* Monoamine oxidase
MAST. *See* Michigan Alcoholism Screening
Test
Matching procedures, 63
Maternal alcoholism, 16
and fetal alcohol effects, 24, 35, 61
and insecure attachment, 157
and prenatal alcohol exposure, 60
Mediational chains, 46–47
Mediators of risk, 52
biochemical, 100
biological, 93
chains of, 46–47
complex models of, 129–33
and family history of alcoholism, 121
and high-risk studies, 53
identification of, 43–47
moderators confused with, 49
multiple, 45–46
overarching model of, 134–38
simple models of, 121–29
and third variables, 50–52
Memory, 89–90
Men
alcohol abuse and dependence in, 14
antisocial behavior in, 75
behavioral undercontrol in, 74
and biological relatives' alcoholism,
19–20
body sway in, 87
in developmental model, 132
emotionality in, 77
fast EEG activity in, 95
and parental modeling of alcohol use, 32
prealcoholic personality traits in, 72
prevalence of alcoholism in, 5
transmissibility of alcoholism in, 6
Michigan Alcoholism Screening Test
(MAST), 56
Milieu-limited alcoholism. *See* Type 1
alcoholism
Minimal brain dysfunction. *See* Attention
deficit hyperactivity disorder
Minnesota Multiphasic Personality Inventory
(MMPI), 73

MMPI. *See* Minnesota Multiphasic
    Personality Inventory
Moderated mediation, 48, 49, 140
Moderators of risk, 47–49, 52
    coping as, 146–47
    mediators confused with, 49
    and third variables, 50–52
    variables of, 140–47
Monoamine oxidase (MAO), 101–3
Monozygotic twins (MZ twins; identical
    · twins)
    concordance rates for alcoholism, 25
    genetic transmission of alcoholism in,
    17–18
Motivation, drinking. *See* Drinking
    motivation
Multiple couple group therapy, 161
Multiple mediators of risk, 45–46
MZ twins. *See* Monozygotic twins

Negative affect alcoholism (Zucker), 9, 132
Negative affect submodel, 137–38
Negative mood states, 125–26
Neuropsychological functioning, 86–92
Neurotransmitter metabolism, 101–3,
    116–17
Nonaversive stimulation, 99–100
Nonfamilial alcoholism (Penick), 8, 9
Novelty seeking, 130–31

Object relations theory, 160–61
Orienting response, 112
Overarching model, 134–38

Panic disorder, 13
Parental alcoholism. *See also* Maternal
    alcoholism; Paternal alcoholism
    assessment of, 58
    and attention deficit hyperactivity disorder,
    36
    and childhood conduct problems, 36
    and cognitive/psychological functioning,
    86–87
    and direction of causality, 50
    and dispositional self-awareness, 144–45
    and emotionality, 77, 78
    and family violence, 26
    and genotype-environment correlation, 51
    and heterogeneity of children of
    alcoholics, 59–60

literature on, 170
    measures of, 56
    and mediators of risk, 46
    and moderators of risk, 48, 140
    and parental modeling of alcohol use, 31–33
    and personality type of offspring, 82
    psychological disorders associated with,
    34
    and race and ethnicity, 173
    and spousal psychopathology, 60–61
    and third variables, 50
Partial mediation, 43, 44, 45
Paternal alcoholism
    and alcohol expectancies, 84
    and alcoholism in offspring, 16
    and fetal alcohol syndrome, 61
    and maternal alcoholism, 60
    and mother's esteem, 142–43
    and reaction to stimulation, 100
    recovering alcoholic fathers, 29
    and stress-response dampening, 113
    and transketolases, 103
PCL. *See* Psychopathy Checklist
Perceptual functioning, 109–10
Perceptual-motor functioning, 88
Perfect mediation, 43, 44
Personality traits
    ascribed to children of alcoholics, 167–68
    and environmental variables, 83
    and later alcoholism, 72–83
    and moderation of risk, 144–45
    and prototypes of alcoholic, 10
Phobic disorder, 13
Placebo control, 67
Platelet MAO, 101, 105, 116–17
Porteus Maze test, 89
Posttraumatic stress disorder (PTSD), 154,
    160
Prenatal alcohol exposure, 60, 61
Prevention, 164–67
Primary alcoholism, 12–14
Prolactin, 103, 104, 115–16
Protective factors, 47–49, 140
Psychological disorders. *See*
    Psychopathology
Psychopathology
    in alcoholics, 11–12
    in children of alcoholics, 34–35
    and control groups, 61–62
    in families of alcoholics, 34–40

and MAO activity, 101
spousal, 60–61
Psychopathy Checklist (PCL), 39
Psychosocial crises, 156, 157, 159
Psychosocial influences in alcoholism,
  25–33
P3 wave, 96–99, 104, 115
PTSD. *See* Posttraumatic stress disorder

Race, 173
Random families, 162
Reactive alcoholism (Knight), 9
Reactivity to aversive stimulation, 100
Reactivity to nonaversive stimulation, 99
Reduction-augmentation, 79
Reinforcing effects of alcohol, 122–24, 129
Research on children of alcoholics, 53–71
  biological, 93–105
  correlational, 50–52
  high-risk design, 53–55
  psychological, 72–92
  underresearched areas, 173–74
Reward maintenance, 130–31
Risk, 41–52. *See also* Mediators of risk;
  Moderators of risk
Role conflict, 154–55
Role reversal, 154–55
Roles
  of adult children of alcoholics, 153–56
  adopted by children of alcoholics, 30–31

Sampling
  and age, 63
  sample size, 63–64
  sources of, 58–59
Schizophrenia, 98
School achievement. *See* Academic
  achievement
Secondary alcoholism, 12–14
Security, 157
Self-awareness, 144–45
Self-esteem, 81, 128
Self-help groups, 163–64
Self-medication, 125
Sensation seeking, 126
Sensorimotor performance, 87–88
Serotonin, 101, 102, 133
Short MAST (SMAST), 56
Simple moderation, 47–48, 49
SMAST. *See* Short MAST

Sociability, 78–79, 130
Social class
  and alcohol-related family violence, 26
  moderation of alcoholism by, 48, 141
Social development theory, 156–59
Social support, 143–44
Sociopathy, 13
SOMAs. *See* Sons of male alcoholics
Somatization disorder, 13
Sons of male alcoholics (SOMAs), 100, 119,
  120, 129, 133
Spontaneous electroencephalographic activ-
  ity, 94–96, 113–14
Spousal psychopathology, 60–61
Spouse abuse, 26
Stimulus-intensity modulation, 79
Strange situation procedure, 157
Stress response, 112–13, 118
Student Assistance Program, 165

Temperament, 130–32, 137, 141
Tension-reduction hypothesis, 110–11
Therapy, 159–66
Third variables, 50–52
Thyrotropin, 104
Tolerance development, 125
Trail Making Test, 89
Transketolase, 103
Triiodothyronine, 103
Twin studies, 17–19
Type A alcoholism (Morey, Skinner, and
  Blashfield), 9
Type B alcoholism (Morey, Skinner, and
  Blashfield), 9
Type C alcoholism (Morey, Skinner, and
  Blashfield), 9
Type V alcoholism (Partington and Johnson),
  9
Type IV alcoholism (Partington and
  Johnson), 9
Type 1 alcoholism (Cloniger), 8, 9
  in adoptees, 19–20
  and dysphoric reactions, 10
  moderation by social class of, 48, 141
  negative affect alcoholism compared to,
    132
  and negative mood states, 126
  and personality disordered versus neurotic
    alcoholism, 15
  and temperament, 130–31

Type I alcoholism (Partington and Johnson),
   9
Type 1 errors, 64–65
Type III alcoholism (Partington and
   Johnson), 9
Type 2 alcoholism (Cloniger), 8, 9
   in adoptees, 19–20
   antisocial alcoholism compared to, 132
   and antisocial personality disorder, 20
   and appetitive effects of alcohol, 10
   and MAO activity, 102
   moderation by social class of, 48
   and personality disordered versus neurotic
      alcoholism, 15
   and sensation seeking, 126
   and temperament, 131
Type II alcoholism (Partington and Johnson), 9
Type 2 errors, 64

Verbal ability, 88–89
Visuospatial ability, 89

Vulnerability, 41–52
   concept of, 41–43
   models of, 121–39
   moderation of, 48, 49
   threshold of, 42
Vulnerability threshold, 42

WAIS. *See* Wechsler Adult Intelligence Scale
Wechsler Adult Intelligence Scale (WAIS),
   88–89, 90
Within-subjects designs, 70
Women
   behavioral undercontrol in, 74
   and biological relatives' alcoholism, 19–20
   and coalcoholism, 151
   in developmental model, 132
   emotionality in, 77
   ethanol challenges with, 70–71
   prealcoholic personality traits in, 72
   prevalence of alcoholism, 5
   transmissibility of alcoholism in, 6